MW01254990

Insects
of
New England
&
New York

By Tom Murray

Kollath+Stensaas
PUBLISHING

Kollath+Stensaas Publishing
394 Lake Avenue South, Suite 406
Duluth, MN 55802
Office: 218.727.1731
Orders: 800.678.7006
info@kollathstensaas.com
www.kollathstensaas.com

INSECTS *of* NEW ENGLAND & NEW YORK

Printed in South Korea by Doosan
10 9 8 7 6 5 4 3 2 1 First Edition

Editorial Director: Mark Sparky Stensaas
Graphic Designer: Rick Kollath

Cover photos by Tom Murray

ISBN-13: 978-1-936571-02-4

Table of Contents

*Dedicated to
my dad, Carl Murray,*

He's always been there with his guidance,
support and encouragement—in nature, sports
and everything else that matters to me.

Acknowledgements

First, thank you Mark Sparky Stensaas for encouraging me and giving me the opportunity to write this book.

When I was first becoming serious about insect photography, Eric Eaton, co-author of the *Kaufman Field Guide to Insects of North America*, would regularly visit my website and identify my photos. With Eric's encouragement I joined www.BugGuide.net in March of 2005. Founded by Troy Bartlett, BugGuide.net has helped me, and many other insect enthusiasts, learn a great deal about all arthropods from the hundreds of online contributors—expert and amateur alike. John VanDyk and Iowa State University have done a great job carrying out the work started by Troy on this ever growing site.

Don Chandler at the University of New Hampshire has been a great mentor and identified many beetles and aquatic insects for me. Vassili Belov tirelessly identifies beetles and true bugs on BugGuide.net, and recruits specialists from all over the world to lend their expertise. Others that have identified many specimens on my behalf are Peter Messer (Carabids), Adam Brunke (Staphylinids), Blaine Mattheson (Elaterids), Bob Carlson (Ichneumons), Dave Smith (Sawflies), Joshua Basham (Buprestids), Kevin Pfeiffer (Arachnids), along with all these others from BugGuide: Thomas Ames Jr., Robert Anderson, John S. Ascher, Thomas H. Atkinson, John & Jane Balaban, Brad Barnd, Troy Bartlett, Joshua P. Basham, Keith Bayless, Vassili Belov, Paul Beuk, Adam Brunke, Boris Buche, Matthias Buck, John Burger, Philip Careless, Bob Carlson, John Carlson, John F. Carr, Donald S. Chandler, Noah Charney, Joe Cicero, S.M. Clark, Patrick Coin, Ben Coulter, Daniel P. Duran, Eric Eaton, Charley Eiseman, K. Taro Eldredge, Chuck Entz, M.J. Epps, William Ericson, Art Evans, Zack Falin, Nick Fensler, David J. Ferguson, Eric Fisher, Steve Gaimari, Matthew L. Gimmel, Lloyd Gonzales, Jeff Gruber, Frank Guarnieri, Andy Hamilton, Phillip Harpootlian, Martin Hauser, Ron Hemberger, Ross Hill, Sam Jaffe, Frans Janssens, Andrew Jensen, Kojun Kanda, WonGun Kim, Joel Kits, Victor Kolyada, Norman & Cheryl Lavers, Jongok Lim, Tim Loh, Stephen Luk, Ted C. MacRae, Christopher Majka, Blaine Mathison, John R. Maxwell, Adriean Mayor, Jim McClarin, Tommy McElrath, Robin McLeod, Peter W. Messer, Laura T. Miller, E.L. Mockford, Beatriz Moisset, Tim R. Moyer, William L. Murphy, Steve Nanz, John D. Oswald, Abigail Parker, Dennis Paulson, S.B. Peck, Gerard Pennards, John Pinto, Dr. Marc Pollet, O. A. Popovici, Mike Quinn, Herschel Raney, Brady Richards, E.G. Riley, J.D. Roberts, Roger

Rohrbeck, Dave Ruiter, Lynette Schimming, Andrew Short, Dave Smith, Villu Soon, M.S. Sweet, William H. Taft, Margaret Thayer, D.B. Thomas, Michael Thomas, James C. Trager, Michael Veit, Richard Vernier, Ferenc Vilisics, John R. Watts, John Weaver, Rob Westerduijn, T.L. Whitworth, Alex Wild, Ken Wolgemuth, Charlene Wood, Norm Woodley, Andrzej Woznica, Doug Yanega, Chen Young, D.K. Young and Diane Young.

Stephen Marshall, Eric Eaton, Ken Kaufman, Dennis Paulson, Sid Dunkle, John Capinera, Charles Covell, Ed Lam, Charley Eiseman, Art Evans, Richard White and Jeffrey Hahn have provided books that were invaluable to my research.

Lastly I have to thank my lovely Julie Lisk for putting up with my obsession with my insects that takes up much of my free time.

Tom Murray
May 9, 2012

The publishers would like to thank Tom Murray for his passion for the "six-leggeds" and his remarkable images. For Tom this is truly a labor of love and we think this comes through in his writing and photography. Even during the layout process, we used Tom's images to identify some insects near our homes.

The publishers
May 11, 2012

ACKNOWLEDGEMENTS

Success

Insects are the most numerous and successful animals on earth. Entomologists have identified about 90,000 different species living in North America and about one million different species in the world. In a typical backyard, there can be as many as 1,000 different insects at any given time. They are successful for several reasons. First, insects occupy essentially all types of habitats except for oceans, using many resources as food. These resources can be divided into three general groups: herbivores, i.e. feeding on plants, carnivores, i.e. feeding on insects and other animals, and saprivores, i.e. feeding on dead or decaying plant or animal material. Insects are also successful because of their small size, their adaptability and their high reproductive rate. As a consequence, there are three times the number of insects compared to all other terrestrial animals in North America combined.

What is an Insect?

Insects belong to a group of animals called arthropods. Arthropods possess segmented bodies, a hard external integument known as an exoskeleton and paired jointed appendages, e.g. legs and antennae. In addition to insects, other common arthropods include arachnids (e.g. ticks, spiders, daddylong-legs, mites), crustaceans (e.g. crayfish, sowbugs, fairyshrimp), millipedes and centipedes.

Insects differ from these other arthropods by possessing three major body parts, the head, thorax and abdomen.

Several important features are found on the head. There is one pair of antennae found on the adult's head, usually found between or in front of the eyes. Antennae vary in form and complexity, and are sometimes referred to as feelers or horns. Antennae are used by insects for many types of sensing, including smelling, hearing, tasting and feeling. Insects also possess compound eyes which are made up of varying numbers of facets. Each facet sees a small part of what the insect is viewing. Together, they comprise what the insect sees. The number of facets in a compound eye varies from as few as several facets as in some subterranean ants and many as 50,000 facets in the large eyes of dragonflies.

Look for insect mouthparts on the head. They are mandibulate, i.e. possessing mandibles, although there is much variation. Mouthparts can be generally divided up into two types: chewing mouthparts, i.e. mandibles (jaws) are prominent, or sucking mouthparts, i.e. the mouthparts are modified into beak-like or tube-like mouthparts. While they differ considerably in appearance, the same basic parts are found in both types.

The second major body part is the thorax. It is divided into three sections, prothorax, mesothorax and metathorax. There is a pair of legs on each thoracic segment, a total of six (a few adult insects possess no legs). Legs vary much in form and function. Legs are used for running and walking, jumping, grasping, swimming and digging. The wings are also attached to the thorax. Most insects have four wings, attached to the second and third thoracic segments (mesothorax and metathorax). Flies have only two wings which are attached to the mesothorax). A few insects lack wings altogether. The wings exhibit a wide variety of modifications.

The last major insect body part is the abdomen which generally possesses eleven segments and usually lacks appendages. The abdomen is relatively simple in structure compared to the head and thorax. Some insects possess a pair of appendages on the last segment of the abdomen known as cerci. Cerci vary in form and usually function as sensory organs. Females typically possess claspers and ovipositors on the abdomen for mating and laying eggs. Some insects, such as bees and wasps, possess a stinger on the abdomen which is a modified ovipositor.

Metamorphosis: Insect Development

Insects are generally oviparous, i.e. they lay eggs. Eggs are generally oval and elongate, although there can be much variation. Eggs can be laid singly or in clusters. Many insects surround their eggs in some sort of protective material. A few insects, e.g. aphids, are viviparous, i.e. eggs develop inside the mother and she gives birth to live young.

Because their hard outer integument does not expand, immature insects must shed their exoskeletons through a process called molting. The stage of the insect between molts is called an instar. Insects often have four or five instars, although this varies with different insect species.

Insect develop through a phenomenon called metamorphosis. Metamorphosis is a change in form during development. Sometimes this change is gradual but many times it is very dramatic. Insect development is broadly divided into two different types, simple and complete metamorphosis.

The life stages of simple metamorphosis are egg, nymph, adult. The immature nymphs look similar to the adults except nymphs are smaller, lack wings and are sexually immature. Their wings develop on the outside of their bodies. The last nymphal instar molts into an adult. There are three types of simple metamorphosis: ametabolous where the adults are wingless and the only difference between nymphs and adults is size, hemimetabolous, where the nymphs (sometimes called naiads) are aquatic differ considerably in form from the adults which live on land and paurometabolous where the nymphs and adults are similar in form, differing chiefly in size, and typically live the same environment.

The life stages for complete metamorphosis, also called holometabolous, are egg, larva, pupa and adult. Larvae look very different from adults, usually feeding on different types of food and living in different habitats. Last instar larvae molt into a pupa or resting stage. In the pupal stage, the insect does not feed and usually does not move. Inside the pupa, the insect changes form through tissue breakdown, tissue reorganization and the development of new structures, such as wings, legs, antennae and mouthparts from masses of specialized cells. Wings develop inside the body. The insect eventually molts one last time with the adult insect emerging from the pupa.

Insect Parts

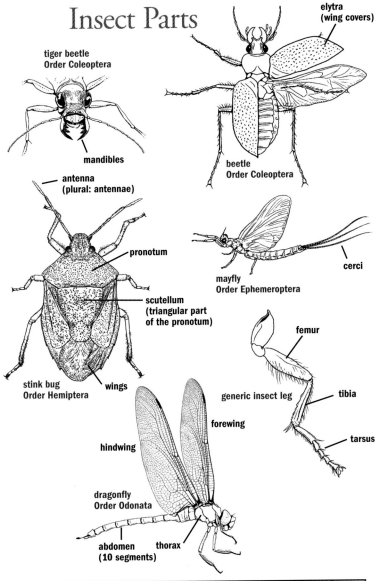

tiger beetle
Order Coleoptera

mandibles

elytra
(wing covers)

beetle
Order Coleoptera

antenna
(plural: antennae)

pronotum

scutellum
(triangular part
of the pronotum)

stink bug
Order Hemiptera

wings

mayfly
Order Ephemeroptera

cerci

femur

generic insect leg

tibia

forewing

hindwing

tarsus

dragonfly
Order Odonata

abdomen
(10 segments)

thorax

How to Enjoy Insects

The great thing about insects is that they occur essentially everywhere in the Northeast. Although they are most common during warm weather, you can find them nearly at all of times of the year. When I am hiking, I like to look on all kinds of plants, especially on the flowers and leaves. Be also sure to examine stems, bark and branches. Don't forget most insects like to be in the warmth and you can often find them sunning themselves in a variety of areas.

Insects are frequently found on the ground, either as they scurry about or are resting after flight. Some insects nest in the soil and you may find them as they are leaving or returning to it. If you encounter logs, give them a good look, especially under any loose bark. It is also worth looking under logs, as well as any loose stones, or similar objects. If you aren't too squeamish, check out dead animals and dung, there is an amazing array of insects that are attracted to these food sources.

Don't forget sources of water, including ponds, lakes, streams, rivers, marshes, bogs for the many species of aquatic insects. Be sure to also check out shorelines for semi-aquatic insects. The immatures of many insects are aquatic and as adults they are found nearby on land on plants and other objects.

Insects are common in and around buildings. Many of these enter inadvertently but there are some species that have adapted to living with people quite nicely.

Getting Closer

If you want to be more proactive in finding insects and observing them up close, you can use different capture methods. One common type, known as sweeping, is done by moving a heavy duty net back and forth through tall plants. This collects a variety of small insects that may otherwise be overlooked.

Another common collecting method is pit fall traps. Sink a tin can or similar container into the ground so the top is even with the ground. Insects walking on the ground fall into the container and become trapped. Drill a small hole into the bottom to prevent water from accumulating. Place a piece of old fruit or other type of material as bait to attract insects. Different baits attract different insects. Place a fine-meshed screen over the bait to make it easier to remove insects that fall into it.

Also check outdoor lights at night which attract a wide variety of different insects. Black (UV) lights are the most attractive. Not all nocturnal insects may be attracted to lights so inspect plants and other nearby sites at night.

You can spend many enjoyable hours watching insects, observing their habits and behavior. You do not need any special equipment to watch them. You can get close to many insects with a slow stealthy approach and practice. If you are fortunate enough to have a device that magnifies images, such as a pair of binoculars that can focus to within six to eight feet, you can increase the number and variety of insects you can observe without the need to get as close.

You will be able to identify many insects to order and even family from your observations and with the common and familiar insects, to species. If you encounter an insect you can not immediately identify, capture it with a jar or insect net so you can examine it more closely without it being able to escape. You can then release the insect after you have an opportunity to look at it more thoroughly.

Photography

Today's digital cameras have improved so much and are inexpensive enough to enable vast numbers of people to photograph nature, including the little critters I enjoy so much. Point and shoot cameras are great for portability and can get excellent pictures of insects that most people notice.

I use Canon digital SLR cameras, the 40D and now the 5D, with Canon 100mm and 65 mm lenses. The 100mm lens is very versatile and gives great quality pictures on subjects larger than 3mm. The 65mm with up to a 5:1 magnification factor does the job for insects under 1mm up to 20mm, but is more difficult to use on moving subjects. A ring flash is needed with the 65mm and I use the Canon MT-24EX dual head flash.

Nearly all my pictures are taken in manual mode and using a flash. That way I can control the depth of field, shutter speed and ISO setting, giving more consistent quality pictures. Everyone has his or her own style, and I'd suggest trying a number of different combinations of camera settings and see which one you're comfortable with. Some pictures come out better without a flash, allowing the background to stay light, but just remember to keep a fast enough shutter speed.

Once you get the images in your computer, don't think that it's cheating to use Photoshop or any other software to enhance your pictures. Even the old film pictures were manipulated when being printed. The color balance was often adjusted as well as the exposure. The only real change with digital is photos can be sharpened, but be careful not to over do it.

Have fun and remember it costs nothing to take extra pictures to make sure you're satisfied with at least one of them.

How to use this Field Guide

Insects of New England & New York includes photos of more than 1250 species in one small guide. We thing that's impressive! Also, by limiting the insects to those found in one geographic area, we have eliminated the need to wade through many hundreds of species, many of which would never be found here.

This book focuses on New York, Connecticut, Rhode Island, Massachussets, Vermont, New Hampshire, Maine and adjacent Canada. But remember, not all species are found in any single area. Habitat preferences tend to spread species out. The Northeast is a mosaic of different habitats from bogs, oak woods, coastal sand dunes and grasslands to lakes, ponds, marshes and rivers; and about everything in between.

Coverage

With tens of thousands of insect species in New England and New York, we obviously could not include all, or even most. Nor would we want to. Only the most common, the most interesting, the really bizarre and the vividly-colored made the cut.

Order

Insects are organized by order and then broken down further into families and genera. We attempted to put closely related species together to further simplify identification. Family name is listed at the bottom of each spread. With experience in the field using this guide, you will gradually learn to identify insect orders and even place the insects you see, collect or photograph into their proper family or even genus.

Insect Names

Like other organisms, insects are given a scientific name. The Latin names tend to be the spoken word of entomologists. The insects with widely accepted common name are few; in cases where there is no common name we simply use the name for that group. For example, the true bug, *Ceresa basalis* has no common name so we call it by the group it belongs to—"Treehopper." But its cousin *Mycrutalis calva* does have an accepted common name so we use it—Honey Locust Treehopper.

And note that it is not always possible to identify insects to species from photos. Many require magnification of certain body parts to separate from superficially similar species. Tom has relied on his vast experience and the feedback from many experts to identify his photos.

Photos

We chose to use photos of free-flying insects—often in their natural habitat—instead of dead pinned speciemens. Amazingly 99.9 percent of the images were provided by the author. Photographing insects is not an easy task! We attempted to use Tom's photos that best illustrated the most distinctive field marks. Sexual dimorphism (different coloration or shape in males and females) is the norm for some species; we label the photos as male or female in cases where it may aid in identification.

Size Scale

Size is relative and often hard to judge in the field, so we've added size-bars to some species' photo. The black bar indicates the actual body length of that species, or in the case of the butterflies and moths, average wingspan. The indicated length does not include antennae nor ovipositor, unless noted. These lengths are averages and may not represent the sexual dimorphism in size of males and females in some species.

Enjoy *Insects of New England & New York*. Take it in the field. Cram it in your pack. Use it. But most importantly, have fun getting to know our fascinating northern insects.

Introductory text for every Order and Family covered

Different header colors are used to quickly access species in that Order

Integrated with each Order intro is an illustration of one member, highlighting features

Color tabs identify each insect order and match to those on the back cover, helping you flip to the right section quickly

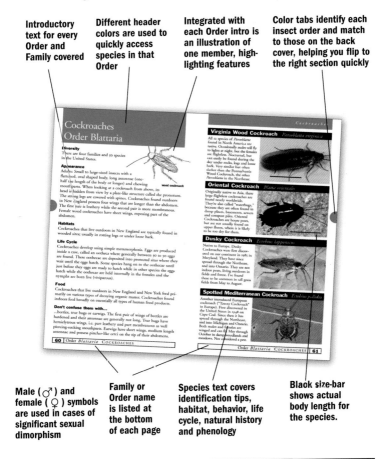

Male (♂) and female (♀) symbols are used in cases of significant sexual dimorphism

Family or Order name is listed at the bottom of each page

Species text covers identification tips, habitat, behavior, life cycle, natural history and phenology

Black size-bar shows actual body length for the species.

Springtails
Order Collembola

Diversity
There are 12 families and 795 species in North America. Springtails are very common in New England and New York.

Appearance
Adults: Very small insects, ranging in size from 1/16 to 1/8 inch long. These wingless insects are usually elongate shaped, although some, like sminthurid springtails, are round and stout. Springtails have short to moderate length antennae with mouthparts generally concealed inside their head and not noticed. Most springtails are dark-colored, brown, grey or black although some species are also white, and some are even iridescent and brightly colored.

Most springtails possess a furcula located on the underside of the abdomen—a few springtails lack such an appendage. A furcula is a forked appendage used for jumping. When not in use, a furcula is tucked up under the body, set like a mouse trap. When it is released, it extends down rapidly propelling the springtail forward. A springtail can jump many times its body length.

Habitats
Springtails are associated with damp conditions and are commonly found in the soil and leaf litter. They are also common under bark, decaying wood and in fungi. At least one species is common in freshwater ponds, even puddles. Another species is common on top of snow during winter and early spring. Occasionally found indoors.

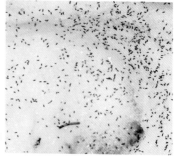

Some springtails are very common on top of the snow on warm winter days. They are known as "snow fleas."

Life Cycle
Springtails develop using ametabolous metamorphosis, a type of simple metamorphosis.

Food
They feed on fungi and decaying plant matter. A few are predaceous on very small invertebrate animals.

Abundance

Despite their small size, springtails can occur in tremendously large numbers and are one of the most abundant insects. One source estimates that millions of springtails occur per hectare (about 2.5 acres).

Regenerating lost body parts

Springtails have the ability to regenerate antennae which are frequently damaged or lost due to attacks by ground beetles and other insects.

Don't confuse them with...

...fleas. Because they are small and jump, people sometimes misidentify springtails with fleas. However, fleas are flattened from side to side while springtails are cylindrical in shape. You would not commonly see fleas in soil, leaf litter, or other places where you would expect springtails.

springtail

Northeast Species Notes

Formerly an order within Entognatha, these hexapods are now considered to be in their own class, consisting of 4 orders, and 20 families in North America, with about 250 described species in the Northeast. The most common springtails are the Elongate-body (Entomobryomorpha), Globular Springtails (Symphypleona) and the order containing Snow Fleas (Poduromorpha).

Springtails are small wingless arthropods ranging in size from under a millimeter to about 5mm. Most species have a furcula, a forked appendage used for jumping like a flea, although there are a few exceptions. Their antennae are short with 4 to 6 segments and a retractable organ called a sensilla located at the tip of the antennae that senses

taste. They have clusters of up to eight eyes, some being fotosensitive, and other eyes sensing polarized light. Mostly they eat decaying plant matter, fungi and micro organisms in the soil.

They can only survive in moist conditions, and are commonly found in soil, leaf litter, moss, under loose bark and under rocks and logs.

Not all springtails are miniscule. Here is one of the largest species—*Tomocerus vulgaris*—at 4mm long next to one of the tiniest—an Isotomidae species—at 0.6mm.

Some may be seen on the surface of puddles and ponds and others on snow. Occasionally springtails are found indoors, especially around house plants. The best way to get rid of them is to remove their source of moisture. With the possible exception of Soil Mites, Springtails are perhaps the most abundant creatures on earth, with densities reported as high as 250 million per acre.

The Greek name *Collembola* means glue wedge, referring to a tube-like structure under its body that is thought to have an important role in maintaining their correct body fluid balance.

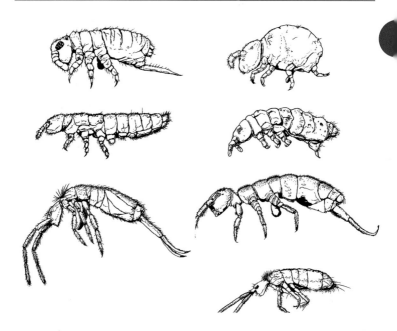

Snow Flea *Hypogastrura harveyi*

This is one of three species in the genus known as "snow fleas." When it gets cold—below 25F—they shelter under the snow's surface, but on warm winter days the snow can appear black with thousands of these tiny springtails. I find them near the bases of trees, and within depressions—like foot tracks in the snow.

During the summer I find them in smaller numbers under loose bark.

Globular Springtail *Janusius sylvestris*

One of the larger and more colorful of the globular springtails, reaching a size of 2.5mm. A forest dwelling species, I typically find them in low vegetation on leaf surfaces. I've found them in May through June. They occur throughout the Northeast. Formerly called *Sminthuris sylvestris*.

Allacma fusca

Allacma purpurescens

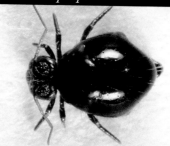

Bourletiella hortensis

Dicyrtomina minuta forma ornata

Pseudobourletiella spinata

Ptenothrix marmorata

Sminthurinus quadrimaculatus

Sminthurus fitchi

Entomobrya clitellaria

Entomobrya nivalis

Orchesella hexfasciata

Orchesella celsa

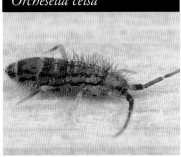

Isotoma viridis

Tomocerus vulgaris

Cyphoderus similis

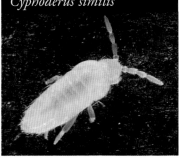

Ceratophysella species

Mayflies
Order Ephemeroptera

Diversity

Twenty families and 614 species in the U.S.. Common in New England and New York.

Appearance

Soft-bodied insects with an elongate body with two or three very long tail-like appendages called cerci at the end of the abdomen. Most possesses four clear membranous wings (some species only two) held upright over its body when at rest. Conspicuous eyes. Mouthparts reduced and non-functional.

Huge, hat-like eyes are characteristic of the males in some mayfly families.

Habitats

Nymphs are aquatic, especially in rivers and streams. Adults are weak flyers and are found on land near water. Adults are particularly attracted to lights at night.

Nymphs are aquatic. Some species emerge *en masse*. This is *Siphlonurus quebecensis.*

Life cycle

Eggs laid in water where the nymphs develop. Mayflies are unique as they have an intermediate preadult stage called a subimago. The nymph rises to the surface where the subimago emerges. It is similar to an adult but is generally sexually immature and duller in color. Adults emerge from the subimago a day or two later and live no more than a few days.

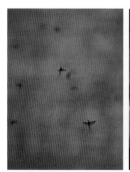

A mass emergence of *Ephemera* mayflies.

mayfly

Food
Because of their short life
span, adult mayflies do not feed.

Abundance
Mayflies often emerge in spectacularly large numbers with homes and
nearby areas inundated with them. There have been times when large
populations of mayflies have coated roads making them slippery—even
requiring snow plows to clear them in rare instances.

Because of their large numbers, mayflies are an important food source
for insects, spiders, fish and birds. Fly fishermen imitate mayflies when
constructing lures—appropriately called "flies"—to catch trout.

Water quality indicators
Mayflies thrive and are abundant in clean aquatic environments. When
these areas become polluted, their number can dramatically decrease.

Don't Confuse Them With...
...ichneumonid wasps. However ichneumonid wasps are harder bodied,
have very long antennae, have elongate forewings and hold their wings
flat when at rest.

Flatheaded Mayfly *Arthroplea bipunctata*

Flathead Mayflies have recently
been elevated to family status.
In North America there's only
one genus, and one species in
that genus represented,
Arthroplea bipunctata. The larvae can be found under rocks
in rivers and streams. The
adults emerge in May and June.

Speckled Dun *Callibaetis ferrugineus ferrugineus*

These small mayflies more than
make up for their lack of size
by their massive and multiple
hatches. Hind wings are very
small and sometimes missing.
The fore wings have a dark
leading edge. Males have
extremely large eyes that are
divided into two parts. Streams,
rivers, ponds and swamps.

Blue-winged Olive *Baetis tricaudatus*

Unlike other Small Minnow Mayflies, I've only found adults of this species in April and May. The larvae I've found have all been in fast moving cool water from small streams to large rocky rivers. Picking up rocks from a river, and looking at its underside is a good way to find some of these larvae.

Sulphur *Ephemerella dorothea*

This is a small species of Spiny Crawler Mayfly that has adults emerging in May and June. The nymphs live in streams and rivers with gravel bottoms and moderate currents. The hatch is usually during the day, but in rivers with water temperatures over 55 degrees, they will emerge at night when the water temperature falls.

Chocolate Dun *Eurylophella prudentalis*

The Chocolate Dun nymphs I've found have all been in submerged vegetation in slow moving rivers. This is a Northeastern species with the adults hatching in June. They're not as abundant as many other Mayflies, so their hatch isn't considered significant by trout fishermen.

Olive-winged Drake *Hexagenia limbata*

Second largest Mayfly in North America, following *Litobrancha recurvata*. Hatch occurs after sunset and continues into the early morning (June and into August in northern locations). May be so numerous that dopplar radar detects them! Found in large silty rivers, ponds and lakes. Throughout North America.

Early Brown Spinner *Leptophlebia cupida*

Also called the Black Quill, these large Mayflies occur throughout the Northeast and Midwest. The adults emerge in April and May. They can be found in rivers, ponds and swamps in submerged leaves and vegetation.

Blue Quill *Paraleptophlebia debilis*

This Pronggilled Mayfly has a late season emergence, hatching out in the fall, when most other Mayfles are gone. Even though it's a small Mayfly, the hatch can be significant, and are important to trout and trout fisherman. They're locally abundant and can be found in rivers across the continent.

Pseudo-Gray Drake *Siphloplecton basale*

This early season large Cleftfooted Minnow Mayfly is found in fast running streams and rivers. They never seem to be abundant in any one location. The adults (imago) are fast graceful flyers that can be seen flying over riffles in the river.

Gray Drake *Siphlonurus typicus*

Nymphs can be found in a variety of wetlands, but most common in slow streams and ponds, usually near weedy vegetation. Adults hatch over a two to three month period starting in May. Found throughout the Northeast, and look very similar in appearance to other species of *Siphlonurus*.

Dragonflies & Damselflies
Order Odonata

Diversity

There are 11 families and 434 species in the United States. Dragonflies and damselflies are very common in New England and New York.

Appearance

Adults: Medium to large insects with four conspicuous wings containing many veins. They have large compound eyes and long, slender abdomens. The Odonata are divided into two suborders, the Zygoptera, the dragonflies and the Anisoptera, the damselflies. Dragonflies hold their wings straight out at rest. The two pairs of wings are similar in length although the hind pair is wider at the base. The compound eyes touch or are separated by a distance shorter than the width of one compound eye. Damselflies hold their wings over their back when they are rest. Both pairs of wings are the same size and are narrowed at the base. The compound eyes are separated by width greater than one compound eye.

Larvae: The immature nymphs (sometimes called naiads) are generally cylindrical and streamlined. Dragonfly nymphs are generally more stout than damselfly nymphs. Damselfly nymphs have three leaf-like gills at the tip of their abdomen while dragonfly nymphs possess inconspicuous gills that are not noticed. The mouthparts are modified into arm-like structures which they keep folded under their head when not in use. They extend these mouthparts forward when they attempt to capture food.

Habitats

The nymphs are aquatic. Adults are often found near water where they nymphs develop but can wander far from any water source.

Biology

Dragonflies and damselflies develop using hemimetabolous metamorphosis, a type of simple metamorphosis. Both adults and nymphs are predaceous feeding primarily on insects. Adults prey on a variety of flying insects. The nymphs feed on a variety of aquatic insects including mayfly nymphs although larger dragonfly nymphs have been known to attack tadpoles and small fish.

Don't confuse them with...

Dragonflies and damselflies are distinctive and would not be confused for other adult insects. Dragonfly and damselfly nymphs could be confused with mayfly and stonefly nymphs although these insects have conspicuous gills on the thorax (stonefly nymphs) or abdomen (mayfly nymphs).

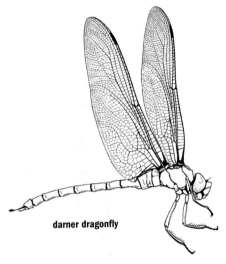

darner dragonfly

Darners
Family Aeshnidae

Appearance

Darners are large dragonflies with compound eyes that touch along a long margin. They usually are brownish with green and blue, sometimes yellow markings on the thorax and abdomen. Their wings are clear.

Biology

Darners have a well-developed ovipositor and lay their eggs in plant stems along the edges of lakes and ponds. Typically the female lays her eggs without a male guarding her. May to October.

Common Green Darner *Anax junius*

One of our first dragonflies of spring, migrants coming up from the south in late April. In October and November, swarms of thousands can be seen migrating south along the coast. It's our only darner species that will often lays eggs with the male attached in tandem. Occurs in every state including Hawaii.

Canada Darner *Aeshna canadensis*

A very common mosaic darner in our area that hunts at forest edges and in late day feeding swarms. Habitat includes almost any boggy or sluggish body of water. Flies from mid June through mid October, transcontinental in northern US and southern Canada.

Shadow Darner *Aeshna umbrosa*

Aptly named, the Shadow Darner is active in the shade and in feeding swarms at dusk. Flies from mid June to mid November, making this one of the latest flying darners. Occurs across North America, except the southern states and Alaska. Habitat includes woodland streams and swampy areas.

Clubtails
Family Gomphidae

Appearance
Clubtails range in size from 1 5/8 to 3 1/3 inches in length. Unlike other dragonflies, their compound eyes do not touch on top. Their wings are clear and the posterior segments of the abdomen of most clubtails are enlarged. Clubtails are usually green or yellow with black markings and have clear wings.

Biology
Clubtails mate for a few minutes before the female goes off to lay eggs; the male does not go with to guard her. Clubtails have an undeveloped ovipositor and they drop their eggs into flowing water and less commonly along the edges of ponds and lakes. Clubtails often like to rest on the ground and other flat surfaces, although they can also be found on foliage. They are present from May to September.

Dragonhunter   *Hagenius brevistylus*

This largest North American clubtail feeds on large insects, including butterflies, wasps and other dragonflies including darners that are its same size. Found around river, streams and rocky lakeshore from June through August. Widespread east of the Rockies.

Black-shouldered Spinyleg   *Dromogomphus spinosus*

Black-shouldered Spinylegs habitats include muddy bottomed streams, rivers and rocky shored lakes, where they often perch on rocks. They're also common in forests where they hunt and will rest in the shade on leaves and the ground. Widespread east of the Rockies from June to September.

Mustached Clubtail *Gomphus adelphus*

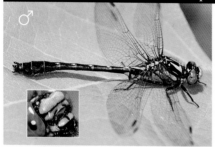

A small clubtail of fast running, clean, rocky streams and rivers. Flies low over the water, especially near riffles, with activity peaking late in the day. Rests on leaves and rocks at the river edge. Occurs in the northeastern U.S. and adjacent Canada from late May through July.

Zebra Clubtail *Stylurus scudderi*

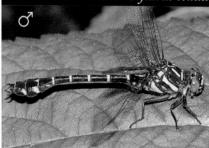

This large yellow ringed clubtail won't be mistaken for any other species. One of our later season clubtails, look near riffles in sandy bottomed rivers and streams from late June through September. Occurs in the northeast U.S. and southeastern Canada. Uncommon.

Arrow Clubtail *Stylurus spiniceps*

Prefers the same habitat and distribution as the Zebra Clubtail and shares the same flight season. Adults spend a lot of time in treetops, but can be seen perched on leaves, rocks and will land on canoes. Most active during the afternoon hours.

Maine Snaketail *Ophiogomphus mainensis*

We have 5 species of Snaketails in the Northeast, all are uncommon and similar looking. Maine Snaketails are found on rocks and leaves at clean rocky streams and rivers from mid May through July. Adults can be found in fields where they do most of their hunting.

Emeralds
Family Corduliidae

Appearance
Moderate sized dragonflies, 1 1/4 to 3 1/4 inches long. They are usually blackish or brown with some species being metallic green. Emeralds have brilliantly colored green eyes and usually have markings on the wings

Biology
They are typically associated with ponds, wooded streams, and bogs. These dragonflies common from May into August.

Racket-tailed Emerald *Dorocordulia libera*

A common inhabitant of forest clearings and edges, flying along trails in dappled sunlight. Like most emeralds, adults hang vertically from branches when resting, but will also rest on top of leaves. Larvae live in marshes, swamps and ponds that are somewhat acidic. Adults fly from mid May to mid August.

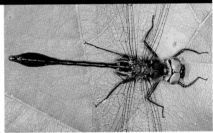

Beaverpond Baskettail *Epitheca canis*

Usually the earliest emerging of our 5 northeastern species of Baskettails, adults fly from early May to mid July. Adults hunt in open sunny areas individually and occasionally in swarms. Males often hover when patrolling along the edge of a mucky bottom wetland.

Ringed Boghaunter *Williamsonia lintneri*

A rare and endangered inhabitant in most of its region from the Great Lakes to southern New England. It's one of the first dragonflies of the season with a short flight period from mid April to mid June. They're weak fliers that commonly perch on the ground in forest trails with dappled light and on tree trunks. Larvae live in sphagnum bogs.

Skimmers
Family Libellulidae

Appearance

Skimmers typically range in size from 1 to 2 inches in length. Their eyes touch on top. Veins in the hindwings form a boot-shape. The wings may be clear but often has spots or bands.

Biology

Skimmers are associated with ponds and swamps where they are commonly found perching nearby on twigs. Mating takes place while in flight. Females dip their abdomens into the water when they lay eggs while males guard them. Skimmers are common from May to October.

Widow Skimmer *Libellula luctuosa*

Mature males are unmistakable with the black wing patches edged in a frosty blue. Immature males resemble females with yellow dorsal stripes. Common in fields from June into September, perching on vertical plant stems. Larvae develop in lentic waters of lakes, ponds and bogs.

Common Whitetail *Plathemis (Libellula) lydia*

These dragonflies really are "common," occurring in all 48 contiguous states and southern Canada. Found in fields and other open sunny areas where they often perch flat on the ground. Male abdomens turn pruinose whitish blue as they mature. Flight is from May to September.

Twelve-spotted Skimmer *Libellula pulchella*

Males are unmistakable in the east (a couple similar species in the western U.S.) Females are similar to Common Whitetails, but they have an unbroken yellow abdominal stripe. Flies May to September. Some join the coastal migration of Common Green Darners.

Four-spotted Skimmer *Libellula quadrimaculata*

A wide ranging dragonfly found in the northern states, Canada, Eurasia and Africa. Larvae develop in acidic bogs, ponds and streams and can tolerate some salinity. Flies from May to August where it hunts in clearings that might be a long distance from water.

Slaty Skimmer *Libellula incesta*

Slaty Skimmers are a common sight perched on vegetation bordering ponds and lakes. Widespread in the east from Texas to Quebec, it flies form mid May through September in the Northeast. Larvae live in muddy bottom ponds and lakes and can tolerate poor water quality.

Chalk-fronted Corporal *Ladona julia*

This is the most common of our 3 Corporal species in the Northeast. It ranges across the northern states and southern Canada. You'll hardly ever find just one of this species, they're very gregarious. Dozens can be seen resting on the same log along wooded trails and logging roads. Flies from May to early August.

Autumn Meadowhawk *Sympetrum vicinum*

In the fall, Meadowhawks are by far the most common dragonflies you'll find. Formerly called Yellow-legged Meadowhawk after its pale legs. It's the latest flying of any of the dragons, going deep into November and in mild years into December. Occurs through most of North America.

White-faced Meadowhawk   *Sympetrum obtrusum*

Most of the Meadowhawks are difficult to tell apart, but the pure white face makes this one easy. It's rare in southern New England but common further north and ranging across the northern states and southern Canada. Adults fly from July through October and often perch on the ground or low vegetation.

Seaside Dragonlet   *Erythrodiplax berenice*

Unique among dragonflies being our only species that breeds in salt water marshes. They inhabit coastal salt marshes in the north, mangrove swamps in the south and saline lakes in the southwest. Often holds wings bent forward when perched on the marsh grasses. Flies from June to September in the north.

Elfin Skimmer   *Nannothemis bella*

It's easy to identify this dragonfly, our smallest North American species; Even most damselflies are larger that Elfin Skimmers. Found around bogs and seeps, adults fly in and out of vegetation very close to the ground. When perched, wings are often held forward. Flies throughout the Northeast from mid May into August.

Eastern Amberwing   *Perithemis tenera*

This tiny ode doesn't just look like a wasp, when it's perched horizontally on vegetation along shorelines and pulses its wings and abdomen in wasp like fashion. It occurs in most of the eastern U.S., except northern New England. A summer species with a flight period of June to early September.

Blue Dasher *Pachydiplax longipennis*

One of our most common summer species distinguished from all other similar northeastern species by the yellow lateral thoracic markings. Found along shorelines, fields and forest edges, wings are often held forward when perched. Occurs throughout the U.S. and southern Canada with adults flying mid May to September.

Eastern Pondhawk *Erythemis simplicicollis*

Voracious feeders, catching butterflies, dragonflies and even buzzing past my head to nab the deer flies circling me. A very common species widespread east of the Rockies, with adults flying in our area from May through September. One of the few skimmers that regularly rests on the ground as well as low vegetation.

Black Saddlebags *Tramea lacerata*

We're at the northern edge of this migratory species that arrives in summer, breeds, then the offspring head south in the fall. Flight is erratic, often hovering at eye level, and most roosting is high in trees on dead branches. Flight period in our area is mid June through September.

Dot-tailed Whiteface *Leucorrhinia intacta*

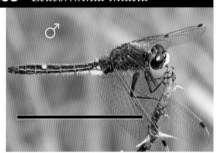

Mature males are easily distinguished by the white dot on the tail. The most widespread and southern flying of our Whitefaces, occurring across southern Canada and the northern half of the U.S. Flies in our area from May through July, preferring ponds and lakes with emergent vegetation.

Frosted Whiteface   *Leucorrhinia frigida*

This is one of the smallest Whitefaces, ranging from the Great Lakes through New England. Flight period is from mid May through August, with adults perching on low vegetation in and around muddy bottom ponds and lakes. Mature males are similar to the larger Red-waisted Whiteface, but lack the red dorsal color.

Crimson-ringed Whiteface   *Leucorrhinia glacialis*

The larger size, bright red thorax and solid black abdomen of mature males is distinctive among our northeast Whitefaces. An uncommon species with a wide range from coast to coast across southern Canada and the northern U.S. Flies from mid May through August near lakes and ponds in forested areas.

Halloween Pennant   *Celithemis eponina*

Our most common Pennant in the Northeast. Found in fields where it flies from one grass top perch to another with a bouncing butterfly like flight. A summertime species flying from mid June to early September, longer flight periods in the south. Widespread east of the Rockies.

Calico Pennant   *Celithemis elisa*

One of our most striking odes with males sporting bright red hearts down the abdomen and red wing patches and females with yellow markings. Found in open fields and along shorelines from May to September. Widespread east of the Rockies.

Damselflies
Suborder Zygoptera

Closely related to dragonflies are the delicate damselflies (suborder Zygoptera). Damsels differ in wing shape (all four wings the same size and shape), resting posture (wings held up over their back—except in the *Lestes* spreadwings), separate eyes, a functional ovipositor and weak, fluttery flight.

River Jewelwing *Calopteryx aequabilis*

River Jewelwings are real attention-getters with their long-winged bouncy butterfly like flight. The similar Sparkling Jewelwing has a smaller black section of the wing tip. Look for these beauties around rivers and streams with fast flowing water and riffles from mid May to mid August.

Ebony Jewelwing *Calopteryx maculata*

Unmistakable, this is the only ode in our area with all black wings. Like all species of Jewelwings, females have a white stigma on the wings. Prefers smaller rivers and streams in forested areas than the River Jewelwing. Common and widespread east of the Rockies, from May into September.

American Rubyspot *Hetaerina americana*

This beautiful broad-winged damselfly's (Calopterygidae) red wing patches are distinctive among northeast damsels, and as males age, the amount of red increases. Occurs throughout the country along rivers and streams. Distribution in our area is spotty with a late season flight in August and September.

Slender Spreadwing   *Lestes rectangularis*

The long slender abdomen, twice the length of the wings, makes this one of the spreadwing damsels (Lestidae). Females make a slice in emergent vegetation in ponds, lakes and marshes to lay eggs inside the stem. Common throughout the east with a flight period from May to October.

Aurora Damsel   *Chromagrion conditum*

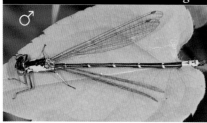

When perched this pond damsel (Coenagrionidae) often holds its wings open like a spreadwing damsel. The coloration is very bluet-like, but Aurora's lack shoulder stripes and eye spots. Common in our area and mostly found on the ground or low vegetation not far from water from May through July.

Eastern Red Damsel   *Amphiagrion saucium*

Despite the bright red coloration these locally common small damsels are hard to find. Most of their time is spent in low vegetation with short flights that hardly ever come out in the open. Occurs near seeps, spring fed bogs and streams throughout the east from May to July.

Violet (Variable) Dancer   *Argia fumipennis violacia*

Also called the Variable Dancer because subspecies from other parts of the country have dark wings and lack the violet body. It's the only violet damsel and the smallest *Argia* in the Northeast. Flight is near the ground along a variety of wetlands and shore lines from June through September. Occurs in most of the country.

Scarlet Bluet *Enallagma pictum*

Limited in range from NJ to southern Maine, this is the only red bluet in our area. Coastal plain and sandy bottom ponds in pine barrens are habitats where this uncommon species inhabits. Adults perch on lily pads and emergent vegetation close to the water. Flight period is mid June through August.

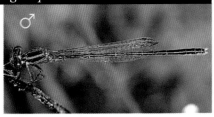

Familiar Bluet *Enallagma civile*

Familiar is an appropriate name for this most common bluet found across the U.S. and southern Canada. Males have the typical blue pattern common to many similar looking bluets. Found in ponds, lakes, slow rivers and even in brackish water. Flies from May to October.

Vesper Bluet
Enallagma vesperum

Orange Bluet
Enallagma signatum

Atlantic Bluet
Enallagma doubledayi

Marsh Bluet
Enallagma ebrium

New England Bluet
Enallagma laterale

Hagen's Bluet
Enallagma hageni

Eastern Forktail *Ischnura verticalis*

Eastern Forktails can be expected around virtually any pond, lake or any still or slow moving water east of the Rockies. Usually stays in dense vegetation and flies from May into November. Immature females are orange and turn blue/gray with maturity.

Sedge Sprite *Nehalennia irene*

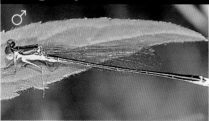

Common in vegetation around bogs, slow streams and grassy ponds, but often overlooked because of its small size. Of the 3 species of sprites in our area, this is the one most often found. Occurs across the northern U.S. and southern Canada from May through August.

Stoneflies
Order Plecoptera

Diversity
There are nine families and 537 species in the United States. Stoneflies are common in New England.

Appearance
Adults: Small to medium sized insects, usually dark-colored, although some, especially spring or summer emerging stoneflies, may be yellowish or greenish. They possess four thin membranous wings containing many veins. The wings are held flat over their backs when at rest, extending a little past the tip of their abdomens. The first pair is a little longer and more narrower than the broader somewhat shorter hind wings. At least a few winter stoneflies, like *Allocapnia*, have very shortened wings. Stoneflies possess moderately long antennae and chewing mouthparts, although in many species the mouthparts are reduced. Stoneflies also have a pair of cerci on the ends of their abdomens.

Nymphs: Nymphs are similar in form to adults except they lack wings. They possess small, inconspicuous gills on their thorax and two long cerci on the tips of their abdomens. They also have two pairs of tarsal claws.

Habitats
Stonefly nymphs are aquatic and are typically found under stones in clean, unpolluted, highly oxygenated water, particularly streams as well as along river and lake shores. Adult stoneflies are poor flyers and are generally found near water.

Large nymphs of the family Perlidae (Common Stoneflies) are beautifully patterned. This is *Acroneuria carolinensis*.

Life Cycle
Stoneflies develop using hemimetabolous metamorphosis, a type of simple metamorphosis. Many stoneflies are active during spring and

Adults of some species emerge in late winter. This is a *Taeniopteryx* species on snow.

summer, although there are a lot of species that are active during fall and winter (sometimes referred to as winter stoneflies).

When a male is looking for a female to mate with, it drums with its abdomen on a surface, such as a log or tree branch. This sends vibrations to which interested females can respond. The specific rhythms of these mating drums are specific to a particular species.

Once mated, females lay eggs on the water surface which sink to the bottom. The nymphs hatch and spend their entire lives in the water. When nymphs are fully developed, they crawl out of the water to emerge as adults. Many species complete their development within one year although there are others that may take several years.

Food
Winter stonefly nymphs generally feed on submerged plant matter and organic debris, while summer stonefly nymphs are usually predaceous on small aquatic organisms, such as midge larvae. Adult winter stoneflies generally feed on algae, lichens, pollen, and fungal hyphae and spores while summer stoneflies typically don't feed.

Water Quality Indicators
Because they prefer clean bodies of waters with a high level of oxygen, stoneflies are good indicators of water quality.

Don't confuse them with...
...mayfly nymphs. Stonefly nymphs are easily confused with mayfly nymphs. Mayfly nymphs, however, possess three caudal filaments, i.e. tails, have obvious gills on their abdomen, and have only one tarsal claw.

Adult stoneflies may be confused with mayflies, caddisflies, or alderflies, dobsonflies, and similar insects. However mayflies hold their triangular wings straight up over their back and possess very short antennae. Caddisflies have very long antennae, lack cerci on the abdomen, and possess hairy wings held tent-like over the body. Alderflies, dobsonflies, and similar insects lack cerci and hold their wings tent-like over their bodies.

stonefly nymph

Small Winter Stoneflies
Family Capniidae

With over 150 species in 10 genera, Capniidae is the largest family of
stoneflies in North America. The Northeast has 3 genera, **Allocapnia**
(most common), **Capnura** and **Paracapnia**. The adults are less than
10mm long, with some species only 4 to 5mm long. From February to
early April they can be found walking on the snow along banks of clear
running rivers and streams. They can be numerous on sunny days over
20 degrees F. They are flightless, and walk around looking for algae to
eat. Nymphs live under rocks and in gravel bottoms of clear streams.

Small Winter Stonefly *Allocapnia pygmaea*

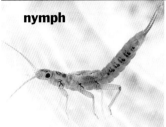

nymph

Green Stoneflies
Family Chloroperlidae

Green Stoneflies are most often green or yellow with a few species
brownish. There are 12 genera of Chloroperlidae in North America,
with over 80 species. In the Northeast we have 5 genera: **Alloperla**,
Haploperla, **Suwallia**, **Sweltsa** and **Utaperla**. Nymphs live in clean,
rocky streams and rivers. The adults are usually found on leaves of trees
and bushes along streams from May to September.

Green Stonefly *Haploperla brevis*

One of the 81 species of Green
Stoneflies, this is our only small
all green stonefly in the
Northeast. Others have markings on their pronotum. It can
be found on tree leaves along
fast moving rocky rivers, with
adults occurring in May and
June.

Rolled-winged Stoneflies
Family Leuctridae

Adults have a distinctive look, with their wings wrapping around their body, giving them a cylindrical shape. Leuctrids are small stoneflies (6 to 10mm). There are 52 species in 8 genera in North America, with only 2 genera in the Northeast. *Leuctra* is the most common genus in our area with 9 to 10 species. The adults of some species start emerging in April, while other species of Leuctrids are out as late as July. The nymphs are under rocks or beneath the substrate of streams and rivers.

Rolled-winged Stonefly *Leuctra laura*

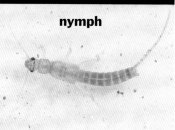

nymph

Spring Stoneflies
Family Nemouridae

These small stoneflies are also called forestflies, and they start emerging from clean cold streams in April. In northern areas, and at higher elevations, adults can be found into July. Nemourids have an X-pattern near the ends of the wings. There are 64 species in 13 genera found in North America, with 8 genera present in the Northeast.

Spring Stonefly *Prostoia completa*

nymph

Common Stoneflies
Family Perlidae

Common Stoneflies tend to be large, ranging in size from 10 to 40mm as adults. Nymphs are found under rocks in rivers, and feed on small aquatic insect larvae of mayflies, caddisflies and midges. The gills of the nymphs are located on their abdomen near each leg. There are 74 species in 14 genera in North America, with 7 genera in the Northeast. Adults are present from April to September, and can have a mass emergence. Early afternoon, immediately following a rainstorm, I witnessed one of these emergences in early June; Hundreds of Common Stones could be seen among the bushes next to the river and flying over it.

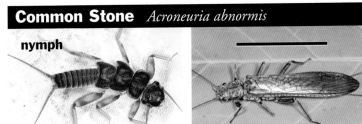

Common Stone *Acroneuria abnormis*

nymph

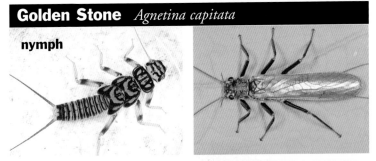

Golden Stone *Agnetina capitata*

nymph

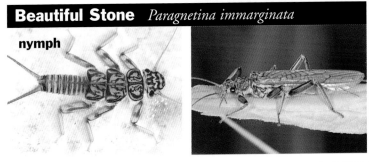

Beautiful Stone *Paragnetina immarginata*

nymph

Perlodid Stoneflies (Springflies) Family Perlodidae

Perlodids are the second largest family of stoneflies in North America, with over 120 species in 30 genera. We have 8 genera in the Northeast, with **Isoperla** being the most common. Adults emerge from May to July, depending on the species. Most range in size from 10-15mm, with a few getting up to 25mm. Subfamily Isoperlinae stoneflies are know as Stripetails, while subfamily Perlodinae are called Springflies.

Perlodid Stonefly *Isoperla similis*

nymph

Giant Stoneflies Family Pteronarcyidae

Giant Stoneflies really are giants, reaching nearly 60mm in size, or almost 2 inches. Nymphs inhabit mid to large rivers and streams where they feed on decaying plant matter. It takes 2 to 3 years for them to emerge as an adult in the spring. Like most other stonefies, the adults do not feed. The nymphs defend themselves from fish by releasing a foul smelling fluid. There are 10 species of Pteronarcyidae in North America, with 4 species in the Northeast.

American Salmonfly *Pteronarcys dorsata*

The American Salmonfly is the most common species in New England. Newly emerged adults are pinkish, thus the name salmonfly. Larvae feed on submerged plant material and take 2 to 3 years to mature into a non-feeding adult. North-central and eastern U.S. and southern Canada. March to June.

Winter Stoneflies
Family Taeniopterygidae

The adults of these medium-sized stoneflies (10-15mm) can be observed walking on the snow, along with Capniidae. They have a long emergence period starting in February and ending in June. Adults are found on rocks, bridges and the sides of buildings. The nymphs inhabit cold water rivers, and can tolerate water quality unsuitable to other stoneflies.

Species of the Winter Stoneflies are found in a variety of river habitats ranging in size, flow and elevation. There's 34 species in 6 genera in North America, with 5 genera present in the Northeast. Only the western genus *Doddsia* isn't found here.

Smoky Willowfly *Bolotoperla rossi*

Nymph Habitat: Fast moving streams as well as slow moving rivers.

Atlantic Willowfly *Taenionema atlanticum*

Nymph Habitat: Prefers higher elevation cold running streams

Eastern Willowfly *Taeniopteryx burksi*

Nymph Habitat: Larger slow-moving rivers.

Grasshoppers, Katydids & Crickets
Order Orthoptera

Diversity
There are 16 families and 1145 species in the United States. Grasshoppers, katydids, and crickets are very common in New England and New York.

Appearance
Adults: Generally medium to large often stout-bodied insects. They possess four wings which they keep folded like a fan behind their backs when at rest. The first pair is leathery, i.e. somewhat thickened, while the second pair is thin, pleated and folded or rolled beneath front pair. Most species possess wings that are as long as the body or longer, although a few species have short wings and some lack wings altogether. Grasshoppers, katydids, and crickets possess chewing mouthparts and large back legs for jumping. This insect group possesses either short or long antennae. Females often have conspicuous ovipositors on the tips of their abdomens (which are often mistaken for stingers).

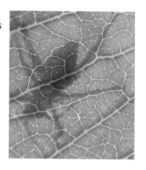

Nymphs: Immature nymphs are similar in form to adults but are smaller and lack fully developed wings or sexual structures, i.e. ovipositors (for females) or cerci (for males). Nymphs sometimes are a different color from the adults.

Habitats
Grasshoppers, katydids, and crickets are found in most types of terrestrial environments, essentially anywhere low growing plants are found such as prairies, fields, meadows, and areas adjacent to wooded sites. Many orthopteran species are found on the ground or a short distance above it on herbaceous plants or low growing shrubs. Other species are associated with trees.

Life Cycle
Grasshoppers, katydids, and crickets develop using paurometabolous metamorphosis, a type of simple metamorphosis. Adult females usually lay eggs at the end of summer or fall. Eggs hatch in spring and nymphs develop during spring and summer before maturing into adults. It usually takes one year to complete their life cycle.

Food

Many orthopterans are plant feeders. Some species are omnivorous, i.e. feeding on both plants and animal matter while others are scavengers on dead or decaying organic material. Some species are even predaceous on insects and other arthropods.

Sound Production

Many orthopterans are capable of producing sound. This is typically accomplished by rubbing specialized structures on two body parts together, a process called stridulation. There are different reasons for grasshoppers, katydids and crickets to make sound. Often males sing to attract females for mating. In other cases, they may signal distress when they are threatened or aggression when a male invades another's territory. Each orthopteran has a song specific to its species. The speed of these songs are dependent on the temperature; the number of beats per second will become slower or faster according to how cool or warm it is.

Don't confuse them with...

...true bugs. While some true bugs have somewhat large back legs and may resemble orthopterans, they have piercing-sucking mouthparts and wings that are folded flat and crosswise over their abdomen.

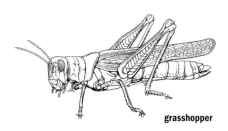

grasshopper

Grasshoppers
Family Acrididae

Appearance

Grasshoppers range in size from ½ to 3 inches long insects and are brownish, grayish, or greenish. They possess short, somewhat thicker antennae, considerably shorter than their body length. Their wings resemble grass blades which are held vertically along the length of the abdomen. They hear with a tympanum which is found on the first segment of the abdomen. Females possess short ovipositors.

Biology

Grasshoppers are active during the day. They are strictly plant feeders usually eating a variety of different species. A grasshopper lays it eggs in the soil by inserting its ovipositor and abdomen into the ground where it deposits a cluster of eggs. Grasshoppers are not as musical as other orthopterans. When they produce sound, they do so by rubbing peg-like structures on their back legs against their forewing producing a low buzzing song or by making a snapping sound with their wings as they fly (called crepitation).

Sulphur-winged Grasshopper *Arphia sulphurea*

A drab grasshopper until it flies, when it flashes bright yellow wings edged in black. Overwinter as nymphs, mature into adults in May and can be observed into July. Fields, roadsides and occasionally grassy areas. Occur all over the eastern half of the country, except southern Florida and northern Maine.

Wingless Mtn. Grasshopper *Booneacris glacialis*

I've found these flightless grasshoppers at forest edges in the mountains of New England. They occur throughout the Northeast, as far south as the Carolinas, and out to the Midwest. July to early September is a good time to look on snowmobile and ski trails for these grasshoppers.

Sprinkled Broad-winged Grasshopper
Chloealtis conspersa

This is the only grasshopper in our area with a black patch on the side of its pronotum. These small grasshoppers can be found from northern New England to the Rockies and south to Oklahoma from July to September. They prefer dry and brushy grass fields.

Marsh Meadow Grasshopper *Chorthippus curtipennis*

These slant-faced grasshoppers are very common throughout our area. They can be found in late summer and fall within damp fields and tall grasses. The wings can be the length of the abdomen or shorter. Females as well as males can be heard stridulating.

Northern Green-striped Grasshopper
Chortophaga viridifasciata

This is the first grasshopper I usually see in spring. Overwintering as nymphs gives them a head start on other species. But by mid summer they're gone. The common color forms are brown and green, or brown wings with a green body and legs. Occasionally I'll find a pink one, usually a nymph. Females noticeably larger than males. Common to abundant.

Short-winged Green Grasshopper
Dichromorpha viridis

Varies from all brown to all green, or a combination. Wings are usually short, but a few are long-winged. Similar to Elegant Grasshopper, but can be distinguished by its two creases in the pronotum (shield behind the head). Mid summer through fall. It can be the most abundant grasshopper in a grassy field.

Carolina Grasshopper *Dissosteira carolina*

Carolina Grasshoppers are active fliers. They make a distinctive crackling noise when they take flight. Their coloration varies from gray to brown, and it has black wings with a yellowish outer edge. These band-winged grasshoppers are very common in sandy areas throughout North America. In our area they can be found June through September, and they are the most common large flying grasshopper.

The hovering, fluttering courtship flight of the Carolina Locust is often seen during late summer.

Two-striped Grasshopper *Melanoplus bivittatus*

With its large size and distinct pair of yellow stripes running from the head to the wingtips, this is one of the easier grasshoppers to identify. But note that there are color variations. Moist weedy areas is its preferred habitat. They can also be found in farm fields, where they may be a pest. It's a common species found throughout most of North America, and can be observed in our area from June into late fall.

Differential Grasshopper *Melanoplus differentialis*

The Differential Grasshopper is similar in size and overall appearance to the Two-striped Grasshopper but lacks the yellow stripes seen in the former, and its hind legs have a black and yellow herringbone pattern. They're found throughout most of North America, although they're absent from northern New England. You can find them in late summer through the fall. Weedy agricultural fields are what these grasshoppers like, and are crop pests in many areas.

Red-leg Grasshopper *Melanoplus femurrubrum*

Be careful...this grasshopper is just one of several species that has red on its hind tibia. They prefer lush vegetation, and are absent from most dry areas. Adults of this hardy species have a long season beginning in June, and I have seen them as late as November, even after a light frost. Abundant throughout most of North America.

Grizzled spur-throated Grasshopper
Melanoplus punctulatus

Pinetree Spur-throated Grasshopper is another name for this species because it is often observed resting on the trunk of a pine or tamarack where its cryptic pattern blends in with the bark. Adults may be seen July to October and are uncommon.

Pasture Grasshopper   *Orphulella speciosa*

As the name implies, this slant-faced grasshopper's preferred habitat is within fields containing short to medium height grasses in sandy soil. They appear in mid summer, and by the fall the population can increase dramatically. Found in most of North America east of the Rockies, except Florida.

Spotted-winged Grasshopper   *Orphulella pelidna*

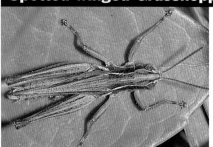

Very similar in appearance and occurrence to the Pasture Grasshopper; but the Spotted-winged has two creases on top of the pronotum, whereas the Pasture has only one. Congregate in small numbers compared to the Pasture. Most of North America, although not documented in Maine. Found in a variety of sunny habitats.

Longhorn Band-winged Grasshopper
Psinidia fenestralis

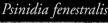
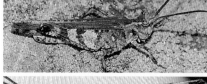

These grasshoppers occur along dirt roads and exposed sandy areas with patches of grass. When disturbed, they fly a short distance and land on the sand, where they blend in almost perfectly. They can be found June to October in the eastern United States, except northern Maine.

Rusty Bird Grasshopper   *Schistocerca rubiginosa*

This large grasshopper's range is in the southeastern United States and its northern limits of Massachusetts. They're a summer to fall species, and rather uncommon in the Northeast. They can be found near woods, especially in damp areas.

Northern Marbled Grasshopper *Spharagemon marmorata*

It likes sandy habitats; more commonly found near the coast and lakes. Late summer to early fall. In flight they're noisy, and show a small orange patch at the base of the wing, surrounded by a broad dark brown band. Great Lakes to New England, and south to Virginia; absent from northern Maine and western New York.

Graceful Sedge Grasshopper *Stethophyma gracile*

Not surprisingly found in wet areas with sedges and grasses, where the males can be heard singing loudly. Ranges across northern North America, throughout the Northeast, except southern New York. Adults found from July to September, and are more common in the northern parts of their range.

Seaside Grasshopper *Trimerotropis maritima*

"Seaside" is an appropriate adjective for this species. It inhabits beaches, dirt roads, lake edges and other sandy areas. When approached, they usually don't move; they count on their sandy color to camouflage and protect them. Found mid summer to October in the eastern half of the United States, except northern Maine.

Crackling Forest Grasshopper *Trimerotropis verruculata*

Similar to the Seaside Grasshopper, but darker. Prefer rocky habitats rather than sandy areas. When in flight, it makes a loud crackling sound, hence the common name. They can be found in the Northeast June to September. They also occur through southern Canada and the western United States.

Pygmy Grasshoppers (Grouse Locusts) Family Tetrigidae

Appearance

The best way to recognize a pygmy grasshopper is by its pronotum which extends past the abdomen, covering the wings and then tapering at the tip. Beware of identifying pygmy grasshoppers by color alone; coloration is highly variable—even between individuals of the same species. They are relatively small, measuring between ½ to ¾ inch long. They have short antennae.

Biology

This is one of the few group of grasshoppers that overwinters as adults. You can see pygmy grasshoppers during spring and early summer. Found along the shores of ponds and streams where there is wet soil.

Awl-shaped Pygmy Grasshopper *Tetrix subulata*

Also know as the Slender Groundhopper, its markings are highly variable, from plain gray or brown, to a variety of white patterns. Found in damp sandy areas around lakes, marshes and woodland trails. Adults appear early in spring, and can be found every month until hard frost. Northeast U.S. to the west coast and south to Mexico.

Black-sided Pygmy Grasshopper *Tettigidea lateralis*

Males easily identified by small squat body and white face and thorax. Females are inconspicuous grayish brown. Adults in spring and again in late summer to fall. Overwinter as adults. Found in a variety of habitats, from sand dunes to forests. Range includes eastern half of North America, through Arizona and into Mexico.

Pygmy Mole Crickets
Family Tridactylidae

Closely resembling the larger Mole Crickets, Pygmy Mole Crickets are not actually crickets, but rather in the same suborder as grasshoppers (Caelifera). Sandy riverbanks, pond and bog margins are where these nocturnal insects live (spend the day in sand burrows). They're good swimmers and fast fliers, and will quickly burrow into the sand to elude capture.

Larger Pygmy Mole Cricket *Neotridactylus apicialis*

Unlike other grasshoppers, its front legs are designed for digging. Found in thinly vegetated sandy areas close to water, where it lives in burrows and feeds on algae. Ranges as far north as Massachusetts, and northern New York. Also known as the Larger Sand Cricket.

Camel Crickets
Family Rhaphidophoridae

Appearance
Brownish, humpbacked insects that range from $1/3$ to $1\frac{1}{3}$ inches in length. Very long, hair-like antennae, about twice the length of their bodies, and conspicuously spiny tibiae. Camel crickets lack wings and females have an elongate ovipositor. Sometimes called cave crickets.

Biology
Active at night in dark, moist places (under logs, stones, in animal burrows, hollow trees, caves). Feed primarily on weakened or dead insects, occasionally feed on plant material. Unlike other orthopterans, they lack any stridulating organs to produce sound.

Camel Cricket *Ceuthophilus species*

Ceuthophilus is the largest genus of Camel Crickets, with 89 described species. It's the most common genus of Camel Crickets in the Northeast. They can be found in damp and dark habitats including basements, caves and under rocks and logs.

Katydids
Family Tettigoniidae

Appearance

Katydids are usually green insects possessing very long, hair-like, antennae that are at least as long as their bodies and often longer. Wings are long and may be narrow or broad and leaf-like and are held tent-like over their bodies. The left hand wing usually lays over the right side wing. Katydids have long, stilt-like hind legs and possess a tympanum, i.e. an ear, in the tibia of their front legs (see photo right). Katydids also have flattened sword-like or blade-like ovipositors.

Note the tympanum on the foreleg; it is the organ which enables katydids to hear.

Biology

Look for katydids in shrubs and trees. Many are plant feeders, although some are omnivorous and a few prey on insects and other invertebrates. Most katydids insert their eggs into leaves or twigs. Katydids are prodigious song makers. Males make sound by rubbing structures on their forewings together which produce a generally raspy song. Listen for them at night when they are active.

Look for katydids along brushy roadsides or along trails in late summer. Key in on their songs.

Short-winged Meadow Katydid *Conocephalus brevipennis*

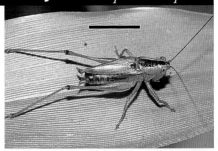

A small katydid that likes moist meadows and marshes, adults occurring from August to October. It can be found throughout our area, and the eastern half of the country. It's not the only short-winged katydid, so a check of the male cerci is helpful in identifying this species.

Slender Meadow Katydid *Conocephalus fasciatus*

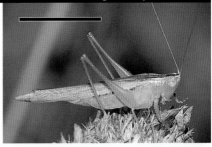

Adults appear in July, earlier than other meadow katydids, and last until October. Its song is a combination of buzzing and clicking noises. This is a small katydid that can be found in open grassy areas. It's found east of the Rockies in the U.S. and southern Canada, and is common all through its range.

Prairie Meadow Katydid *Conocephalus saltans*

A widespread species covering most of the country east of the Rockies, but absent from the northern parts of the Northeast. This small katydid is less common and later than most other meadow katydids, and can be found on low vegetation.

Oblong-winged Katydid *Amblycorypha oblongifolia*

A common species found in the eastern half of the country, except Florida and northernmost Maine. Found in shrubs, and moist weedy patches at the margins of deciduous forests. Females lay eggs in the ground, and it can take up to two years for them to hatch. Adults are active from July to September.

Fork-tailed Bush Katydid *Scudderia furcata*

Look for this large katydid in damp weedy fields and trees from August to October. Common across the U.S. and southern Canada. The nymphs are colorful with long banded antennae. They call day and night with 3 or 4 raspy chirps usually from high perches.

Protean Shieldback *Atlanticus testaceus*

A ground dwelling katydid found in forest openings and borders. In our region, they are only present from coastal New York to eastern Massachusetts. Not commonly seen, the adults start showing up in late spring, and linger into fall.

Roesel's Katydid *Metrioptera roeselii*

An introduced species from Europe that was first found in Montreal in 1953, and has been expanding its range ever since. Easily found in grassy fields all over New England, and recently as far west as Iowa. Adults are out in June, and linger into September.

Common True Katydid *Pterophylla camellifolia*

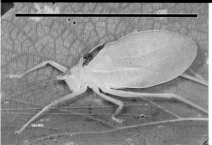

A robust katydid that's usually high up in trees. Unlike other katydids, they don't fly, but will glide to a lower branch and run rather than hop. Only males give the classic *"katy-did"* call, females give a short reply. The noise of many calling at once can be extremely loud. July to October. Absent from northern New York, and north of Massachusetts.

Crickets
Family Gryllidae

Appearance

Crickets possess very long, hair-like antennae that are at least as long as their bodies. Their wings are held flat over their abdomens. Crickets have three tarsal segments in their legs and have needle-like ovipositors. Like katydids, crickets possess a tympanum on each of their front legs.

Biology

Common in fields, roadside ditches and other open areas where they are found on the ground or on low vegetation. Tree crickets be found in trees and shrubs. They are often omnivorous, feeding on both animal and plant matter, while some are strictly plant feeders and a few are just predaceous. Crickets lay their eggs in the soil or in plants. Many crickets are quite musical producing songs, like katydids, by rubbing their front wings together. Unlike katydids, the right hand wing of a cricket lays over the left one.

Fall Field Cricket · *Gryllus pennsylvanicus*

Late summer and fall are when mature Fall Field Crickets are around. They can be found in good numbers under rocks, logs and boards in grassy fields. Virtually identical to Spring Field Crickets, but adults of Fall Field Cricket are only found in the fall. Found throughout the Northeast, and most of North America.

Carolina Ground Cricket · *Eunemobius carolinus*

Look for this cricket moving around in grassy fields and lawns. They're out in late summer and fall throughout the Northeast, and all across the central part of North America. Their song is a constant set of short buzzy calls.

Two-spotted Tree Cricket *Neoxabea bipunctata*

You can find these crickets from June to October usually high up in trees or bushes and occasionally on low vegetation. I've also commonly seen them at lights. They occur throughout our area, and most of the eastern United States.

Snowy Tree Cricket *Oecanthus fultoni*

♂

You could call them "thermometer crickets." As the temperature rises, the cricket's steady chirp accelerates. One can estimate the temperature in Fahrenheit by counting the number of chirps in 13 seconds and adding 40. July to September in most vegetation, but rarely grass. Throughout most of the country, but absent from northern Maine.

Blackhorned Tree Cricket *Oecanthus nigricornis*

♀

This tree cricket isn't found up in trees, but rather on low branches and vegetation. Their diet consists of aphids and other small plant feeding insects. Eggs are laid in the soft center of plant stems. They mature by August and can be found into October. Northeast quarter of the country, and through our area.

Narrow-winged Tree Cricket *Oecanthus niveus*

Closely related to the Snowy Tree Cricket, sharing many of the same characteristics, but its call is a trill instead of a series of chirps. Their range is in the eastern half of the country, but absent from northern New York and northern New England. Adults can be found from August to October.

Pine Tree Cricket   *Oecanthus pini*

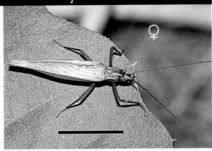

Like its name implies, the Pine Tree Cricket is found exclusively on coniferous trees and shrubs, especially White Pine. Its brown head, pronotum and legs make this an easily recognizable species. Absent from the northernmost parts of our region. Closely related to the Black-horned Tree Cricket.

Say's Trig   *Anaxipha exigua*

Also called Say's Bush Cricket, this species can be found in most of eastern half of the country. Adults active August to October. Most are short winged, but I've found a few females with extremely long wings. Most commonly found on shrubs and low tree branches. Attracted to lights.

Red-headed Bush Cricket   *Phyllopalpus pulchellus*

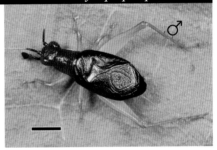

A colorful southern species that has recently extended its range as far north as Massachusetts. It's said to inhabit ground vegetation about a yard from the ground, however I have also found them close to the ground on clover, and at eye level in a fruit tree. The best time to find them is August and September. Also called the Handsome Trig.

Walkingsticks
Order Phasmida

Diversity

There are four families and 41 species in the United States. Only two species of the common walkingsticks (family Heteronemiidae) are found in New England and New York.

Appearance

Adults: Walkingsticks are large twig-like insects with very long, slender brownish or greenish bodies. They have long antennae and chewing mouthparts that point forward. These slow moving insects lack wings. Males are usually smaller and more slender compared to females.

Nymphs: The immature nymphs are very similar to adults only smaller.

Habitats

They are found in wooded areas, associated with hardwood trees and shrubs. They are normally not found in urban landscapes.

Life Cycle

Walkingsticks develop using paurometabolous metamorphosis, a type of simple metamorphosis. Adult females typically drop their eggs from trees, letting them fall down to the forest floor. When nymphs hatch, they climb up shrubs and small trees to feed. Once they mature into adults, they typically move into larger trees.

Food

Both adults and nymphs feed on the leaves of a variety of hardwood trees and shrubs. Sometimes their feeding can severely defoliate plants.

Protection From Enemies

Walkingsticks protect themselves by using mimicry. They are hard to see, especially when they hold still, because of their resemblance to sticks and twigs. They will also sway to mimic a twig in the wind. This helps protect them from natural enemies, like birds. Interestingly, walkingsticks are one of the few insects that can regenerate lost legs, although this ability is restricted to immature nymphs.

Don't confuse them with...

...stilt bugs. Stilt bugs are slender and twig-like but have piercing-sucking mouthparts. They are also much smaller than walkingsticks. Otherwise walkingsticks are distinctive and you are unlikely to confuse them with other insects.

Northern Walkingstick *Diapheromera femorata*

Walkingsticks in New England? Also called the Common Stick Insect, this is the most common and widespread walkingstick in North America. They occur from Quebec to Florida, and into the southwest. They're usually high up in the trees, and are not commonly seen.

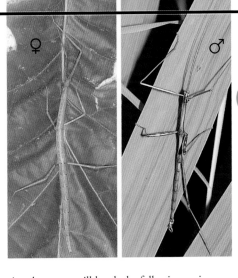

It feeds on a variety of hardwood leaves, but oak, cherry and linden are their favorites. Adults mature in late summer, and in the fall, I've seen females down low on tree trunks, sunning themselves. Fall is when eggs are laid in leaf litter, and some may hatch in the spring, but most will hatch the following spring. With over 40 species of walkingsticks in North America, only two species are found in the Northeast. The Slender-bodied Walkingstick *(Manomera blatchleyi)* occurs in parts of New York and Connecticut.

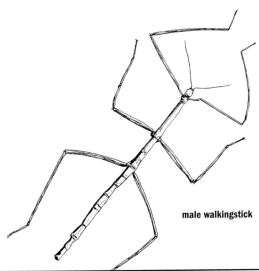

male walkingstick

Earwigs
Order Dermaptera

Diversity
There are six families and 22 species in the United States. Earwigs are uncommon in New England and New York.

Appearance
Adults: Earwigs are medium-sized, brownish to blackish beetle-like insects with somewhat flattened bodies. They have medium length antennae and chewing mouthparts. Their first pair of wings are typically leathery and very short with a pair of rounded membranous wings hidden underneath.

They are distinctive because they possess a pair of strong pinchers (cerci) on the tip of their abdomen. You can distinguish between the sexes as males have stout, strongly curved cerci that are widely separated at the base while females possess slender, straight pinchers that are close together. Earwigs use these cerci to protect themselves and to grab and hold prey. You can also distinguish between males and females as males possess ten abdominal segments while female only have eight.

Nymphs: Nymphs are similar to adults except they are smaller. They will also lack wing pads when they first hatch. All immature earwigs have female-like, slender straight cerci. Young earwigs are generally lighter in color than adults.

Habitats
Earwigs are nocturnal and hide during the day in cracks and crevices as well as under objects and debris, such as leaves, mulch, stones, bark, and logs. Earwigs are also commonly found on plants, especially flower blossoms.

Life Cycle
Earwigs develop using paurometabolous metamorphosis, a type of simple metamorphosis. Eggs are typically laid in small constructed nests in the soil. Female earwigs are very maternal, an unusual trait for insects. They guard and protect their eggs and newly hatched young.

Food
Earwigs are generally scavengers feeding on damaged and decaying plant matter as well as weakened or dead insects and other small organisms. Some earwigs also feed on healthy plant material.

Protecting Themselves

There is an old story that claims that earwigs climb into people's ear while they are sleeping. This of course is untrue! However, they will try to pinch with their cerci. Fortunately most earwigs are not capable of inflicting anything painful. Some earwigs can also secrete a foul-smelling liquid from their abdomen to ward off enemies.

Don't confuse them with...

...beetles with short wings, especially rove beetles. These odd true beetles could be confused with earwigs. However, beetles lack strong pinchers on the abdomen.

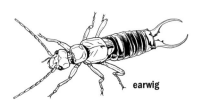

earwig

earwig attempting to pinch with cerci

European Earwig *Forficula auricularia*

In the early 1900s, European Earwigs were introduced into Rhode Island, and quickly spread across the country. Predatory on aphids and other small insects, they can be a garden pest, feeding on plants. Love cool, damp places, and can be a nuisance in basements. Female protects the nest until her nymphs are able to live on their own.

Maritime Earwig *Anisolabis maritime*

These large wingless earwigs occur above high tide lines along coastlines all around the country. During the day they hide under logs and weeds within the wrack line. At night they scavenge for eggs and dead insects, but will also catch sand fleas. The female makes a nest chamber in the sand under driftwood, where she feeds the young.

Cockroaches
Order Blattaria

Diversity
There are four families and 50 species in the United States.

Appearance
Adults: Small to large-sized insects with a flattened, oval shaped body, long antennae (one-half the length of the body or longer) and chewing

wood cockroach

mouthparts. When looking at a cockroach from above, its head is hidden from view by a plate-like structure called the pronotum. The strong legs are covered with spines. Cockroaches found outdoors in New England possess four wings that are longer than the abdomen. The first pair is leathery while the second pair is more membranous. Female wood cockroaches have short wings, exposing part of the abdomen.

Habitats
Cockroaches that live outdoors in New England are typically found in wooded sites; usually in rotting logs or under loose bark.

Life Cycle
Cockroaches develop using simple metamorphosis. Eggs are produced inside a case, called an ootheca where generally between 30 to 50 eggs are found. These oothecae are deposited into protected sites where they wait until the eggs hatch. Some species hang on to the oothecae until just before they eggs are ready to hatch while in other species the eggs hatch while the oothecae are held internally in the females and the nymphs are born live (viviparous).

Food
Cockroaches that live outdoors in New England and New York feed primarily on various types of decaying organic matter. Cockroaches found indoors feed broadly on essentially all types of human food products.

Don't confuse them with...
...beetles, true bugs or earwigs. The first pair of wings of beetles are hardened and their antennae are generally not long. True bugs have hemielytrous wings, i.e. part leathery and part membranous as well piercing-sucking mouthparts. Earwigs have short wings, medium length antennae and possess pincher-like cerci on the tip of their abdomens.

Virginia Wood Cockroach *Parcoblatta virginica*

All 12 species of *Parcoblatta* found in North America are native. Occasionally males will fly to lights at night, but the females are flightless. Nocturnal, but can easily be found during the day under rocks, logs and loose bark. Very similar but often darker than the Pennsylvania Wood Cockroach, the other *Parcoblatta* in the Northeast.

Oriental Cockroach *Blatta orientalis*

Originally native to Asia, these large flightless cockroaches are found nearly worldwide. They're also called "waterbugs," because they are often found in damp places, basements, sewers and compost piles. Oriental Cockroaches are house pests, but are not usually found on upper floors, where it is likely to be too dry for them.

Dusky Cockroach *Ectobius lapponicus*

Native to Europe, Dusky Cockroaches were first discovered on our continent in 1985 in Maryland. They have since spread through the Northeast, and into Ontario. They are not indoor pests, living outdoors in fields and forest. I've found these to be common in tall grass fields from May to August.

Spotted Mediterranean Cockroach *Ectobius pallidus*

Another introduced European cockroach ("Tawny Cockroach" in Europe). First discovered in the United States in 1948 on Cape Cod. Since then it has spread through the Northeast, and into Michigan and Ontario. Both males and females are winged and can fly. May through October in damp woodlands and meadows. Not considered a pest.

Mantids
Order Mantodea

Mantids are ambush predators that will eat anything they can catch with their raptorial front legs, even other mantids. Some large species of mantids have even been known to capture and eat hummingbirds. 20 species occur north of Mexico, but only 2 species are well established in the Northeast.

Females are larger than males, and will occasionally eat a male trying to mate, or even after mating. In the fall frothy egg cases that later harden; called oothecae are laid on branches, buildings, rocks or other solid surfaces. The ootheca overwinters, and in the spring up to 100 baby mantids emerge. Cannibalism is common among the hatchlings if other food isn't found. Six to nine molts occur before the mantids are fully mature.

European Mantis *Mantis religiosa*

Introduced from Europe in 1899 by gardeners, this is the common mantid of the Northeast. Its effectiveness as a pest control agent is very limited, because of cannibalism and its generalist feeding choices. A white spot ringed in black on the inside of the front femur is distinctive to the European Mantis, also called the Praying Mantis. Both  green and brown forms are common. Until recent years they were only in the Northeast, but are now being reported from most of North America.

Chinese Mantid *Tenodera aridifolia*

Native to China, these mantids were introduced to the United States in 1896 for pest control. Their effectiveness is questionable since they eat both harmful and beneficial insects, but oothecae (egg cases) are still introduced by farmers. Their range has expanded from throughout the east to include California. Chinese Mantids are much larger than the European Mantis, and also have green and brown forms. Look near flowers for these mantids, especially late summer when females need plenty of food for egg development.

body length

True Bugs, Cicadas, Aphids, etc. Order Hemiptera

Diversity
There are 90 families and 11,298 species in North America. True bugs are very common in New England and New York.

Appearance
Adults: Form, size and color are quite variable and diverse. They possess piercing-sucking mouthparts which can be very short and beak-like or long and slender. They have short to moderate length slender antennae. They usually possess four wings. The first pair of wings can be hemelytrous, i.e. partly leathery and part membranous (the true bugs) or uniformly thickened or membranous, (cicadas, hoppers, aphids and others). The second pair of wings is membranous. Some species lack wings (Some populations and even some individual adults can have the wings reduced or absent.). Many hemipterans have sawlike or piercing ovipositors for laying eggs in plant tissue or bark.

Nymphs: Similar in form to adults except they are smaller and lack wings. Wings pads are present in older nymphs. It is common for the nymphs to be different colors from adults. True bugs use simple metamorphosis to develop.

Habitats
Most hemipterans are terrestrial, inhabiting a wide variety of different habitats. They are often found associated with plants. Some are aquatic living in or on the surface of water or are semiaquatic living on shores.

Life Cycle
The hemipterans develop using paurometabolous metamorphosis, a type of simple metamorphosis. The life cycle varies with the particular insect. Some have complex life cycles requiring multiple plant hosts. Some hemipterans overwinter as adults and lay eggs in the spring while others overwinter as eggs.

Food
Most are plant feeders, although a few are predacious, a few omnivorous, and a few are even parasitic on the blood of animals or birds.

Don't confuse them with...

...beetles. The first pair of wings of beetles are modified into a hard shell known as elytra. Beetles also have mandibles and chewing mouthparts. Some hemipterans can be confused with grasshoppers, crickets, or katydids. However, they have chewing mouthparts and large back legs. Hemipterans either fold their wings roof-like over their abdomens or cross them flat on their backs.

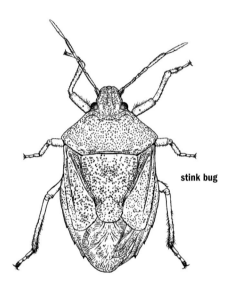

stink bug

Water Scorpions
Family Nepidae

Appearance

Most are slender brownish walkingstick-like insects ranging up to 1½ inches long with an elongate prothorax. All water scorpions have modified front legs, called raptorial legs, that allow them to capture and hold their prey. They possess a pair of long breathing tubes, as long as

Modified front legs are used to capture prey.

their body, protruding from the tips of their abdomen. Water scorpions have very short antennae which are rarely noticed.

Biology

Water scorpions are aquatic, living in ponds and along the shores of lakes, amongst aquatic weeds. They obtain oxygen at the water surface using a pair of long breathing tubes. Water scorpions can store air under their wings if they wish to swim under the surface. They are not good swimmers and spend much of their time clinging to submerged plants. They swim by rowing with their middle and back legs, stroking them alternatively, although if they wish to swim more quickly, they use these legs in unison. They are predacious, feeding on insects and other aquatic invertebrate animals. If threatened, water scorpions will play dead. Water scorpions overwinter as adults and typically insert eggs into aquatic plants in the spring. Adults are active throughout spring and most of the summer.

Brown Water Scorpion *Ranatra fusca*

Out of the 10 species of *Ranatra*, *R. fusca* is the most widespread and common. They occur across the northern U.S. and southern Canada, from spring until fall. Even though it's a large insect—up to 1¾ inches—they often go unnoticed. They sit motionless on submerged vegetation, ambushing aquatic insects that pass by.

Giant Water Bugs
Family Belostomatidae

Appearance
These large, one to two and a half inch, brown insects are broadly oval and somewhat flattened. Their front legs are raptorial, i.e. they are modified for grabbing prey. Their hind legs are broad and oar-like. They swim with their middle and hind legs, using them alternately but will use them together when swimming more quickly.

Biology
Common in ponds and lakes where they breathe using a pair of small retractable

Some species deposit their eggs on the back of the male. This is *Belostoma testaceum*

flap-like organs on the tip of their abdomen. They are predators, feeding on other insects, tadpoles, snails and even small fish. Eggs are generally laid on stones, logs, plants and other inanimate objects. It is common for giant water bugs to leave the water and fly to lights and because of this, they are sometimes called "electric light bugs." They can bite if handled carelessly. Overwinter as adults and lay eggs in spring. One generation a year and adults are seen during spring and most of the summer.

Giant Water Bug *Lethocerus americanus*

One of our largest bugs at 2½ inches. They live in muddy bottoms of ponds and are voracious predators of tadpoles, small fish and even salamanders. One of five North American species in the genus. Eggs are laid on vegetation above the water line, and are protected by the male.

Toe Biter *Belostoma testaceum*

One of the smaller giant water bugs, but it can still deliver a good bite if handled. In spring, females place their eggs on the back on a male, where they develop and hatch (see photo above). It occurs across the east coast, and lives near vegetation in slow moving or standing water.

Water Boatmen
Family Corixidae

Appearance

No larger than ½ inch long and generally dark brown with dark crosslines. Commonly confused with Backswimmers (Notonectidae) but water boatmen swim right side up, are usually smaller and have uniformly textured wings, lacking veins in the membranous part of hte wing. It possesses short scoop-like front legs and long paddle-like back legs. They are very agile swimmers, moving their back legs synchronously.

Biology

Found in freshwater ponds and lakes and less commonly in slow moving streams and small stagnant bodies of water. They breathe at the water surface through the thorax but can also carry a bubble of air under its wings and around its abdomen. May occur in large numbers, moving erratically under the water's surface. Most feed on algae, diatoms, nematodes and other tiny aquatic animals. Some are predacious on small insects, especially midge and mosquito larvae. Water boatmen overwinter as adults and are active spring and most of the summer.

Water Boatman *Sigara ornata*

Sigara is our largest genus of Corixidae, comprised of 51 species, but small in size (5-9mm). This one pictured is a dark form of *S. ornata*. Identification to species is difficult in this large genus, where wing pattern alone usually isn't enough to determine species.

Water Boatman *Hesperocorixa lobata*

Hesperocorixa is one of our largest genera of Corixidae in both size (9-11mm) and number of species (19). They have been reported in ponds from Massachusetts, Ontario and Michigan, and most likely can be found in adjacent states.

Backswimmers
Family Notonectidae

Appearance

Oval, elongate insects with a convex dorsum (top surface). The first pair of legs are normal-sized while the last pair of legs are long, broad and oar-like. The antennae are very short and inconspicuous. Most backswimmers are about ³/₅ inch long. They are generally light colored on their dorsal surface, lacking dark crosslines and dark underneath. This camouflages them from fish that swim below.

Biology

Backswimmers spend much of their time near the surface of ponds, swimming mostly on their backs. They breathe at the surface of the water through the tip of their abdomen. Backswimmers can carry a store of oxygen on the underside of their abdomen as well as under their wings.

Backswimmers do the backstroke! Hind legs row in tandem.

Their pattern of movement is less erratic than water boatmen. They commonly rest with their body at a 45 degree angle with their head down and their hind legs stretched out. They are ready to swim away quickly if necessary. Like water boatmen, backswimmers "row" with their back legs moving in tandem. They are predacious, feeding on small aquatic invertebrate animals and even occasionally on tadpoles and small fish and can bite people if handled carelessly. Backswimmers lay their eggs on or into submerged plant tissue as well as on rocks. Backswimmers overwinter as adults and lay eggs in the spring. Watch for them from spring through summer.

Backswimmer *Notonecta undulata*

These medium-sized (10-12mm) backswimmers are commonly found throughout the U.S. and southern Canada. The scutellum (triangular part behind the head) is usually black, but a few have varying amounts of orange like the one pictured. That makes this one very similar to *N. lunata*, which has very few markings on its pale body.

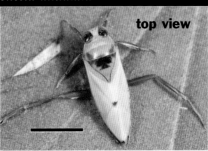

top view

Toad Bugs
Family Gelastocoridae

Toad Bugs are rough-textured and cryptic, and usually only seen when they move. We have 8 species in 2 genera that occur north of Mexico. These flat bodied bugs have reduced antennae that are hidden under its head, and large eyes. Their habitat is along pond edges and shorelines, where they feed on small insects.

Toad Bug *Gelastocoris oculatus*

G. oculatus is our most common and widespread Toad Bug. It's the only northern species, and is variable in color and pattern. Dark ones blend in well with mud, while tan speckled ones are hard to see on sand. They occur from Mexico to southern Ontario, spring through fall, with both adults and mature nymphs overwintering.

Water Measurers
Family Hydrometridae

Water Measurers or Marsh Treaders look like miniature walking sticks. Look carefully for these small (7-12mm) insects at the edge of ponds and marshes, on floating vegetation. Their movements are slow and deliberate while they walk on the surface of the water, hunting mosquito larvae, springtails and other small insects. Most of our 9 species occur in the eastern U.S. and Canada.

Water Measurer *Hydrometra martini*

A common water treader in the Northeast, *H. martini* is a difficult bug to find. Its thin body and slow movements keep it from being spotted by predators. Look where there's duckweed floating at the edges of still ponds and marshes. You can find them from early spring through the fall.

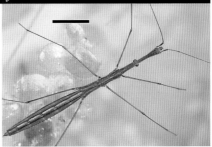

Water Striders
Family Gerridae

Appearance

Slender bodied insects ranging in size from ¼ to over ½ inch long. The second and third of pairs of legs are long and slender while the first pair is short. Water striders possess slender, moderate length antennae. They typically have black or brown bodies with many of them lacking wings.

In shallow clear waters, the water strider creates a unique shadow of its body and the depression in the water's surface its legs create.

Biology

Water striders are common on the surface of ponds and slow moving steams, sometimes occurring in large numbers. The tarsi are covered with very fine hairs which allows a water strider to skate over the surface of the water. It is difficult for those hairs get wet, but if they do a water strider will

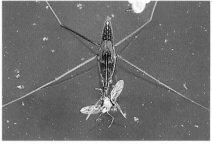

sink. Only the middle and hind pair of legs touch the water. The first set of legs are held in front of them and above the water. Adults spend the winter in protected sites, e.g under rocks or leaves on land near the water.

This water strider has captured an insect.

Common Water Strider *Aquarius species*

The 6 species of *Aquarius* are the most common and widespread water striders we have. Formerly considered part of the genus *Gerris*, these are larger (over 11mm) and the hind femur is longer in proportion to the hind tarsi (foot). Found throughout the continent from early spring through the fall, with *A. remigis* being the most common species in the genus.

Shore Bugs
Family Saldidae

Appearance

Small, usually between ⅛ to ¼ inch long, oval, flattened insects. Shore bugs are dark-colored insects, typically brown or black and white markings. They have moderate length antennae and large eyes. Shore bugs are distinctive because they possess four to five closed cells in the membrane of the wing.

Biology

Shore bugs are found on the shores of streams, rivers, ponds and lakes. They can run quickly and like to hide under plant debris, small stones and other objects. They can also jump and sustain short bursts of flight. Shore bugs are usually predacious on other small insects and other invertebrates, although they may occasionally scavenge on dead specimens. They overwinter as adults and lay eggs in the spring. You can find adults during spring and most of the summer.

Shore Bug *Pentacora ligata*

Penta refers to the 5 closed cells in the membrane part of the wing, unique to our 5 species in this genus. These large (6mm) shore bugs are most often found resting on exposed rocks in rivers. Sometimes they are on the firm sandy shore.

Shore Bug *Salda anthracina*

When I first saw this black bug running non-stop, I thought it was a ground beetle. This one was on damp sandy soil with sparse vegetation. Three of the eight species of *Salda* occur in New England. *S. anthracina*, like most of this uncommon genus, is large and all black.

Flat Bugs
Family Aradidae

Flat Bugs are wafer thin true bugs that live under bark. These small (3-11mm) bugs have a four segmented beak and antennae, lack ocelli and the wings do not cover the abdomen. They feed on fungi using their long thin mouthparts. Occurring throughout North America there are more than 120 species in 10 genera, with ***Aradus*** containing over 80 species. In the Northeast, four or more genera can be found; ***Aneurus, Aradus, Neuroctenus*** and ***Quilnus***.

Flat Bug *Aradus similis*

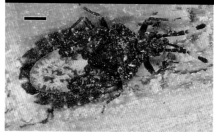

This small (6mm) flat bug, despite having stubby wings, can easily fly. The white band on the antennae separates this from most of the other small *Aradus* in the Northeast, and this species is associated with oak *(Quercus)*.

Bed Bugs
Family Cimicidae

North America hosts 15 species of Cimicidae, but just a couple feed on human blood. Most hosts are birds and bats. Bed bugs have a flat, oval body and short wing stubs. Despite bedbugs disgusting blood diet, they are not thought to transmit disease. Mating is brutally rough, with the male's external genitalia ripping a hole in the female's abdomen, inseminating her. This mating behavior is known as traumatic insemination.

Common Bed Bug *Cimex lectularius*

Reports of bed bugs are on the rise in the last decade, especially in motels. During the day they hide in bedding and furniture, and come out at night to feed. Bites are painless, and not noticed until later when welts form. Originally from Europe. Multiple generations a year, their numbers can reach several thousand in a house.

Soft Scale Insects
Family Coccidae

Scales use their piercing mouthparts to suck juices from plants. Females start off being somewhat mobile, and as they mature, become sedentary. They lose their legs, and a protective surface develops over them, hiding their bodies. Males are winged, but are rarely observed.

Non native species like the Brown Soft Scales *(Coccus hesperidum)*, are a common ornamental tree pest. They secrete large amounts of honeydew that covers tree leaves, and causes sooty mold. This activity can kill younger trees, and weaken larger trees.

Cottony Scale   *Pulvinaria species*

Cottony Scales can occur on either leaves of plants and trees, or directly on stems during the summer months. Native species like this *Pulvinaria* rarely occur in large enough numbers to damage plants and trees. We have 22 species of *Pulvinaria* north of Mexico, and knowing the host plant helps with identification. Some of these scales can resemble *Microdon* larvae (Syrphid flies). The cottony appearance and habitat preferences are distinctive.

Lace Bugs
Family Tingidae

Appearance

These are small insects, measuring about ⅛ to ¼ inch long. The head is concealed under an expanded hood-like pronotum. Their pronotum and wings are sculptured giving them a lacy appearance. They are often brownish or grayish, often mottled with black spots.

Biology

Lace bugs are slow-moving insects, feeding gregariously on the underside of deciduous tree and shrub leaves, especially oak, hackberry, willow, chokecherry and hawthorn and other plants in the rose family. This feeding causes a speckled discoloration on the upper surface of leaves. Lace bugs overwinter as adults and lay eggs on leaves in the spring.

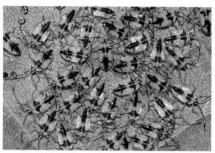

Nymphs, like adults, congregate in masses on their preferred host plant.

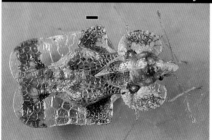

Hawthorn Lace Bug   *Corythucha cydoniae*

Look on the UNDERSIDES of tree leaves for these bizarre insects. Visible veins on flat transparent wings give it a lacy look. And they are often found in groups with nymphs. Leaves of hawthorn, juneberry, crab apple, chokeberry and other trees and shrubs in the rose family are its primary food. Active spring and summer.

Cherry Lace Bug *Corythucha pruni*

Corythucha lacebugs are difficult to identify to species. Host plant association is important, but in this genus of 49 species, other factors are needed. A low and elongate shaped hood helps distinguish this from other similar species. Look under cherry leaves *(Prunis)* to find congregations of both nymphs and adults feeding on the leaf.

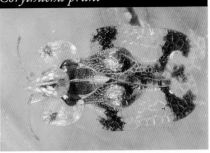

Linden Lace Bug *Gargaphia tiliae*

These elegant looking lace bugs only feed on linden (basswood), so the host plant is important for distinguishing this species from the other 14 that occur north of Mexico. Look for these on the underside of linden leaves through the summer and early fall. They occur across the east.

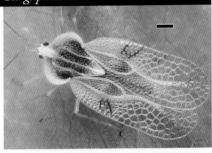

Fringetree Lace Bug *Leptoypha mutica*

A small (3mm) narrow lace bug, *L. mutica* occurs across the eastern U.S. and Canada. Feeds on the underside of ash, fringetree and privet leaves. Of the 9 species of *Leptoypha* north of Mexico, this is the most common, and the only one in the Northeast. Adults hibernate in leaf litter. Active from May through September.

Willow Lace Bug *Physatocheila variegata*

The oval shape, lack of a hood and spines on the head, identify this small (3.5mm) lace bug as one of the 4 species of *Physatocheila*. In the Northeast, we have 2 other species, *P. brevirostris* and *P. plexa*. Look on willows and alders for these lace bugs.

Plant Bugs
Family Miridae

Appearance

Small to medium-sized insects, ⅙ to ⅜ inch long, with moderate length antennae and usually an oval or elongate body, although the shape is variable. Many are green or brown and blend in with their surroundings but some can be brightly colored, e.g. red or yellow. Plant bugs possess a cuneus, a triangular segment of the thickened portion of the wings and one or two closed cells in the membranous part of the wings. This membranous section of the wings is characteristically bent down. A few plant bugs lack wings or have shortened wing.

nymph

Nymph of the Fourlined Plant Bug, *Poecilocapus lineatus*.

Biology

This is the most common group of true bugs. They are typically found on plants where most species are herbivores. Some are scavengers and a few are predacious on other insects. Plant bugs spend the winter as eggs, typically laid into plant tissue.

Northeast Species Notes

Plant bugs are a very diverse group of insects. They range in appearance from the small northeastern ant mimic **Pilophorus strobicola**, that feeds on pines to the ubiquitous **Tarnished Plant Bug (*Lygus lineolaris*)**, that's found throughout the U.S. and southern Canada on a wide variety of plants. If you like colorful bugs, Mirids won't disappoint, with the bright reds and orange coloration of the *Lopidea* species, the contrasting lines of the **Four-lined Plant Bug (*Poecilocapsus lineatus*)**, to the jet black with orange highlights of *Prepops* and *Taedia* species.

They come in all kinds of shapes and sizes like the wasp-like **Pseudoxenetus regalis**, to the tiny fleahoppers like **Halticus intermedius**, the alien looking **Myiomma cixiiformis** and the **Phytocoris** species with the cricket-like hind legs.

Tarnished Plant Bug *Lygus lineolaris*

"Tarnished" probably refers to this abundant insect's brown with yellow, white and black markings, but it could also refer to its damage to plants it feeds on. Color is variable as demonstrated in these two photos. But no matter what base color the specimen is, it will always show a yellowish heart-shaped marking on the anterior of its wings (sometimes looks more like a Y). Unlike most other plant bugs, Tarnished Plant Bugs feed on a wide variety of herbaceous plants as well as some trees and shrubs. Tarnished plant bugs are active spring, summer and into fall.

Four-lined Plant Bug *Poecilocapus lineatus*

Gardens are where you may encounter Fourlined Plant Bugs as they feed on many types of perennials as well as on fruits such as gooseberry; Also feed occasionally on trees and shrubs including dogwood, viburnum and sumac. They are greenish yellow with four black stripes down the wings. Fourlined plant bugs overwinter as eggs

laid in clusters into slits near the tops of canes of currants, brambles and other woody plants. Eggs hatch in May. Fourlined Plant Bugs are active into early July.

Plant bug *Metriorrhynchomiris dislocatus*

This striking red and black plant bug is most often seen along woodland trails; In some areas mostly found on species of *Iris, Lychnis* or *Geranium*. But don't be fooled by this photo—Several color variations can occur: all black, red pronotum with black wings, orange and black, etc.

Alfalfa Plant Bug *Adelphocoris lineolatus*

Another alien from Europe that has gained pest status; The Alfalfa Plant Bug made its North American appearance in the mid 20th century and has become a problem in seed alfalfa fields. It is also found on wildflowers in summer.

Meadow Plant Bug *Stenotus binotatus*

Originally a European species, they were accidentally introduced into North America a century ago. Like the Latin specific epithet *binotatus* suggests, it has two bold spots on the prothorax. The similar Alfalfa Plant Bug lacks these. Commonly found in meadows, fields and ditches on a variety of grasses during July and August.

Plant Bug *Collaria meilleurii*

You may get your feet wet trying to find this plant bug; It prefers wet sedge meadows. But it can also be found in dryer fields of grasses (*Poa* species). Found throughout our area from June through August.

Plant Bug *Capsus ater*

Roadside grasses are the microhabitat of *Capsus ater*. Like the Alfalfa Plant Bug above, it is an introduced species from Europe. The all black form is most common but individuals with a red pronotum (seen here) are also encountered. The second antennal segment is swollen near the end. May to July.

Adelphocoris rapidus
Rapid Plant Bug

Coccobaphes frontifer

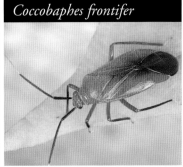

Dicyphus famelicus

Halticus bractatus
Garden Fleahopper

Ilnacora malina

Leptopterna dolabrata
Meadow Plant Bug

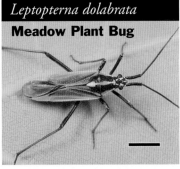

Lopidea media

Lopidea species
Scarlet Plant Bug

Family *Miridae* PLANT BUGS | **81**

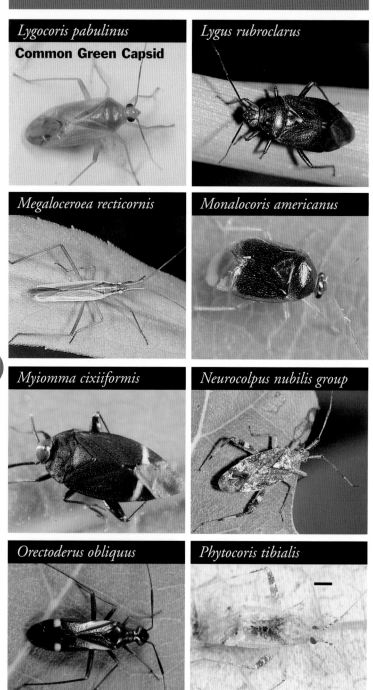

Lygocoris pabulinus
Common Green Capsid

Lygus rubroclarus

Megaloceroea recticornis

Monalocoris americanus

Myiomma cixiiformis

Neurocolpus nubilis group

Orectoderus obliquus

Phytocoris tibialis

Pilophorus strobicola

Pinalitus approximatus

Plagiognathus alboradialis

Plagiognathus obscurus

Polymerus fulvipes

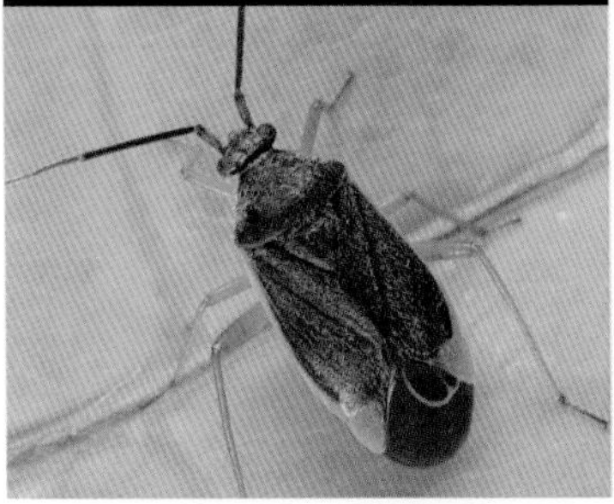

Prepops borealis

Prepops insitivus

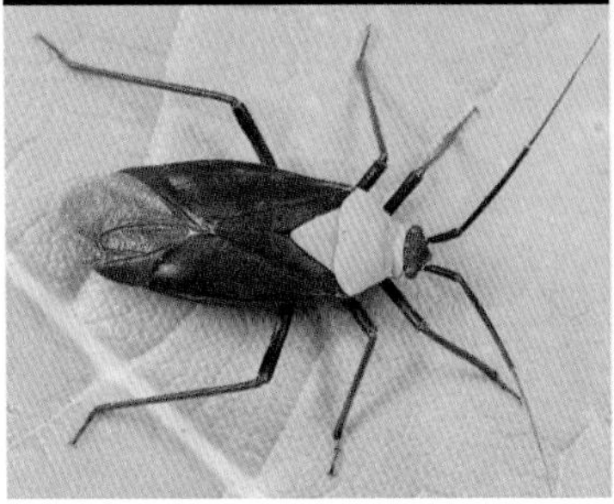

Pseudoxenetus regalis
color variations

Damsel Bugs
Family Nabidae

Nymph of a damsel bug.

Appearance
They have a somewhat enlarged femur on their front leg as well as many small closed cells around the edge of the membrane of the hemelytra. Some species possess very short wings.

Biology
Look for them on plants where they feed on aphids, leafhoppers, spider mites, insect eggs and small larvae, including caterpillars. They overwinter as adults and can have several generations in a year.

Banded-legged Damsel Bug *Hoplistoscelis pallescens*

Usually short-winged, but fully-winged individuals are occasionally found. These banded-legged damsel bugs are one of 5 members of it's genus in North America, and the only one found in the Northeast. They range throughout the eastern U.S. and Midwest. Mid spring to late fall.

Common Damsel Bug *Nabis species*

There are 9 species of *Nabis* in North America, with *Nabis americoferus* being our most common. They often overwinter as adults, and can be found any month of the year. On warm winter days, I occasionally find them walking on the snow in meadows.

Black Damsel Bug *Nabis (Nabicula) subcoleoptrata*

Glossy black and usually short-winged, these bugs are good ant mimics. This native species feeds on a variety of small bugs, including the introduced Meadow Plant Bug. They range across the northern half of the U.S. and southern Canada. June through August. Formerly *Nabicula subcoleoptrata*.

Minute Pirate Bugs
Family Anthocoridae

Appearance

Very small, between ¹/₁₆ to ¹/₅ inch long flattened insects. Minute pirate bugs are typically shiny black with whitish wings and somewhat diamond-shaped.

Biology

Minute pirate bugs usually occur on flowers and occasionally on trees where they are predacious on small insects, insect eggs and mites. These small insects can bite people if they land on them, administering a surprisingly painful bite. Fortunately this is just accidental and they do not leave lasting injuries. Swarms of migrating minute pirate bugs can be encountered during September and early October. They are strongly attracted to blue. Minute pirate bugs overwinter as adults.

Minute Pirate Bug   *Elatophilus inimicus*

This colorful little bug preys on scale insects that feed on Red Pine and Pitch Pine. It's not commonly found, and its been recorded from Canada, Colorado, Michigan, North Carolina, New York and now Massachusetts. I found this one on the underside of an oak leaf in a mixed forest of Pitch Pine and oak on Cape Cod.

Insidious Flower Bug   *Orius insidiosus*

These bugs are abundant on flowers, but most people never see them because of their very small size of 2mm. They're a welcome guest in gardens, because they prey on thrips, aphids and other small garden pests. Despite their tiny size, they can deliver a bite that gets your attention. They overwinter as adults, and can be found most of the year across the country.

Assassin Bugs & Ambush Bugs Family Reduviidae

Appearance

Slender to stout-bodied insects, usually medium-sized. They possess a short beak which fits into a groove on the underside of the head. The abdomen of many species widen in the middle often extending beyond the wings. They are generally colored green or brown although some can be brightly colored. Some of these insects have raptorial front legs.

Some species, like this *Barce uhleri*, have raptorial front legs for catching and holding prey.

Biology

Assassin bugs and ambush bugs are predacious, feeding on other insects. They are typically found on plants as well as in leaf litter, under stones and debris. Ambush bugs are commonly found on flowers where they use camouflage to hide and feed on insects that land there, some twice their size. They paralyze prey by toxins in their saliva which acts in seconds.

The distinctive nymph of the Wheel Bug *Arilus cristatus*

The male Jagged Ambush Bug (*Phymata pennsylvanica*) is much darker than the female.

No family love; The nymph of one species of ambush bug eats an adult Jagged Ambush Bug.

Thread-legged Bug *Barce species*

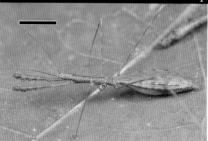

Barce fraterna is the more common of the 2 northeastern species, with 6 species occurring in North America. These assassin bugs live in tall grasses. Note the raptorial front legs for catching and holding small insect prey. Adults can be found in the summer and early fall and will come to lights.

Assassin Bug *Acholla multispinosa*

Often confused with the more common and widespread *Sinea* assassin bugs, *A. multispinosa* lack the spines on its front legs. Woodland habitats are preferred as opposed to open fields for *Sinea diadema*. Northeastern U.S. and adjacent Canada, from June until frost. It's the only eastern species in the genus.

Wheel Bug *Arilus cristatus*

Our largest assassin bugs (28-36mm). A wheel-shaped crest makes them unmistakable. Nymphs have a bright red abdomen that they hold erect (photo on previous page). A common bug of the South, it's now been found as far north as New York and southern Ontario. Will come to lights at night. Careless handling results in a painful bite.

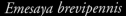

Thread-legged Bug *Emesaya brevipennis*

Even though this is the largest thread-legged bug in the East (35mm), seeing them can be difficult. The long dull-colored body and spindly legs help it blend in. One of five species in the genus, they occur in most of the U.S. and southern Canada. Sometimes found in spider webs, steeling captured insects (kleptoparasite).

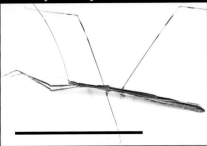

Assassin Bug *Fitchia aptera*

An uncommonly encountered bug, *F. aptera's* wings are very short, exposing the yellow abdomen, with its wide dark stripe down the center. Spends most of its life on the ground around grasses but occasionally found in low vegetation. They occur in most of the country. Adults overwintering under bark.

Jagged Ambush Bug *Phymata pennsylvanica*

Ambush predators that are common on flowers during summer. Females are light colored and always larger than the males. Powerful front legs are used to grasp prey, often much larger than itself (even Bald-faced Hornets!), before its piercing mouth injects toxic saliva that paralyzes the victim almost instantly.

Assassin Bug *Pselliopus cinctus*

During the summer months look for this assassin on flowers, where unsuspecting insects are its prey—Even other ambush bugs can be victims! One of six species in the genus, it can only be confused with the other eastern species, *P. barberi*, which is usually a brighter orange.

Spined Assassin Bug *Sinea diadema*

The jagged spines on the inner part of the front legs distinguish this assassin from the similar *Acholla multispinosa*. The other *Sinea* species in the Northeast, the Spiny Assassin Bug *(S. spinipes)* has a more rounded abdomen and blunt tubercles on the pronotum. Open weedy areas throughout most of North America. July until October in the Northeast.

Assassin Bug *Zelus luridus*

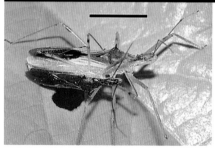

Look for these slender green assassins on tree and shrub leaves. Sticky hairs on the front legs help catch prey. Nymphs are green, and easily found in spring and fall. Adult males have black wings, while larger females have two-toned wings. 11 species in the genus. Of two found in Northeast, this is our most common—*Zelus tetracanthus* is darker.

Seed Bugs
Family Lygaeidae

Appearance
Most are orange and black while a few are brownish. Five conspicuous veins in the wings. Abdominal spiracles found on top of the body.

Biology
Found especially on milkweeds where they feed on seeds. Bright colors warn predators that they taste bad. Winter as adults.

Small Milkweed Bug *Lygaeus kalmii*

Very common in weedy fields containing milkweed throughout most of North America. Feed on flower nectar, and also milkweed seeds. Western populations have white spots on the black membranous portion of the wings. Adults overwinter. Nymph in inset.

Large Milkweed Bug *Oncopeltus fasciatus*

Bright coloration is a warning to predators that it tastes noxious from the toxins it acquires from its diet of milkweed seeds. Much larger than its cousin, the Small Milkweed Bug (above). In female's lifespan (about a month), she can lay up to 2,000 eggs. Adults and nymphs can be found in large aggregations on the milkweed seedpods (inset).

Birch Catkin Bug *Kleidocerys resedae*

This small (3-4mm) bug is an introduced species native to Europe and Asia, which now occurs throughout North America. They feed on seeds from a variety of trees and shrubs, with birch being their favorite. Despite their small size, they have a pungent odor.

Leaf-footed Bugs
Family Coreidae

Appearance

Moderate to large stout-bodied insects, leaf-footed bugs are typically dark colored. They have moderate length antennae with a head narrower than the pronotum. They possess well developed scent glands on their thorax which allows them to give off a distinctive odor to deter predators. The membrane of their wings possesses many veins. Some species have a leaf-like expansion on their hind legs.

Biology

Leaf-footed bugs are plant-feeders, usually on the seed-bearing fruit or on the exposed seeds or cones. Some species are general feeders while others feeds on a particular group of plants. Leaf-footed bugs overwinter as adults, often in plant debris. Leaf-footed bugs are active during spring and summer.

 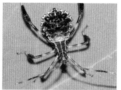 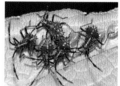

Nymph of the Squash Bug, *Anasa tristis*

The distinctive nymph of the leaf-footed bug, *Acanthocephala terminalis*

Congregation of Helmeted Squash Bug nymphs (*Euthochtha galeator*).

Helmeted Squash Bug *Euthochtha galeator*

nymph

This is the only species of *Euthochtha* in North America, and can be distinguished from *Anasa* species by the spines on the thick hind legs. The nymphs are very spiny (see photo above), and are our only leaf-footed bug with the third antennal segment swollen in all instar stages. They occur throughout the eastern U.S. with adults active from late spring into the fall.

Leaf-footed Bug *Acanthocephala terminalis*

Of the five species of *Acanthocephala* in North America, *A. terminalis* is the only one occurring in the Northeast. The orange antennae tips distinguishes this large (22mm) bug from others in the genus. Adults found in weedy fields east of the Rockies from spring to early fall.

Squash Bug *Anasa tristis*

The Squash Bug lacks the flattened hind legs that are typical of the family. The most common and widespread of the six *Anasa* species in North America, occurring from southern Canada to South America. They feed on leaves, stems and fruit of plants in the squash family, causing noticeable damage from the toxins they inject while feeding.

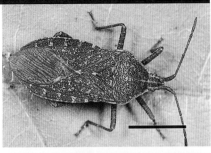

Western Conifer Seed Bug *Leptoglossus occidentalis*

Originally a native to the western U.S. pine forests, this bug has expanded its range in the last few decades to become very common throughout the east. Adults are most noticeable in the fall when they congregate, and enter homes to overwinter. They don't bite, and are harmless to people and pets, but when handled they can give off a foul odor.

Distinct Leaf-footed Bug *Merocoris distinctus*

This is one of our smallest Coreids (9mm). Of the 3 *Merocoris* species in North America, this is the only one found in the Northeast. These little, fuzzy bugs can be found on flowers throughout the eastern U.S., except Florida, where *M. typhaeus* occurs.

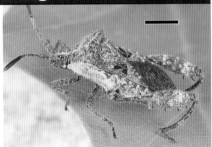

Broad-headed Bugs
Family Alydidae

Appearance
Medium-sized insects with a long, narrow brownish or blackish body and medium length antennae. They have a large head that is as wide or wider than the thorax and nearly as long. The membrane of the wings has numerous veins. Broad-headed bugs have well developed scent glands on the thorax which gives off a foul odor.

Biology
Broad-headed bugs are plant feeders and are found on herbaceous plants, grasses and weeds in woodlands, grassy fields and roadsides. Some broad-head bugs mimic ants. They also use odors to protect themselves from would be predators. Adults are active during summer.

Some nymphs are very convincing ant mimics.

Broad-headed Bug   *Alydus eurinus*

nymph

The nymphs are great ant mimics, but when they reach the adult stage, *A. eurinus* look like spider wasps. A secondary chemical defense used, is to exude allomones (butyric and hexanoic acids) from scent glands. This is the most common of the 6 species of *Alydus* in North America, ranging from the east coast to the Rockies. They're found from June through October, on goldenrod, and can be abundant on bush clover in the fall.

Lupine Bug   *Megalotomus quinquespinosus*

This assassin bug mimic is the only species of *Megalotomus* we have, and it occurs throughout most of North America. It feeds on a wide variety of plant species, and can be found in weedy openings of forests and along roadsides from June through October. The white band on the antennae is a distinctive feature.

Broad-headed Bug *Protenor belfragei*

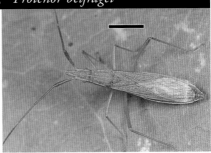

This Broad-headed Bug defies its name, having a rather narrow tapering head. It feeds on grasses and sedges, and is found in damp habitats. One of just 2 species of *Protenor* in North America, *P. belfragei* is the only species in the Northeast. Adults occur from July through September, and range as far west as the Rockies.

Stilt Bugs
Family Berytidae

Appearance
Slender, slow moving, insects with long thread-like antennae and legs. Winter as adults and lay eggs in the spring. Adults mature by summer.

Biology
Typically found on plants. Most feed on plant sap, although a few are predacious on insects.

Stilt Bug *Neoneides muticus*

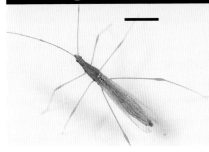

These spindly-legged bugs can be easily recognized as stilt bugs, rather than the similar looking thread-legged bugs, by the knobs on the antennae, and lack of mantis-like forelegs. This is the most common and widespread of the twelve species found in North America. Adults can be found during the summer months in weedy fields throughout the U.S. and southern Canada.

Scentless Plant Bugs
Family Rhopalidae

Appearance

Small to medium, moderately oval insects. Generally brownish or light colored, although some species are brightly colored. They have an average-sized head with medium length antennae. Scentless plant bugs have many veins in the membrane of their wings. They lack scent glands.

Biology

Scentless? The name is from the lack of a large scent gland opening by the hind legs that most bugs have. They are plant feeders and are primarily found on weeds and other herbaceous plants. A few feed on trees. Look for scentless plant bugs during mid to late summer.

Eastern Boxelder Bug *Boisea trivittata*

Common throughout North America, except West Coast. By summer, they're feeding on box elders and maples. Eggs laid in bark crevices of host tree. During fall, they congregate on the sunny side of buildings, and can be a nuisance when entering houses, looking for a place to overwinter.

Scentless Plant Bug *Harmostes reflexulus*

Often on flowers in fields. Throughout the continent, this is the most common and widespread of the 7 species in the genus. *Harmostes* are distinguished from other scentless plant bugs by the spines on their hind legs and front thorax. Highly variable in color.

Scentless Plant Bug *Stictopleurus punctiventris*

Our most common scentless plant bug, *S. punctiventris* occurs across southern Canada, and the northern U.S.. A close look behind the head will reveal a pair of dark lines that terminate in a loop. Look for these bugs in fields and wet meadows during the summer and fall.

Pachygronthid Bugs
Family Pachygronthidae

The 7 North American species were once a subfamily of Lygaeidae. They're found throughout the tropical regions of the world, and occur over most of the country. You can find them in meadows and marshes, where they feed on grasses and sedges.

Seed Bug   *Phlegyas abbreviatus*

A common bug throughout eastern North America, these grass feeders can be abundant in the north. With only 2 species in the genus, this is the only one in New England. They can be found from early spring through the fall, with adults overwintering in leaf litter.

Big-eyed Bugs
Family Geocoridae

Large eyes that bulge from the sides of the head are a distinctive feature of the approximately 30 species north of Mexico. These predatory little bugs (3-5mm) dash about in open dry areas looking for springtails, aphids, leafhoppers and whatever other small bugs they can catch, making them beneficial to the agriculture industry. They were formerly considered part of the Lygaeidae.

Big-eyed Bug   *Geocoris discopterus*

Look for these small bugs in dry sandy areas with sparse vegetation. This eastern species has a disjunct population in the Yukon, thought to be a relict population from the last ice age. They're active in the spring and summer, and overwinter as adults.

Chinch Bugs
Family Blissidae

Blissidae are a group of grass-feeding true bugs with about 30 species in 3 genera in North America. Some are considered pests of ornamental grasses and lawns.

Chinch bugs are small (4-5mm), have black bodies, wings with white markings, red legs and clubbed antennae. They occur throughout the continent, with adults active from spring through fall.

Saltmarsh Chinch Bug *Ischnodemus falicus*

These small bugs occur in *Spartina pectinata* in the prairies, and on *Carex* along ponds, lakes and saltwater marshes. Its range includes southern Canada, and most of the eastern half of the U.S. It's not known to be a significant pest like the Hairy Chinch Bug *(Blissus leucopterus)* that kills patches of grass on lawns.

Ebony Bugs (Negro Bugs)
Family Thyreocoridae

Small, oval, black and shiny. Their scutellum is enlarged, covering the wings and most of the abdomen, giving them a beetle-like appearance. Negro bugs are common on flowers, weeds and grasses in open fields.

Ebony Bug *Corimelaena pulicaria*

A small beetle lookalike, this tiny 3mm bug doesn't have a line down the back, separating the wing covers like beetles have. Of the 20 species of *Corimelaena* north of Mexico, it's our most common species. Can be abundant on goldenrod and sunflowers. Most of the U.S. and southern Canada.

Ebony Bug *Galgupha nitiduloides*

Most of the ebony bugs in the genus *Galgupha* are easy to recognize by their large size (5-6mm) and all black appearance. But distinguishing species is difficult, with at least 3 occurring in the Northeast. Look in flowers from spring through the fall for these large ebony bugs.

Burrowing Bugs
Family Cydnidae

Burrowing Bugs are small (3-8mm) bugs that resemble Stink Bugs, but have middle and hind legs heavily spined. Some have scoop-like front legs designed for digging. There are 43 species in North America, and most of them are subterranean, and they feed on plant juices. Adults overwinter under leaf litter.

White-margined Burrowing Bug *Sehirus cinctus*

This glossy blue/black bug margined in white, unlike most others in the family, is commonly seen above ground on flowers. White-margined Burrowing Bugs occur throughout the U.S. and southern Canada, where they feed on seeds of plants in the mint family. Females care for the young, and stock the nest with mint seeds.

nymph

Stink Bugs
Family Pentatomidae

Appearance

Moderate to large insects that are ovoid or triangular in shape. Typically green or brown (some brightly colored or metallic). They possess a long, broad scutellum (the triangular segment between their "shoulders."

Biology

Stink bugs, like their name implies, have well developed scent glands and can produce a bad odor. Primarily plant feeders (especially immature fruit and seeds) but a few species eat insects. Eggs laid in clusters on plants. They are typically barrel shaped and armed

This colorful nymph of the predacious stink bug *Apateticus cynicus* has captured a caterpillar and is feeding on it. Not all stink bugs are carnivores; in fact, most are plant feeders.

with spines. Females of many species protect their eggs and sometimes even the newly emerged young. Common spring and summer.

Stink Bug *Banasa calva*

Eastern Hemlock is the host for this two-toned stink bug that occurs in the eastern U.S. Although 11 species in the genus occur north of Mexico, *B. dimiata* is the only one this can be confused with. Look for the black spots on the edge of the abdomen, and the dividing line on the pronotum has a dark notch.

Banasa Stink Bug *Banasa dimiata*

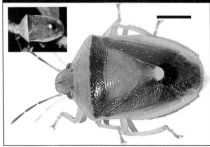

Found across North America, this is one of our most common stink bugs. Birch, currants, bearberry and many other plants make up its diet. Often attracted to lights. May be two-toned brown, like *B. calva*, or green and red. Look for the smooth line dividing the colors on the pronotum and the lack of spotting on the edge of the abdomen.

Four-humped Stink Bug *Brochymena quadripustulata*

Usually found on tree trunks, these large bugs are difficult to see, with their rough appearance blending in with the bark. Their diet consists of a wide variety of trees, and occasionally will eat insects. Adults overwinter under tree bark, and occur through most of the U.S. and southern Canada.

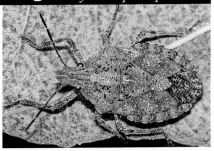

Green Stink Bug *Chinavia hilaris (Acrosternum hilare)*

Formerly called *Acrosternum hilare*, the nymphs have a colorful contrast of dark and light colors. As an adult, they blend in with the wide variety of green vegetation they feed on. It's one of our most common stink bugs, and occurs throughout most of North America.

nymph

Stink Bug *Dendrocoris humeralis*

Like the photo shows, this rounded stink bug is often found on leaves where it feeds on oak, hickory, hazel and others. The scutellum is more rounded, evenly merging with the wings than in other stink bugs. Also note the even coloration and myriad of tiny black pits.

Twice-stabbed Stink Bug *Cosmopepla lintneriana*

Most of North America in fields and gardens, they feed on a variety of plants including grapes, potatoes, mint and thistle, but are rarely considered a pest. A small bug (6mm) with distinctive markings, it's also known as Wee Harlequin Bug, Black-and-Red Stink Bug and Two-spotted Stink Bug. Formerly *Cosmopepla bimaculata*.

Brown Stink Bug *Euschistus servus*

One of our most common stink bugs, it's not particular about what it feeds on, such as trees, grains, fruit, flowers and many others. It inhabits grassy fields throughout the eastern U.S. and southern Canada. Adults can be found from late spring until the fall frost.

Stink Bug *Menecles insertus*

A widespread, but seldom seen stink bug, *M. insertus* is thought to spend most of its time in the canopy of hardwoods, where it feeds. They're active at night and are attracted to lights, where they're most commonly found. The appearance is similar to *Euschistus* species, but the shoulders are rounded rather than pointed.

Harlequin Bug *Murgantia histrionica*

adults   nymph

While this is one of our most striking stink bugs, it's considered a crop pest on cabbage, mustard and related plants. A native to Central America and Mexico, it started spreading across the southern U.S. about the time of the Civil War, and is now found as far north as New England. Southern populations can have up to 5 broods a year.

Predatory Stink Bug *Perillus circumcinctus*

Look for this uncommon stink bug that occurs from Ontario and New England, south to Missouri in weedy fields during the summer. The chestnut brown color with white markings distinguishes this from our other 6 species of *Perillus*, which are more of a black color with orange lines.

Striped Predatory Stink Bug *Perillus strigipes*

White stripes on the middle and hind femurs, plus the distinctive pattern of this beautiful bug identify it as *P. strigipes*. Sometimes included in the genus *Mineus*. It can be found in fields during late spring through fall in the north, and most of the year in the south. Maine south to Oklahoma.

Predatory Stink Bug *Picromerus bidens*

A recently introduced species from Europe, *P. bidens* now occurs throughout New England, New York and adjacent Canadian provinces. A spine on the front legs distinguishes this from similar looking stink bugs with large spines projecting from the corners of the pronotum. Its diet consists of many species of caterpillars.

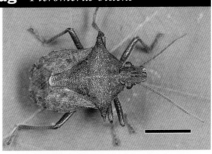

Spined Soldier Bug *Podisus maculiventris*

Of the nine species of *Podisus*, this one has the most pronounced spines. Spined Soldier Bugs prey on many different types of arthropods, like this sawfly larva, thus making them undesirable as a biological control agent. Its range includes most of North America, where it's one of our most common predatory stink bugs.

Anchor Stink Bug *Stiretrus anchorago*

Highly variable in appearance, the Anchor Stink Bug can be white, pink, yellow, orange or red, usually with diagnostic black markings. Found in the eastern U.S. and southern Canada. They feed on larvae and adults of butterflies, moths and beetles, making them a beneficial agricultural insect. Adults overwinter.

nymph

Family *Pentatomidae* STINK BUGS | **101**

Shield Bugs
Family Acanthosomatidae

Appearance
Very similar to the pentatomid stink bugs. Also called "Parent Bugs."

Biology
Parent bugs are, indeed, very good parents. Once their barrel-shaped eggs hatch, the adults lead the nymphs to their feeding grounds.

Red-crossed Stink Bug *Elasmostethus cruciatus*

Named for the distinct red **X** on its back. Only 3 species of *Elasmostethus* in North America, and just 2 species in our region. The similar *E. atricornis* has black antennae. Adults overwinter in leaf litter or under bark, and can be found most of the year, especially near alder, their preferred food. Northern half of the U.S. and southern Canada.

Parent Bug *Elasmucha lateralis*

nymphs

Rare among bugs, the female watches over her brood until the young are able to fend for themselves, and hence the name "parent but." One observer has noted the female flicking her wings at passing insects, presumably to scare them away. This is the only species of *Elasmucha* in North America. Some entomologists prefer to place this species with the stink bugs in family Pentatomidae. It can be found up and down the east coast and across southern Canada. They are herbivores, feeding on birch catkins.

Shield-backed Bugs
Family Scutelleridae

Appearance
Very similar to stink bugs but with a "shield" that covers their entire back (actually an extension of the thorax).

Biology
One generation per year in the north. Overwinters as an adult.

Shield-backed Bug *Eurygaster alternata*

Wet meadows with sedges are the habitat these bugs can be found in. Its color and pattern are variable. The scutellum of our 5 species of *Eurygaster* is narrow, exposing more of the anterior wing. They're not encountered often, but they do occur throughout most of North America.

Shield-backed Bug *Homaemus aeneifrons*

I've found these bugs very common in northern New England in the summer and fall, when using a sweep net through tall grass meadows that are either damp or dry. They occur across Canada and the northern U.S. and overwinter as adults. Not much is known about its diet, but from the habitat it's found in, there's reason to believe it's a generalist feeder.

Cicadas
Family Cicadidae

Appearance

Large, stout insects with green or brown bodies and black markings. Four membranous wings longer than the abdomen which they hold tent-like over their abdomens. Very short antennae between bulging eyes.

Empty larval case still clings to the tree after the cidada has emerged.

Biology

They insert eggs in tree twigs during late summer. Twigs wilt and drop. The nymphs hatch and tunnel into the ground where they remain feeding on the roots of trees for four to eight years. Adults start to emerge in July and are active into September. Cicadas are well known for their ability to produce sound. The males use sound organs (tymbals) located on the sides of the base of their abdomen which vibrate and resonate into a cavity located inside parts of the thorax and abdomen. This produces a powerline type hum which is used to attract females. Each species creates its own unique sound.

Dog-day Cicada *Tibicen canicularis*

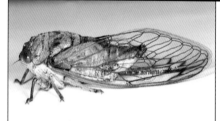

The most common cicada in the Northeast. Name comes from their habit of singing during the hottest "dog-days" of summer. Larva spend an average of 3 years underground, feeding on tree roots. Unlike periodic cicadas, their broods overlap, so adults emerge every year. Adults sing August through September.

Cicada *Okanagana rimosa*

Most of the roughly 50 species of *Okanagana* live in the west, with just two species in New England; *O. rimosa* and *O. canadensis*. They are called small-headed cicadas, since their head is narrower than the thorax. Their emergence is earlier in the summer than the more common Dog-day Cicada, where their ranges overlap.

Acanaloniid Planthoppers
Family Acanaloniidae

Often green with broad short wings held vertically, possibly to mimic a leaf. Some consider this group to be a subfamily of Issidae called Acanaloniinae.

Nymph

Two-striped Planthopper *Acanalonia bivittata*

A great leaf mimic. Nymphs are squat, high domed bugs with a white waxy tail. Adults can be found feeding on a variety of trees and shrubs from June until September throughout eastern North America.

Flatid Planthoppers
Family Flatidae

They have short antennae positioned below the compound eyes. Moth-like with triangular, wedge-shaped wings held tent-like over the body. They feed on trees, shrubs and vines gregariously in nonsocial groups.

Citrus Flatid Planthopper *Metcalfa pruinosa*

Citrus trees are just one of many plants fed upon by *M. pruinosa*. Not much damage is done from their feeding, so they're not considered pests. Both nymphs and adults are covered with a coating of wax. Mid summer to fall. Quebec to Mexico.

Northern Flatid Planthopper *Anormenis chloris*

Throughout the eastern U.S. and into southern Ontario, but absent from northern New England. Formerly called *A. septentrionalis*. Often found feeding in groups under leaves. Adults can be found from July until frost season.

Achilid Planthoppers
Family Achilidae

Distinctive among planthoppers, Achilids have wings that overlap. Adults are often in tree foliage, and may be attracted to lights. Family is comprised of 55 species in 8 genera, and occurs throughout North America.

Dwarf Catonia *Catonia pumila*

Look for this diminutive planthopper that can be found in the Northeast and down to Texas, in the fall. The head is narrow, and the face has two brown bands (inset photo). Maple has been recorded as a food plant, but not much is known about what else it might feed on.

Achilid Planthopper *Synecdoche dimidiata*

The even brown coloration and lack of black spots on the head and thorax distinguishes this from other similar species. Not much is known about the diet, but I found this one on a beech leaf on August 1. Maine to Florida, with inland reports from Ohio and West Virginia.

Dictyopharid Planthoppers
Family Dictyopharidae

Most of our nearly 70 species of Dictyopharidae are easily recognized by their long snout. Two genera can be found in the Northeast, **Scolops** being very common, and **Phylloscelis** which lacks any horn.

Partridge Bug *Scolops sulcipes*

By far the most common Dictyopharid in the Northeast, Partridge Bugs can be found across the continent from July into September. They're most commonly found in meadows, where they feeding on sap from many types of plants. The intricate network of veins on the tip of the wings distinguishes this from other Scolops which have simpler veins.

Derbid Planthoppers
Family Derbidae

Primarily a tropical family of planthoppers, Derbid variety is greatest in the south. Comprised of 70 species in North America, only about a dozen are found in New England. Nymphs feed on fungi, and adults are usually on plants and can show up at lights.

Derbid Planthopper   *Cedusa maculata*

Of our 32 species of *Cedusa*, this one is easily recognizable from its color pattern, unlike most of the genus that are a solid blue-black. This is a rarely found bug with a range from Ontario to Texas. One unique character of the genus is big ear-like lobes on the head that wrap around the antennae.

Derbid Planthopper   *Otiocerus degeeri*

Our 10 species of *Otiocerus* are characterized by having long wings, and antennae that are otiose, meaning ridiculous. The antennae curve around the side of the face, giving the appearance of a grimacing mouth. *O. degeeri* is the pinkish one that occurs throughout eastern North America. The adults are most often found at lights from July to September.

Derbid Planthopper   *Otiocerus wolfii*

Not as common as *O. degeeri*, this yellowish *Otiocerus* also occurs in the same Eastern North America range. It too will go to lights during the months of July through September. A small black line on the tip of the face distinguishes this from the very similar *O. amyotii*.

Cixiid Planthoppers
Family Cixiidae

Cixiids are a diverse family with over 170 species in North America. Adults have a flattened appearance, and can be found on leaves and tree trunks. Nymphs feed on plant roots, and overwinter underground.

Cixiid Planthopper *Cixius coloepeum*

We have 28 species of *Cixius*, and this one is limited to the eastern U.S. and southern Canada. *Cixius coloepeum* can be distinguished from the similar *C. misellus* by its narrower head, and black face divided by an orange vertical line.

Cixiid Planthopper *Oliarus cinnamoneus*

Oliarus is our largest genera of Cixiids with 51 species. These dark-winged planthoppers of the northeastern North America are rarely encountered. I've found them in a grassy field and on a rocky coastline. They have been recorded coming to lights.

Piglet Bugs
Family Caliscelidae

Until recently, Caliscelidae was considered a subfamily of Issidae. Easily confused for a beetle, these small (about 3mm) shiny bugs are a type of planthopper. Four genera in North America. Adults are usually short-winged.

Piglet Bug *Bruchomorpha oculata*

Easily overlooked, these small bugs occur in weedy fields throughout eastern North America. Adults have a distinctive long nose, and occur in the summer months in its northern range, and can be found all year in the southern U.S.

Delphacid Planthoppers
Family Delphacidae

Delphacids are one of our largest groups of planthoppers with 149 species. Most are short-winged and small, making them look like immature bugs. Their unique antennae and a flexible spur on the hind leg distinguish this family from other Fulgoroidea. Grasses and sedges are the preferred habitat, where they can be found in abundance.

Ornate Planthopper · *Liburniella ornata*

In my opinion, this is our most spectacular Delphacid. The only member of its genus, it occurs across the eastern U.S. and southern Canada, with adults active from June until October. They can be abundant in grassy fields, where most often long-winged adults are found.

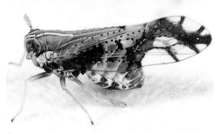

Delphacid Planthopper · *Sogatella kolophon*

A coastal species that's common in the south, *S. kolophon* has been found as far north as Nova Scotia. It also occurs in Australasia. It's one of two species in the genus, and can easily be confused with some *Muirodelphax* species.

Delphacid Planthopper · *Pissonotus basalis*

Our 31 species of *Pissonotus* are very similar in appearance. This one can be identified by the combination of a brown face and two white bands on its back. They are found in wet meadows through the summer months, and into the fall. Long-winged adults occur, but short-winged adults are most commonly found.

Treehoppers
Family Membracidae

Appearance

Small insects, most are between ⅕ to ⅓ inch long, with a large pronotum that extends back over the abdomen. The pronotum can assume a variety of different shapes, e.g. thorns and horns. Treehoppers are typically brown or green. Four membranous wings are partially exposed or hidden underneath the pronotum. The legs of treehoppers are all similarly sized with the hind legs slightly larger. Treehoppers possess very short, inconspicuous antennae.

Biology

Treehoppers are plant feeders, feeding on either trees and shrubs or herbaceous plants (some species will feed on herbaceous plants when immature and then woody plants as adults). Some treehoppers feed gregariously. Ants often tend certain species for their honeydew excretions. They have one or two generations a year. Treehoppers spend the winter as eggs inserted into plant tissue.

Northeast Species Notes

We have about 260 species of treehoppers in North America. The **Honeylocust Treehopper (*Micrutalis calva*)** is a common species that feeds on locust trees. ***Ceresa alta*** is one of the 20 species in the genus referred to as **Buffalo Treehoppers**, because of their horns. ***Entylia carinata*** are very common on goldenrod and other herbaceous plants. They're extremely variable in their coloration. ***Telamona monticola*** is a common oak feeder in a genus recognizable by its blunt shaped hump. ***Enchenopa*** has two described species and a number yet to be described.

Microcentrus caryae was formerly considered in a subfamily of Membracidae, but recently have been classified in its own family Aetalionidae, which lacks the large pronotum, but has ear-like lobes.

Treehopper *Atymna querci*

Associated with White Oaks (*querci* from genus *Quercus* for oaks), this treehopper is commonly found at lights from May to August. This species is dimorphic, with all green females and black males with yellow markings. One of 6 species of *Atymna*. *A. querci* is widespread across the east.

Treehopper *Glossonotus univittatus*

This common oak-feeding tree-hopper is one of our 5 species of *Glossonotus* sporting an impressive horn. Distinguished from similar species by the stouter horn. They blend in well with the tree branches and are hard to find. I've used a sweep net through oak saplings and found them from July to October.

Treehopper *Ceresa basalis*

Ceresa basalis is an often encountered treehopper with a very broad pronotum. Color can vary wildly in this species but note the characteristic black body and face on top specimen. The dark legs, black undersides and brown patches on the sides of the pronotum, are distinctive. Feeds on willows.

Treehopper *Smilia camelus*

A distinctively humped green striped treehopper, it's the only one in the genus found in the Northeast. The other species, *S. faciata* is only found in the southeast. Look on oak leaves during June when they're most commonly found.

Treehopper *Telamona molaris*

The "molar"-like crest on this attractive treehopper and bright red feet are diagnostic on this oak feeding species. This species ranges north to Saskatchewan, Manitoba and Ontario. June to hard frost.

Acutalis brunnea

Acutalis tartarea

Atymna helena

Atymna inornata

Campylenchia latipes

Carynota marmorata

Marbled Treehopper

Carynota mera

Ceresa alta

Buffalo Treehopper

Ceresa diceros

Ceresa lutea

Ceresa palmeri

Cyrtolobus griseus

Cyrtolobus maculifrontis

Cyrtolobus muticus

Cyrtolobus ovatus

Cyrtolobus puritanus

Enchenopa sp. (E. binotata?)

Entylia carinata

Glossonotus acuminatus

Micrutalis calva
Honey Locust Treehopper

Ophiderma definita

Ophiderma flava

Ophiderma pubescens

Ophiderma salamandra

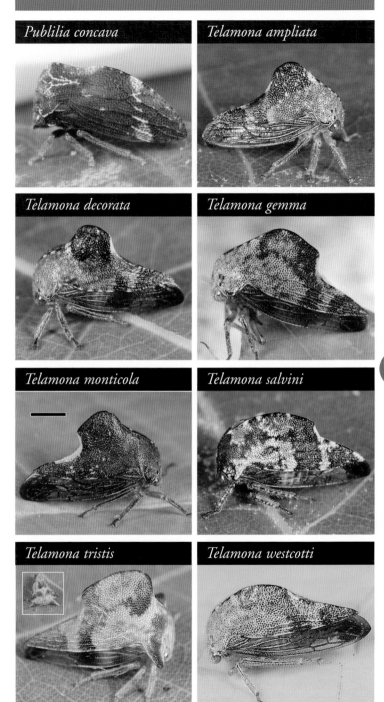

Publilia concava

Telamona ampliata

Telamona decorata

Telamona gemma

Telamona monticola

Telamona salvini

Telamona tristis

Telamona westcotti

Froghoppers (Spittlebugs) Family Cercopidae

Appearance

Small insects, most between ⅕ and ⅝ inch long. The back legs are enlarged for jumping. Froghoppers are recognized by the circle of short spines on the hind leg. They have short antennae. Forewings are longer than the abdomen, and are leathery and held tent-like over their body. Hindwings are large and membranous.

This is a nymph taken from the spittle.

Biology

Feed on plant sap. Immature nymphs are known as "spittlebugs." They create a frothy, bubbly mass around their body by mixing air with fluid secreted from the anus. They use this froth to protect themselves from drying out and to deter predators and parasitoids. Froghoppers overwinter as eggs inserted into plant stems.

This is the "spittle" that the nymphs create by mixing air with a fluid secreted from their anus. It deters predators and parasitoids.

Meadow Spittlebug *Philaenus spumarius*

dark form

This introduced species from Europe is one of our most common spittlebugs. Its color and pattern are extremely variable, but raised wing veins and two tiny black spots at the tip of the head are distinctive. An all black form also occurs. They're considered a crop pest, because they feed on strawberries, alfalfa, oats and over 400 other plants. Most of North America. May until the first frost.

Pine Spittlebug *Aphrophora cribrata*

The nymphs make frothy masses on several types of pine, with White Pine being the preferred sap ingested. Analysis of the froth has found a chemical mixture that repells ants, but doesn't appear to contain any irritants. Quebec to North Carolina, and west through the Great Lakes region. Adults mature in June.

Alder Spittlebug *Clastoptera obtusa*

Alder is one of about 20 species of trees and shrubs that hosts these spittlebugs. Unlike many other spittlebugs, this species does not go through its final molt inside the spittle, but molts to adulthood out in the open. They vary in color, so the best character used to identify them is the dark lower half of the face. June until the first frost.

Dogwood Spittlebug *Clastoptera proteus*

These colorful spittlebugs have light and dark forms (inset). Normally it's hard enough to tell which end is the front on *Clastoptera*, but these also have a pair of false eyes on the hind end to confuse predators. They occur from southeastern Canada to Tennessee and west to the Mississippi River. June through August.

Diamond-backed Spittlebug *Lepyronia quadrangularis*

The name comes from the dark diamond shape on the front wings of this flat-topped spittlebug. It's found in weedy fields, where it can be very common. They occur in the U.S. and southern Canada, east of the Rockies, and adults can be found from May until the first frost.

Red-legged Spittlebug *Prosapia ignipectus*

Difficult to separate from the black form of the Two-lined Spittlebug. The coxae of the Red-legged is red, and the venter is black. Little Bluestem is the host plant of this uncommon spittlebug. In northern New England, most likely any *Prosapia* species would be the Red-legged Spittlebug.

Leafhoppers
Family Cicadellidae

Appearance

Small slender insects, most are between ⅛ and ½ inch long. Leafhoppers have large back legs that have a row of small spines on lower part of the hind legs. They are typically green or brown, although some are brightly colored. They have short antennae located between their compound eyes. Their forewings are leathery while their hindwings are membranous.

Biology

Leafhoppers are plant feeders on a wide range of trees, shrubs and herbaceous plants. They can go through more than one generation a year. They lay eggs into plant tissue. Most leafhoppers overwinter as eggs or adults.

Nymphs can be as brightly colored as the adults (top: *Coelidia olitoria*; bottom: *Eutettix* species).

Northeast Species Notes

With about 3,000 species of leafhoppers in North America, comes a great deal of diversity. The widespread but uncommon **Flexamia areolata** found as far north as Massachusetts, is a specialist on Lovegrass *(Eragrostis spectabilis)*. The **Speckled Sharpshooter** is one of our largest leafhoppers, while the colorful species of **Arboridia** are among our smaller ones. **Grape Leafhoppers** are another small and colorful species that when in numbers, can damage grape leaves. The imported **Japanese Maple Leafhopper** has adapted to feeding on native maples, in addition to it's original food, Japanese Maples. **Red-banded Leafhoppers** are one of our 18 species of colorful **Graphocephala**, and while most of our 50 species of **Gyponana** are green, **Gyponana octolineata** stands out with a beautiful pink pattern. Most leafhoppers are readily recognizable to the family, but a few like **Penthimia americana** look like spittlebugs.

Red-banded Leafhopper *Graphocephala coccinea*

Quite common, the Candy-striped Leafhopper is also quite beautiful. It is red and green/blue with a yellow head and legs. It is found in fields and the edge of wooded areas. Candy-striped leafhoppers feed on blackberry (*Ribes* sp.) and a variety of other plants. Watch for them during mid to late summer.

Silver Leafhopper *Athysanus argentarius*

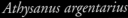

The Silver Leafhopper is an immigrant from Europe that has spread across North America. It is quite common and often on alfalfa (though this specimen was photographed on a milkweed). Light colored with dark colored veins. They are common from June to August.

Striped Leafhopper *Cuerna striata*

The colors of the Striped Leafhopper are stunning. Also note in this photo, the hitch-hiking red mite on the leafhopper's back. Congregations of adults overwinter together. They are commonly found on herbaceous plants, including thistles, May through September.

Grape Leafhopper *Erythroneura comes*

A beautiful pest of grape plants, the Grape Leafhopper lays its eggs inside the leaf. Nymphs feed on the underside of the leaves sucking out cell liquids, eventually damaging the leaf. If enough leafhoppers are present the grapes themselves could be damaged with increased acidity and lower sugar content. May to October.

Agallia quadripunctata

Amblysellus curtisii

Arboridia plena

Athysanus argentarius
Silver Leafhopper

Balclutha confluens

Balclutha impicta

Bandara johnsoni

Coelidia olitoria

Colladonus brunneus

Colladonus clitellarius
Saddled Leafhopper

Colladonus setaceus

Cuerna striata
Striped Leafhopper

Dikrella cruentata

Draeculacephala antica

Empoasca fabae
Potato Leafhopper

Erythroneura comes
Grape Leafhopper

Erythroneura elegans

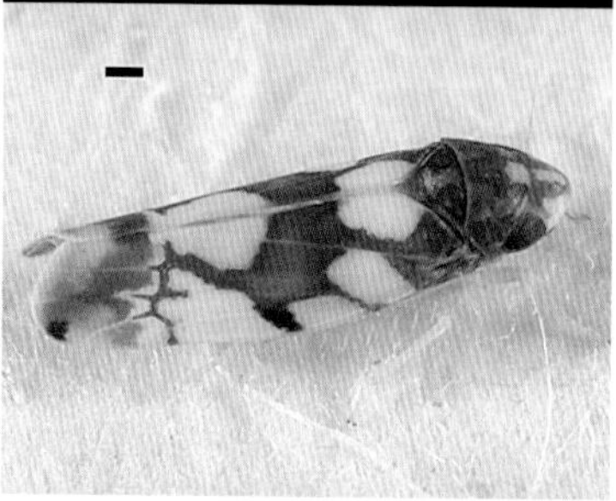

Erythroneura vulnerata

Eupteryx atropunctata

Eutettix borealis

Flexamia areolata

Gyponana octolineata

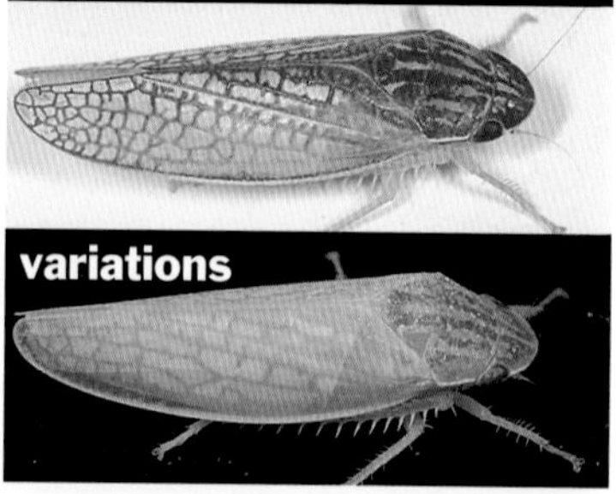

variations

Helochara communis

Idiocerus formosus

Idiocerus lunaris

Idiodonus kennecottii

Kyboasca splendida

Latalus ocellaris

Limotettix nigrax

Macrosteles quadrilineatus
Aster Leafhopper

Macrosteles slossonae

Neokolla hieroglyphica

variations

Norvellina seminuda

Oncometopia orbona
Broad-headed Sharpshooter

Oncopsis abietis

Oncopsis citrella

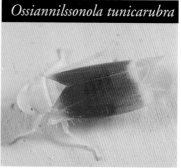

Orientus ishidae
Japanese Maple Leafhopper

Ossiannilssonola tunicarubra

Paraphlepsius irroratus
Bespeckled Leafhopper

Paraulacizes irrorata
Speckled Sharpshooter

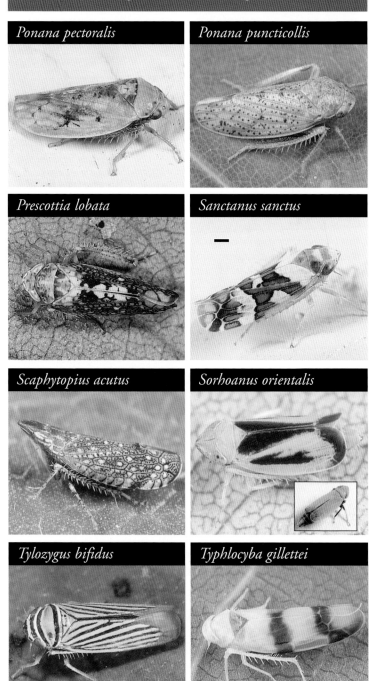

Ponana pectoralis

Ponana puncticollis

Prescottia lobata

Sanctanus sanctus

Scaphytopius acutus

Sorhoanus orientalis

Tylozygus bifidus

Typhlocyba gillettei

Aphids
Family Aphididae

Winged and wingless adults are often found feeding together as in this group of Brown Ambrosia Aphids.

Appearance

Tiny, $^1/_{25}$ to $^1/_5$ inch long, soft-bodied pear-shaped insects with long antennae and a pair of tube-like structures on the abdomen called cornicles. Aphids occur in many colors including green, red, yellow, orange, black and gray. Most are wingless, although some possess four membranous wings.

Biology

All aphids are plant feeders, feeding on all types of woody and herbaceous plants. They usually overwinter as eggs which hatch into females. Aphids reproduce parthenogenetically, i.e. eggs develop without being fertilized. The eggs hatch inside the females and are born live. Several generations can be produced like this. These individuals are wingless. Eventually winged aphids are formed which will fly to alternate plant hosts. During late summer, a generation of reproductive males and females are formed. They mate and females lay eggs which remain until the following spring. Aphids produce honeydew, a sugary sticky waste material. Honeydew can be a food source of other insects, especially ants.

White-banded Dogwood Aphid *Anoecia cornicola*

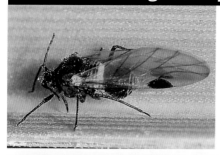

Look for this white banded aphid on dogwood leaves. Less commonly it will also feed on grasses, like the one in this picture. There are six other species of *Anoecia* in North America, with *A. cornicola* occuring throughout most of the country, and adults are found in the fall.

Oleander Aphid *Aphis nerii*

Bright orange color is a warning to potential predators, just like the Monarch butterfly, which also ingest toxins from milkweed sap. Introduced from Europe, with only females in North America, so reproduction is done by parthenogenesis. Feed on members of the dogbane family, at times nearly covering milkweed plants. June until October.

Foxglove Aphid *Aulacorthum solani*

This non native aphid is an agricultural pest. It feeds on a variety of plants, including foxglove, potato, lettuce and many other cultivated plants. Being polyphagous, the Foxglove Aphid is a vector of potato leaf roll virus, cucumber mosaic virus and beet yellows virus. Found throughout the country.

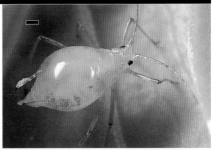

Poplar Leaf Aphid *Chaitophorus populicola*

As their common name implies, these aphids feed only on poplar and cottonwood. Heavy infestations can damage new shoots on *Populus* trees, causing deformities in the branches. Ants can be found tending the aphids, for the honeydew. Overwinter as eggs in cracks in tree bark.

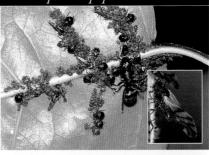

Woolly Alder Aphid *Paraprociphilus tessellatus*

The white woolly stuff on these aphids is a waxy substance for insulation and protection from predators. Large masses of them will congregate on alder branches. Harvester butterfly larva—one of our few carnivorous caterpillars—feed exclusively on Woolly Alder Aphids. In the fall winged reproductive aphids will move from alder to maple.

Goldenglow Aphid *Uroleucon rudbeckiae*

This genus of nearly 100 species feeds mostly on varieties of plants in the aster/composite family. Goldenglow Aphid feeds on black-eyed Susan *(Rudbeckia)*. In *Uroleucon*, over 20 species reported to feed on goldenrod *(Solidago)*. Most of North America. Native.

Booklice & Barklice
Order Psocoptera

Diversity
There are 23 families and about 340 species in North America. Psocids are common in the New England and New York.

Appearance
Adults: Psocids are small, most are less than 1/4 inch long, and soft-bodied insects. They are generally colored gray or brown, although a few can be brightly colored. Most psocids (barklice) possess four membranous wings which are held roof-like over their bodies. The forewings are a little larger than the hind wings. Some psocids (booklice) lack wings. Psocids have moderately long antennae, chewing mouthparts and an enlarged, bulb-like clypeus (nose).

Nymphs: The immature nymphs are very similar to adults but are smaller and lack wings.

Habitats
Many psocids (barklice) are found outdoors on or under bark, on tree and shrub leaves and under stones or dead leaves. Some species live inside buildings (booklice) where they are found associated with books and paper.

Life cycle
Psocids develop using paurometabolous metamorphosis, a type of simple metamorphosis. Some species cover their eggs with silk.

Food
Barklice feed on fungi, lichen, pollen, decaying plants and other organic material. Booklice feed on molds as well as fungi, grains, insect fragments and other starchy material, including glue from book bindings.

What's In a Name
Despite being called barklice and booklice, psocids do not resemble head lice and other true lice nor are related to them. Psocids do not bite people and are harmless to humans.

Don't confuse them with...
...members of the Hemiptera, especially froghoppers, treehoppers and leafhoppers. These insects have piercing-sucking mouthparts, have short antennae and lack a conspicuous clypeus (nose). Barklice may be confused for true lice. True lice have short antennae, lack a conspicuous clypeus (nose) and are parasitic on animals.

Common Barklouse *Cerastipsocus venosus*

One of the most conspicuous barklice. They are commonly found in "heards" on tree trunks with smooth bark. Adults and nymphs occur in the same clusters, where they move in unison when threatened, like a flock of birds. Found throughout the east where they feed on lichens. July and August.

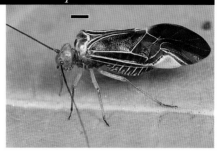

Common Barklouse *Psocus leidyi*

This clear-winged barklouse can be identified by the 3 black dots on the forewing, and the black dots on the nose and over the ocelli. It's one of 62 species we have in the family Psocidae. They're often attracted to lights, and are associated with White Pine. August to October.

Mouse-like Barklouse *Lichenomima species*

Mouse-like Barklice (Myopsocidae) are represented in North America by two genera with only 6 described species. 12 species of *Lichenomima* are thought to be in North America, but only 3 are described. This is one of the undescribed ones. During late summer look on tree trunks for these algae and lichen feeders.

barklouse

Beetles
Order Coleoptera

Diversity
This is the most abundant group of insects for total number of species. Roughly 40 percent of all insects are beetles! There are as many beetles as there all plant species combined. There are 128 families and about 30,000 species in North America.

Appearance
Adults: Beetles are generally elongate, cylindrical, or hemispherical in shape. Most are black or brown, although there are many that brightly colored. Beetles have four wings. They are distinguished from other insects by the first pair, called elytra, which are hardened or leathery and typically cover the abdomen. The second pair of wings are membranous and used for flight. Beetles possess well developed mandibles and have chewing mouthparts. The antennae are quite variable in form and size. Species range from very small, 1/20th inch to large, three inches long.

Larvae: Beetle larvae generally have conspicuous heads and elongate and flattened bodies, although others can be worm-like, cylindrical, or curled into a C-shaped body. Most beetle larvae possess legs although a few species lack them.

Habitats
Beetles are found in essentially all habitats in the Northeast, including terrestrial sites, e.g forests and prairies. They occupy open areas, are found on flowers, in fungi, on carrion, in the leaf litter and even under bark or in the wood of trees and shrubs. Some beetles are subterranean. Others are found in aquatic or semiaquatic areas.

Biology
Very diverse. Many beetles are plant feeders, including leaf feeders and tree borers. Others are predaceous, especially on other insects. Yet others are scavengers on decaying animal or plant matter.

Life Cycle
Beetles are holometabolous insects, going through complete metamorphosis to develop. Most beetles take one year to go through their life cycle once. Some beetles, particularly those living in wood or soil can take more than one year, some as long as seven years. Other beetles can complete more than one generation in a year.

Food

Very diverse. Many beetles are plant feeders, feeding completely on plant parts—leaves, fruits, flower blossoms, roots, branches and trunks. Others are predaceous, especially on other insects. Yet others are scavengers on decaying animal or plant matter. And some are fungus feeders.

Sound Production

Many beetles produce sound, especially by stridulation, i.e. rubbing different body parts together. In many cases, beetles produce sounds for defensive reasons.

Don't confuse them with...

...true bugs. You can distinguish between them as true bugs have hemelytrous wings and needle-like mouthparts.

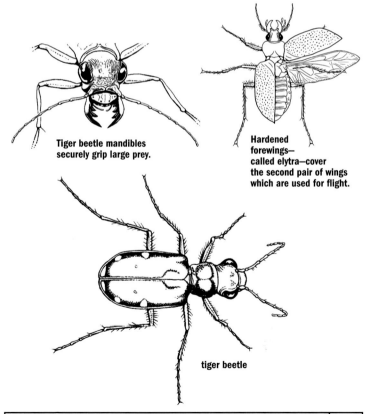

Tiger beetle mandibles securely grip large prey.

Hardened forewings— called elytra—cover the second pair of wings which are used for flight.

tiger beetle

Ground Beetles
Family Carabidae

Appearance

Small to moderate sized beetles, generally between 1/8 to 1/2 inches long with flattened bodies and parallel sided wing covers. The head is narrower than the pronotum with moderate length thread-like antennae. These beetles possess long, slender legs with a large trochanter on each of the last pair of legs. This group of beetles contains the third largest number of beetle species in North America.

Biology

Ground beetles are active at night and are occasionally attracted to lights. They hide during the day and are typically found on the ground under leaves, logs, stones, loose bark, in grassy areas, although a few can be found in trees. When exposed, ground beetles typically move quickly to find shelter but rarely fly. Tiger beetles, however, are active during the day and are usually found in sunny areas. Ground beetles and tiger beetles are predaceous, feeding on other insects as well as other invertebrate animals. Some species are scavengers and a few eat seeds. You can find ground beetles during spring and summer.

Bombardier Beetles
Subfamily Brachininae

All 48 species of North American Bombardier Beetles are in the genus *Brachinus*, with at least 12 occurring in the Northeast. Their defense mechanism is a sudden release of a foul smelling hot chemical mixture over 200F from the tip of the abdomen that gives an audible "poof." They even have the ability to swivel the tip of their abdomen like a turret to aim the chemical mixture. Found under bark, boards, logs and rocks near water, especially swampy habitats. Larvae are external parasites of Predacious Water Beetles and Whirligig Beetles.

Bombardier Beetle *Brachinus cyanochroaticus*

This species superficially looks just like every other *Brachinus* species. Small details are needed to differentiate the species, such as the third antenna segment being orange at the basal half, legs entirely orange and other minor details.
Throughout the northern U.S. and across Canada.

Ground Beetles
Subfamily Carabinae

Subfamily Carabinae is comprised of about 150 species with most being uniformly dark, heavy bodied beetles. Roughly 20 species occur in the Northeast, with the bulk of the species in the west and south. Adults of the different species feed on various prey, including caterpillars, worms, slugs and snails.

European Ground Beetle *Carabus nemoralis*

Imported from Europe and introduced on both coasts, its North American range has expanded over most of the continent, except for the deep south. Common in gardens and damp wooded areas where they feed on slugs, caterpillars and other soft invertebrates. Adults can be found from early spring to late fall.

Searcher *Carabus maeander*

The wing covers have a series welts between the ridges of this searcher that's associated with moist vegetated ground. It's found from the Northeast and through most of Canada, being more common in the east, with adults active May through August. Most often found under bark or on dirt paths near wetlands.

Fiery Searcher *Calosoma scrutator*

Occurring through most of the U.S. and southern Canada, these large beautiful beetles hunt caterpillars as both larvae and adults. These ground beetles will even go up into trees to find caterpillars. Usually found near hardwood forests in open areas from spring until fall. The long-lived adults (up to 3 years) will come to lights, and are most common in the spring.

Tiger Beetles
Subfamily Cicindelinae

Tiger Beetles have large eyes and formidable mandibles that can deliver a painful bite. They dash around quickly in short bursts looking for insect prey, with ants at the top of the list. Open sunny areas with plenty of sand, like beaches, river banks and sand pits are where most tiger beetles can be found. Others prefer dappled light in forests, rocky/pebble riverbanks or muddy areas. Most are active only during the day. Larvae are large jawed ambush predators, living in burrows. We have 109 North American species in 12 genera, with about 20 species (all in the genus *Cicindela*) in the Northeast. The **Eastern Red-bellied Tiger Beetle** is a summer species that has a distinctive red abdomen and prefers clay/gravel soil. **Green-margined Tiger Beetles** can be found on sloping bare clay soil, and is active in the spring, then again in late summer. *C. patruela* occurs spring through fall in pine barrens.

A tiger beetle larva waits for prey in its circular pit trap in the sand.

Tiger beetles have formidable jaws. These beetles were formerly placed in their own family (Cicindelidae).

Common Shore Tiger Beetle *Cicindela repanda*

Look for our most common tiger beetle on sandy riverbanks, shores, and dirt roads near water. Found in most of North America, commonly seen in spring then again in late summer. Like all tiger beetles it's a voracious predator of small insects, but it's also the only one reported to eat fruit.

Six-spotted Tiger Beetle *Cicindela sexguttata*

Brilliant metallic green. Some Six-spotted Tiger Beetles have less than 6 spots, and some have none. Adults overwinter, so as soon as the snow melts in spring, you'll start seeing them in dappled sun on woodland trails and woodland edges. By midsummer they will become scarce.

Twelve-spotted T. B.
Cicindela duodecimguttata

Big Sand Tiger Beetle
Cicindela formosa generosa

Hairy-necked T. B.
Cicindela hirticollis

Green-margined T. B.
Cicindela limbalis

Barrens Tiger Beetle
Cicindela patruela

Sidewalk Tiger Beetle
Cicindela punctulata

E. Red-bellied T. B.
Cicindela rufiventris

Oblique-lined T. B.
Cicindela tranquebarica

Subfamily Elaphrinae *Elaphrus americanus*

Looking and moving like tiny (6-8mm) tiger beetles, our 19 species of *Elaphrus* are mostly northern/boreal. Watch for them along muddy river banks, shorelines, marshes and even temporary mud, dashing about April to June. *Elaphrus ruscarius* is one of the widest ranging in the genus. *Elaphrus americanus* is usually found on mud along woodland marshes.

Ground Beetles
Subfamily Harpalinae

The diversity is vast in our largest Carabid subfamily Harpalinae, with almost 1,400 species in over 100 genera in 20 tribes that occur through-out North America. It contains ground beetles that are found under logs, rocks, bark, leaf litter, on foliage, in forests, along rivers, in arid sandy areas and ranges in size from tiny to large. A whole book could be dedicated to this one subfamily.

Vivid Metallic Ground Beetle *Chlaenius sericeus*

Don't let the good looks fool you. This beauty is a real stinker; When disturbed it lets off a foul odor. During the day these gems hide under rocks, logs and boards close to rivers and lakes. Both larvae and adults are preda-cious. Adults overwinter and are found most of the year, but scarce in mid summer.

False Bombardier Beetle *Galerita bicolor*

False Bombardier Beetles are larger and possess no weapons like the *Brachinus* species they mimic. They occur in open forests but can also occur along shorelines with the bombardier beetles. *Galerita bicolor* is distin-guished from our other north-eastern species, *G. janus*, by the shape of the head and pronotum.

Colorful Foliage Ground Beetle *Lebia pectita*

Ground beetles in the genus *Lebia* are day active on flowers and foliage, looking for small insects to eat. Most of our 48 species are small (3-10mm) and colorful, with the tip of the abdomen extending beyond the square-tipped elytra, like this *L. pectita*, that's widespread in the eastern U.S. Larvae of many *Lebia* species parasitize leaf beetles.

Lebia fuscata

Lebia tricolor

Lebia viridis

Calleida punctata

Long-necked Ground Beetle *Colliuris pensylvanica*

Another name for these odd looking beetles could be "giraffe beetles" with that very long neck. *Colliuris pensylvanica* is the most common of the 4 North American species, and the only one in the Northeast. Usually near damp areas under logs and in short grasses. Adults are thought to overwinter and are found spring through fall.

Ground Beetle *Agonum cupripenne*

Agonum with its 72 species of mostly dark shiny beetles that should be named "*Agony*" because of their difficulty to identify. Of the 50 species in the Northeast, this is one of the few easy ones to identify with its oval body and purplish/green sheen. Under rocks in damp areas or running across dirt trails from May to September. The green *A. octopunctatum* (inset) has 8 dimples on the dorsal surface.

Woodland Ground Beetle *Poecilus chalcites*

Most of the Woodland Ground Beetles are black, larvae and adults predacious. *Poecilus* only has 9 representatives, all medium sized forest dwellers. *Poecilus chalcites* can be easily recognized when it is iridescent green or bronze, but it's occasionally black. *Pterostichus* is the largest genus containing 180 North American species, (*P. commutablis*, inset).

Constricted-necked Ground Beetles Subfamily Scaritinae

The Scaritinae are constricted-necked ground beetles usually found under logs and other objects around farm fields or other areas with rich soil. Their large jaws used for catching small insects, make them look similar to stag beetles. The larger of the 2 tribes, Clivinini with 120 species is made up of small beetles. Tribe Scaritini is small, containing 17 large species. Found across the continent from spring to fall.

Big-headed Ground Beetle *Scarites subterraneus*

These large beetles (25mm) use their formidable jaws to capture insects as large as caterpillars during their nocturnal hunting. Often found under logs, rocks and boards around gardens and farm fields from spring to fall. Occurs through most of the U.S. and parts of southern Canada.

Ground Beetles
Subfamily Trechinae

Trechinae contains about 680 species north of Mexico made up of 5 tribes. Bembidiini is the largest with about 360 species, most of which are 3-6mm. Trechini is another large tribe with about 300 species, most being only about 3mm, and a few species that have no eyes. Most beetles in this subfamily are small, brown or black, not brightly colored and are associated with moist habitats.

4-spotted Ground Beetle *Bembidion quadrimaculatum*

Most of our 260 species of *Bembidion* aren't as well marked as the Four-spotted Ground Beetle. But you'll need keen eyesight to see the 4 orange dorsal marks on these day active, small (3mm) fast moving beetles as they race across a muddy riverbank. Adults can be found spring through fall across most of North America, and Europe.

Bembidion americanum

Bembidion castor

Round Sand Beetles *Subfamily Omophroninae*

Round Sand Beetle   *Omophron americanum*

Our most common round sand beetle. At night these predacious beetles emerge from burrows along sandy shorelines, sometimes in large numbers. Adults rarely fly; they prefer to run across the sand. They can be flushed from their burrows during the day by splashing water on the shoreline where they hide.

Predaceous Diving Beetles
Family Dytiscidae

Appearance

Elongate oval, convex beetles that are moderate in size, most measuring between 3/16 to 1 1/2 inches long. They are generally dark-colored, although they are sometimes yellow-

larva

ish, or have light colored markings. The antennae are thread-like and moderate in length. The back pair of legs are flattened and fringed with hair.

Biology

Predaceous diving beetles live in ponds, lakes, and streams. They are good swimmers, moving their hind legs in unison. They float at the surface of water, their head pointed down. They store air underneath their wing covers which allows them to swim underwater for a long time. Predaceous diving beetles feed on other insects and other small creatures, including small fish. They typically overwinter as larvae burrowed into the mud at the bottom of the water. Eggs are laid on aquatic plants or dropped loose into the water. They pupate in earthen cells on shore.

Predacious Diving Beetle *Acilius mediatus*

One of our most common Dytiscids in the Northeast, it can be found in almost any pond, swamp, vernal pool or even a tire track puddle. Both larvae and adults a predatory, feeding on aquatic invertebrates, small fish and even frog and salamander eggs. Adults are active spring to early summer.

Vertical Diving Beetle *Dytiscus verticalis*

Dytiscus species are among our largest diving beetles, and this is no exception at 35mm. Males have a suction cup disc on each front leg used for holding onto the female's smooth elytra during mating. Adults of this northeastern species are active March to November.

Crawling Water Beetles
Family Haliplidae

Appearance

This large family with 68 species is small in stature (2-5mm). In New England 2 genera occur; *Haliplus* containing 45 North American species, and *Peltodytes* with 18 species.

Biology

These aquatic beetles are awkward swimmers, flailing their legs alternately in a crawling motion. Needing air to breath, they carry an extra supply underwater several ways; under their wings, between the large base of each hind leg and their abdomen and at their tail. Larvae feed exclusively on algae, while adults dine on small aquatic arthropods, larvae, eggs and some algae.

Crawling Water Beetle   *Haliplus fasciatus*

Most species of crawling water beetles live in still water found in ponds, lakes and swamps. But the only place I've found *Haliplus fasciatus* is along the edge of a large river with slow moving water. It's one of the larger species of *Haliplus* at over 4mm and one of the darkest with all the black patches.

Whirligig Beetles
Family Gyrinidae

Appearance

Moderate sized beetles, 1/8 to 5/8 inch long. They are dark-colored, elongate oval, and somewhat flattened beetles. The first pair of legs are long and slender while the second and third pairs of legs are short and inconspicuous. They have two pairs of compound eyes and short clubbed antennae.

Biology

These are the aquatic beetles that make crazy loop-the-loops on the surface of lakes, ponds and streams—often in large groups—in a seemingly random pattern.

Large groups of Whirligig Beetles can be found in quiet waters.

How do they avoid each other? They sense and react to the ripples made by the other beetles. They can dive below the surface if necessary. They are able to see above and below the surface of the water simultaneously. Whirligig beetles are opportunistic, feeding on small insects that have fallen into water. They overwinter as adults and lay their eggs on the underside of the leaves of aquatic plants.

Whirligig Beetles *Dineutus & Gyrinus species*

Dineutus discolor

Dineutus is made up of 11 species of large (9-15mm) whirligig beetles. When at rest, their aggregations can number in the hundreds on lakes, ponds, rivers and streams. When threatened, a milky fluid that smells like apple is emitted. *Dineutus discolor* has light undersides and legs and are found in slow moving rivers.

Gyrinus dichrous

Gyrinus is a large genus of small whirligigs (4-7mm) with over 20 species in the Northeast. Usually found in small numbers and prefer lakes, ponds and swamps, but I found this *Gyrinus dichrous* at the edge of a large river. It is only about 4mm and has a distinctive black and orange color pattern on its belly.

Clown Beetles
Family Histeridae

Appearance

A diverse beetle family with almost 450 North American species. The wing covers on these squat beetles are shorter than the abdomen, and the short antennae with a 3 segmented club can be tucked away into cavities beneath the pronotum. The front legs are designed for digging, and the middle and hind legs often are spiny. Some are mere specks of dirt at 1mm while the largest species get up to 20mm.

Biology

Both adults and larvae prey on other insects, and they can be found in many different habitats such as; under bark, rotting fungi, beaches, leaf litter, ant nests and more.

Clown Beetle *Hololepta aequalis*

One look at those jaws and you know this beetle isn't a vegetarian. This is one of our largest Histerids in the Northeast measuring in around 10mm, and one of just 2 *Hololepta* species in the Northeast. Its flattened body is perfect for navigating under recently felled hardwood trees with tight bark. If you flip one over, you'll probably find it's carrying a load of mites.

Carrion Beetles
Family Silphidae

Appearance

Elongate to broadly oval and generally flattened beetles, carrion beetles are moderate sized with many over 1/2 inch long. The antennae are moderate length and clubbed. The elytra can be long, covering the abdomen, or short and squared off, exposing part of the abdomen. Many carrion beetles are black or black with orange or red markings while a few are black and yellow.

Biology

Carrion beetles are typically associated with dead animals, while others are found on dung or decaying plant matter. Some species bury small, freshly deceased animals they find, providing their young with food. This strategy reduces competition with flies that also seek out dead animals. Other carrion beetles are attracted to carcasses that have been dead longer and have started to dry out which also reduces competition with necrophorous flies.

A dead White-tailed Deer is irresistible to Margined Carrion Beetles (*Oiceoptoma noveboracense*). They are often seen mating on such carcasses, the male holding on to the female until she lays her eggs.

American Carrion Beetle *Necrophila americana*

larva

American Carrion Beetles are visually distinct from all the other 29 carrion beetles, and the only one we have in the genus. Both the roach-like black larvae and adults consume carrion, fly larvae and rotting fungi. Commonly found in damp forest habitats throughout the eastern half of the continent, the adults overwinter and are active from May to October.

Sexton Beetles (Burying Beetles) *Genus Nicrophorus*

In the Northeast we have 9 of the 15 Burying Beetle species. Adults bury the carcass of a small mammal or bird, and then lay eggs on it and are dedicated parents, feeding the larvae bits of carrion. Adults also feed on carrion, and often carry a large load of mites that help eliminate some of the fly larvae competing for food on the carrion. Adults are most common in the summer, but do occur from April to October.

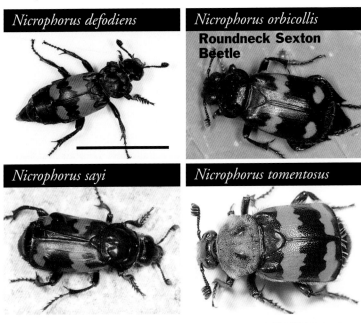

Nicrophorus defodiens

Nicrophorus orbicollis
Roundneck Sexton Beetle

Nicrophorus sayi

Nicrophorus tomentosus

Carrion Beetles *Genus Oiceoptoma*

We have 2 species of *Oiceoptoma* in the Northeast that are forest dwellers. Adults overwinter and emerge in the spring to mate and feed on carrion, fly maggots on the carrion and rotting fungi. Often they're seen in pairs with the male holding the female's antennae until she finishes laying her eggs. Larvae feeding alongside the adults have an orange edge to their roach-like dark bodies.

Oiceoptoma inaequale
Ridged Carrion Beetle

Oiceoptoma noveboracense
Margined Carrion Beetle

Rove Beetles
Family Staphylinidae

Appearance

Slender, flat beetles ranging considerably in size from 1/16 to 1 inch long. Vast majority of species are tiny. They are conspicuous because their elytra are very short, exposing most of the abdomen which is flexible. Rove beetles have fully developed hind wings which they fold underneath the short elytra. Most rove beetles are blackish or brownish. Often mistaken for earwigs but lack distinct forceps at tip of abdomen. With over 55,000 described species worldwide is the largest animal family on the planet. North America has 4,400 described species.

Biology

Rove beetles are found in many types of habitats, especially decaying organic material, including dead animals and dung. They are also associated with fungus and found on the ground under stones, leaves, loose bark and along shorelines. Most rove beetles are nocturnal and are predaceous on other insects.

Cross-toothed Rove Beetle *Oxyporus vittatus*

Oxyporus vittatus is a fall species with adults active in September and October. Look for them on mushrooms, especially *Boletus* species. This Cross-toothed Rove Beetle (Oxyporinae) is one of 14 North American *Oxyporus* species, with 6 occurring in New England, like the *Oxyporus quinquemaculatus* also a fungi feeder.

Ant-loving Beetle *Ctenisodes piceus*

The rove beetle subfamily Pselaphinae formerly treated as a family contains over 700 North American species of tiny beetles that don't look like a typical rove beetle. This *Ctenisodes piceus* is just 2mm with the clubbed antennae nearly as long as the body. Adults are found in leaf litter and under boards in the spring.

Gold and Brown Rove Beetle (May-Sept) has larvae that feed on carrion and fungi. *Platydracus violaceus* is found under hardwood bark, while *Platydracus fossator* develops in rotting fungi and carrion. *Homaeotarsus cribratus* is found along shorelines. *Scaphisoma rubens* is tiny (2mm). The **Hairy Rove Beetle** is found under carrion feeding on fly larvae. *Philonthus caeruleipennis* is found in mushroom gills May-Sept.

Creophilus maxillosus
Hairy Rove Beetle

Ontholestes cingulatus
Gold and Brown Rove Beetle

Philonthus caeruleipennis

Platydracus fossator
Red-spotted Rove Beetle

Platydracus violaceous

Homaeotarsus cribratus

Paederus littorarius

Scaphisoma rubens
Shining Fungus Beetle

Scarab Beetles
Family Scarabaeidae

Appearance

A large and variable group of beetles. They range from small to large, most between 1/4 to 1 inch long. They are slender to broadly oval and heavy bodied. Most scarabs are generally convex. They possess short antennae that usually end with three asymmetrical lobes. Unlike stag beetles, scarab beetles can compress these lobes into a club or fan them out to detect smells. Many scarab beetles are dark-colored, black or brown, but some are more brightly colored orange, gold or green.

Biology

Their habits are quite varied. Many are scavengers feeding on a variety of decaying organic matter while others feed on dung. Some feed on plants, including leaves and fruit and some feed on pollen. A few are fungus feeders and a few even live in the burrows or nests of animals. Many scarabs take one year to complete their life cycle but there are some species than can take three years. Look for them at lights at night.

Fruit & Flower Chafers *Subfamily Cetoniinae*

Bumble Flower Beetle *Euphoria inda*

Bumble Flower Beetles start flying on the first warm sunny days in April looking to mate after overwintering. They stay low to the ground and look and sound like bumble bees. Larvae are reported to live in rotting wood, dung, compost piles, haystacks and even ant nests, with adults emerging in late summer.

Green June Beetle *Cotinis nitida*

This large emerald of a beetle is often considered a pest. Larvae are root eaters, and can damage grasses, ornamental plants and a variety of cash crops. Adults will feed on ripe fruit, especially peaches, and can damage the fruit. It's found across the east as far north as southern New England and New York during summer.

Hairy Flower Scarab *Trichiotinus affinis*

Trichiotinus affinis and *Trichiotinus assimilis* are a common sight on flowers June to August. Adults feed on flower pollen, and larvae develop in decaying wood. They're very similar and have some overlap in range. *T. affinis* occurs all over the east from Maine to Florida, while *T. assimilis* is found coast to coast from New Hampshire and further north.

Trichiotinus affinis

Trichiotinus assimilis

Rhinoceros Beetles *Subfamily Dynastinae*

Rhinoceros Beetle *Aphonus species*

Not all Rhinoceros Beetles are large and have impressive horns. The 6 species of *Aphonus* are all in the eastern states, 10-15mm in length and neither males nor females have any horns. Differs from similar genera by the pronotum narrowing towards the front, and the shape of the face (clypeus).

May Beetles & Junebugs *Subfamily Melolonthinae*

Rose Chafer *Macrodactylus subspinosus*

Rose Chafers are a common sight on flowers throughout the east during June and July. Mating pairs are often more conspicuous on flowers than individuals. Areas with sandy soil are where the larvae develop, feeding on roots of plants including grasses. Adults have the same defensive chemical cantharidin, as blister beetles.

Junebug *Phyllophaga tristis* complex

May beetles (junebugs) are a common site around lights. The genus *Phyllophaga* has over 400 North American species of large beetles, often heard bouncing off window screens at night. Smaller relatives like the 109 *Serica* species often with an oily iridescence on its ridged elytra and the 212 species of *Diplotaxis,* join the *Phyllophaga* at lights.

Dichelonyx elongatula

Hoplia trifasciata

Three-lined Hoplia

Maladera castanea

Asiatic Garden Beetle

Serica iricolor

Shining Leaf Chafers *Subfamily Rutelinae*

Oriental Beetle   *Anomala orientalis*

This introduced Asian species is common on foliage and at lights all along the east coast from June to August. The grubs live in the ground under grass where they feed on the roots. Adults are variable in their dark brown and tan pattern, and sometimes can be all black. There are 48 species of *Anomala* in North America.

Grapevine Beetle   *Pelidnota punctata*

Also called the Spotted June Bug, adults are found on grape vines from June to August, where they feed on the leaves and fruit. Larvae feed on tree stumps and their rotting roots. Found across the east, it's not as common in northern New England as it is in southern states.

Japanese Beetle   *Popillia japonica*

Japanese Beetles were accidentally brought into New Jersey from Asia with nursery plants almost a century ago. Their range has expanded to include the eastern half of the continent. Adults are most abundant in June and July, and will last into October, skeletonizing leaves of hundreds of different plants. Grubs feed on a wide variety of roots.

Dung Beetles & Tumble Bugs *Subfamily Scarabaeinae*

Rainbow Scarab   *Phanaeus vindex*

Rainbow Scarabs are as colorful as the name implies. *Phanaeus vindex* is the only one of the 7 species to reach the Northeast, where it can be found in southern New England and New York. Males look like a miniature Triceratops dinosaur. Females are just as colorful as males but lack the horn. Adults active in summer.

Scooped Scarab   *Onthophagus hecate*

The Scooped Scarab is a common dung beetle found in dung and carrion from spring through fall. The genus contains 40 species of small scarabs like the 12mm *Copris minutus*, the colorful little (6mm) *Onthophagus orpheus* and the 10mm *Onthophagus taurus*).

Copris minutus
Small Black Dung Beetle

Onthophagus orpheus

Onthophagus taurus
Bull-headed Dung Beetle

Onthophagus striatulus

Earth-boring Dung Beetles Family Geotrupidae

Appearance
Oval, convex stout beetles, measuring 3/16 to 1 inch long with wing covers covering their abdomen. They are typically black or dark brown.

Biology
Typically found in and around dung while some are associated with carrion, rotting wood or fungi. They construct tunnels for the larvae (up to several feet long) which is provisioned with dung or plant material.

Earth-boring Dung Beetle *Geotrupes splendidus*

Most of the time these beetles are a foot or more underground, beneath cow patties and carrion. But when they are above ground, they look drunk, falling all over the place. Their color varies from purple, green, blue or bronze on these shiny beetles. Found spring through fall across eastern North America.

Bumble Bee Scarab Beetles Family Glaphyridae

Recently elevated to family status, they were a subfamily of Scarabaeidae. There are 8 species north of Mexico, found along the both coasts. These hairy day flyers resemble bumble bees, and often visit flowers or hover over sandy areas. Larvae feed on decaying leaves and other organic matter.

Cranberry Root Grub *Lichnanthe vulpina*

The Cranberry Root Grub is a native species that's a pest in cranberry bogs. Larvae feed on the roots of the plants, reducing cranberry yield. Studies with Massachusetts cranberry growers have shown that over 60 percent of the bogs were infested with this pest.

Stag Beetles
Family Lucanidae

Appearance

Elongate oval medium to large beetles, with most measuring between 1/2 to 1 inch long. They have short antennae that end in three asymmetrical lobes. Males particularly have large mandibles. Stag beetles are black or dark brown, though a few species are iridescent blue or green.

Biology

Stag beetles are usually associated with trees because the larvae inhabit the decaying wood of stumps and logs of both hardwood and evergreen trees. Adults feed on sap that exudes from plants. They lay their eggs into

Jaws of male *Ceruchus piceus*

the cracks and crevices of bark or logs. Stag beetles are often attracted to lights at night.

Oak Stag Beetle *Platycerus virescens*

♂

♀

Platycerus consists of 5 species here that are some of the smaller stag beetles. *P. virescens* is sexually dimorphic with the female being small jawed, broader and brown. Males are black and sometimes have a bluish to greenish sheen, hence the name. Occurring east of the Rockies, adults are active in the spring. Males are often seen on low vegetation.

Soldier Beetles
Family Cantharidae

Appearance

Flattened, oval bodies, long antennae and legs, and the first pair of wings are soft and leathery. Similar to fireflies but lack light-producing organs and their heads are visible from above.

Cantharis livida is native to Europe, but is now found all through the Northeast.

Biology

Common on flowers where they feed on pollen and nectar during the day. Some are predaceous, feeding on insects, especially aphids. Very active and readily fly plant to plant. Many species can protect themselves by secreting defensive chemical compounds to make them distasteful.

Two-lined Leather-wing *Atalantycha bilineata*

Formerly *Cantharis bilineatus* and *Ancistronycha bilineata*. This is one of just 3 species in the genus north of Mexico. Adults visit a variety of April and May flowers including viburnum, daffodil, violets and dandelions. Eastern half of North America.

Goldenrod Soldier Beetle *Chauliognathus pensylvanicus*

Very common in blooming meadows in August and September. Nectar and pollen are taken from many flowers, but goldenrod is their favorite. 19 species of *Chauliognathus* on the continent, but only this one and *C. marginatus* (spring to early summer) occur in the Northeast.

Soldier Beetle *Podabrus punctatus*

We have 108 species of *Podabrus* throughout North America. They look like *Cantharis* but without the pronotum shielding any of the head. Most species feed on aphids like this *P. punctatus*, that's widespread in the east. May and June.

Fireflies (Lightning Bugs) Family Lampyridae

Appearance

Flattened beetles with soft wing covers, often with orangish, yellowish or reddish markings on their pronotum. The head is generally hidden underneath the pronotum.

Biology

Fireflies are associated with damp areas on foliage. Some adult fireflies are predacious, while others feed on pollen and nectar. Fireflies

produce light (biolumines-cence) on the tip of abdomen on the underside. Oxygen combines with a chemical called luciferin producing luciferase. This bioluminescence is used to

Larval fireflies are well-protected predators of snails, slugs and worms.

Different species produce different light flash patterns and colors (top). It is the tip of the abdomen that bioluminesces.

communicate to members of the opposite sex through a series of light flashes at night, each species creating a unique pattern. Not all fireflies can produce light, especially the smaller species.

Northeast Species Notes

With about 170 firefly species in North America, there's plenty of diversity. For instance, ***Ellychnia corrusca*** is one of the diurnal fireflies that has no light. They can be found year round on tree trunks, even mid winter on sunny days above freezing. The **Black Firefly** (***Lucidota atra***) is another day flyer, but has light organs that are smaller than nocturnal species. The nearly 50 species of ***Photinus***, like this *P. obscurellus* employ chemical defenses (lucibufagins) that make them distasteful. Females in the genus ***Photuris*** are known to lure in male ***Photinus*** by mimicking their signal, in order to consume the male to obtain his defensive chemicals. Larvae of the 16 species of ***Pyractomena*** feed on snails, and are often seen on tree trunks in damp habitats. ***Pyropyga decipiens*** is one of 5 species in the genus that has reduced or no light organs. Pheromones emitted by the female are used to attract a mate instead of light signals.

Ellychnia corrusca

Lucidota atra

Black Firefly

Photinus obscurellus

Photuris species

Pyractomena angulata

Pyractomena borealis

Pyractomena linearis

Pyropyga decipiens

Net-wing Beetles
Family Lycidae

Appearance

Moderate sized beetles that have soft wing covers with raised ridges. The wing covers are fan-shaped and soft. The head is partially hidden underneath the pronotum. Many net-winged beetles are black, although some can be brightly colored orange or red. They have moderately long antennae with broad, flat segments.

Biology

Common on foliage, flowers and trees in wooded areas. They feed on other insects as well as juices from decaying plants, nectar and honeydew. Net-winged beetles are distasteful to potential predators and they apparently do not have any known natural enemies.

Northeast Species Notes

In the Northeast about half of the 80 species of net-wing beetles occur. *Caenia dimidiata* is one of just 2 species in the genus and has huge comb-like antennae. The **Banded Net-wing Beetle** (*Calopteron reticulatum*) can be found in small groups on foliage June to September. The bright colors of the **Golden Net-wing Beetle** (*Dictyoptera aurora*) really stand out on tree trunks in the spring when trees are starting to leaf out. Its larvae are predacious under bark. *Leptoceletes basalis* with its large comb antennae is the only species in the genus found in the Northeast. The colors on the pronotum of *Lopheros fraternus* are reversed from the norm, with the orange in the center bordered by black. *Plateros* is a large genus with more than half the 30 similar looking species occurring in the Northeast.

Calopteron reticulatum
Banded Net-wing Beetle

Calopteron terminale
End Band Net-wing Beetle

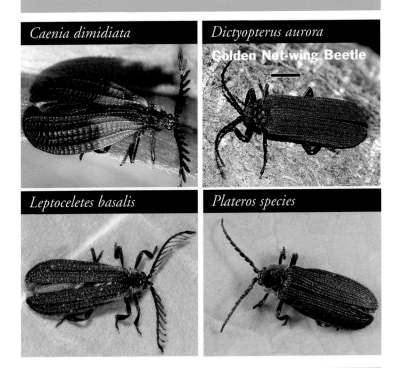

Caenia dimidiata

Dictyopterus aurora
Golden Net-wing Beetle

Leptoceletes basalis

Plateros species

Click Beetles
Family Elateridae

Appearance

Small to moderate sized beetles, they are typically between 1/8 to 1/2 inch long (one species is up to 1 3/4 inches long). They are elongate oval and flattened beetles and are typically dark brown or black. The prothorax appears "loose" from the rest of the body. The back corners of the prothorax are prolonged into sharp points. Click beetles have moderate length antennae.

Biology

Click beetles are found on foliage and flowers as well as under bark. Some species are predaceous on aphids while others feed on pollen, nectar and decaying fruit. A click beetle is unique because it can right itself when it is on its back. It arches the area between the prothorax and mesothorax and then snaps it back (usually producing an audible "click"). If it fails the first time, it will keep trying until it succeeds. Click beetles commonly are attracted to lights. The larvae are commonly called wireworms and can take five to seven years to develop.

Northeast Species Notes

Subfamily Cardiophorinae is made up of about 120 smallish beetles like this squat all black ***Cardiophorus gagates***. The Prosterninae have some of the more ornate beetles like ***Selatosomus pulcher*** and ***Pseudanostirus hieroglyphicus***, both northeastern species. The 34 northeastern species of Elaterinae sport quite a few orange and black beetles like ***Ampedus areolatus***, ***Ampedus rubricus***, ***Ampedus sanguinipennis*** and ***Melanotus leonardi***, all of them widespread in the east. Another Elaterinae, ***Agriotes collaris*** occurs in northern New England and Canada in May and June.

Eyed Click Beetle *Alaus oculatus*

Besides being one of our largest click beetles, it has a spooky "face" staring back at you. In the Northeast it can only be confused with the Small-eyed Elater (*Alaus myops*) which has perfectly round smaller eyes. Spring and summer adults feed on nectar and plant juice, while larvae live in decaying wood and are predatory on wood-boring beetle larvae.

Click Beetle *Denticollis denticornis*

The sole member of the genus in North America, this click beetle mimics a distasteful and highly toxic firefly to avoid predation. Found in forested areas, larvae develop in rotting wood, and adults can be seen on leaves and other low vegetation during the early part of summer.

Danosoma brevicorne

Lacon discoideus

Cardiophorus gagates

Agriotes collaris

Ampedus areolatus

Ampedus nigricollis

Ampedus sanguinipennis

Melanotus leonardi

Selatosomus pulcher

Pseudanostirus hieroglyphicus

Checkered Beetles
Family Cleridae

Appearance

Small to moderate very hairy beetles, most between 3/16 to 1/2 inch long. They are elongate and cylindrical in shape. The prothorax narrower than the base of the wing covers while the head is as wide or wider than the pronotum. They have moderate length antennae which are often clubbed. Checkered beetles are often brightly colored.

Biology

Checkered beetles are typically found on or under the bark of trees and logs where they are predaceous chiefly on other insects, such as bark beetles. Other species are common on flowers and feed on pollen. A few species are associated with dead animals. Larvae of some species are parasites of solitary bee larvae.

Checkered Beetle *Enoclerus rosmarus*

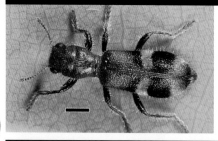

You need to take a good look, because this looks and acts just like a velvet ant that can deliver a painful sting. An eastern species often found on the ground and in weedy vegetation around damp areas. Adults can be seen on flowers from May to July.

Red-Blue Checkered Beetle *Trichodes nuttalli*

Adults are nectar feeders that are active from June to August, but the larvae prey in leaf-cutter bee nests. Also called Nuttall's Shaggy Beetle, this beautiful beetle was named after British naturalist Thomas Nuttall. Widespread across southern Canada and the northern states.

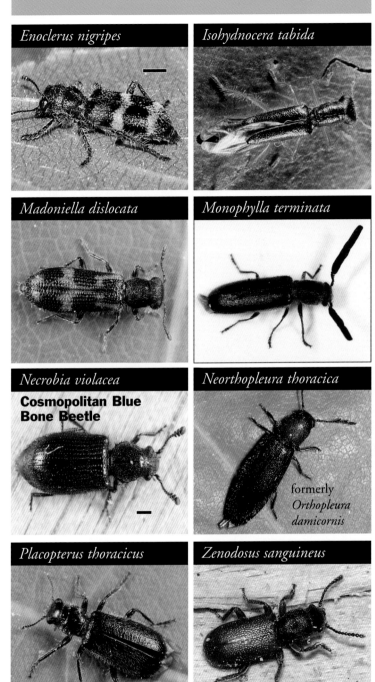

Enoclerus nigripes

Isohydnocera tabida

Madoniella dislocata

Monophylla terminata

Necrobia violacea
**Cosmopolitan Blue
Bone Beetle**

Neorthopleura thoracica

formerly
*Orthopleura
damicornis*

Placopterus thoracicus

Zenodosus sanguineus

Soft-winged Flower Beetles Family Melyridae

We have 520 species of these small (2-7mm) colorful beetles. Many species congregate on flowers, but adults and larvae are omnivores—scavenging, preying on small arthropods and feeding on pollen and nectar. Males of some species like this **Collops tricolor** have modified antennae thought to aid in mating. Other males like **Hypebaeus oblitus** have modified elytral tips where glandular secretions are emitted for females to consume before mating. **Anthocomus equestris** is native to Europe and this aphid eater is now well established in the Northeast. **Nodopus flavilabris** is a rarely encountered forest dweller from eastern Canada to Florida that is attracted to lights.

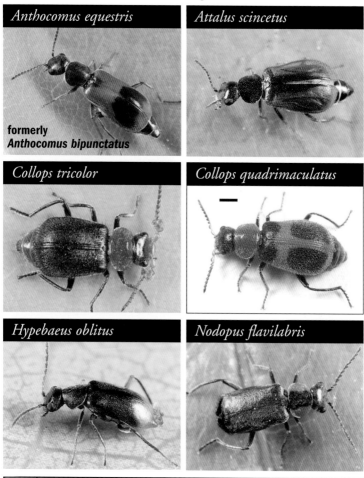

Anthocomus equestris

formerly Anthocomus bipunctatus

Attalus scincetus

Collops tricolor

Collops quadrimaculatus

Hypebaeus oblitus

Nodopus flavilabris

Metallic Wood-boring Beetles Family Buprestidae

Appearance

Small to moderate sized beetles, most are between 1/8 to 1 inch long. They are bullet to elongate oval shaped beetles and flattened. The head is somewhat retracted into the prothorax with moderate length antennae. They are iridescent or metallic—bronze, black or green—some with yellow or red markings.

Biology

Metallic wood boring beetles are typically borers in deciduous trees and shrubs. A few species occur in other plants, including evergreens and berries. They generally overwinter as larvae under the bark. Adults emerge in spring and lay eggs on trunks or branches. Adults feed on leaves of the host plant. Some may also be found on flowers where they feed on pollen.

Bronze Birch Borer *Agrilus anxius*

Agrilus is the largest genus in the family with over 170 North American species. Bronze Birch Borers are pests of many species of birch and have been found on beech. The larvae live under the bark where they make tunnels (galleries). Adults emerge from their pupal stage by chewing through the bark in June. Found throughout the Northeast and adjacent Canada.

Flatheaded Hardwood Borer *Dicerca divaricata*

Our 24 species of *Dicerca* have a characteristic flaring of the tail, similar to the *Poecilonota* but without their metallic sheen. Of the 16 species found in the Northeast, this species is most commonly encountered. Larvae feed in hardwood trees that are sick or already dead. They can enter from an injury and mine through the heartwood, killing the tree. Adults active from April through June.

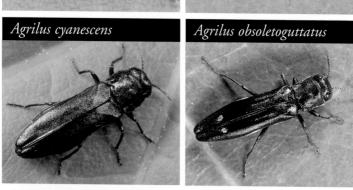

Acmaeodera tubulus

Agrilus bilineatus
Two-lined Chestnut Borer

Agrilus cyanescens

Agrilus obsoletoguttatus

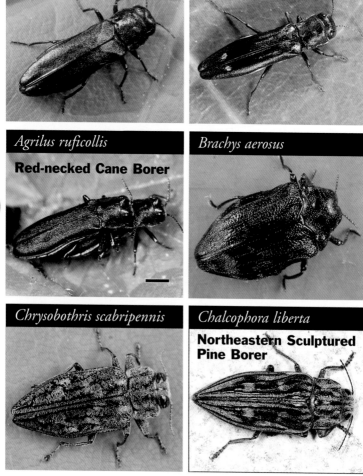

Agrilus ruficollis
Red-necked Cane Borer

Brachys aerosus

Chrysobothris scabripennis

Chalcophora liberta
Northeastern Sculptured Pine Borer

Wedge-shaped Beetles
Family Ripiphoridae

Appearance .

Small to moderate sized beetles ranging from 1/8 to 3/5 inch long. They have a humpbacked shape with a blunt, squared off abdomen, giving them a wedge-shaped appearance. The elytra are short and pointed, exposing part of the abdomen. They possess moderately short, fan-like or comb-like antennae. They are black and orange.

Biology

Wedge-shaped beetles are typically found on flowers where they presumably feed on pollen. They also lay eggs there. After hatching, larvae attach themselves to certain types of wasps or bees and carried back to their nests where they are parasitic on the wasp or bee larvae. Adult wedge-shaped beetles are short-lived and are active during August.

Wedge-shaped Beetle *Macrosiagon dimidiata*

This beetle looks like a large brightly colored tumbling flower beetle that's also usually found on flowers. But that's where the similarity ends. Females lay eggs on flowers where the larvae attach to nectarring wasps. Once back to the nest, the larvae is a parasite, feeding on the host larvae. Adults are active June to September but they only live a day or two.

Wedge-shaped Beetle *Ripiphorus walshi*

In the case of *Ripiphorus*, the old saying you are what you eat holds true. Larvae of these bee look a likes are parasites of solitary bees. The genus is in need of revision, with many species unidentifiable even with a specimen. Females visit flowers to lay eggs, and males only live a day or two apparently don't feed. Adults are active from June to September.

Blister Beetles
Family Meloidae

Appearance

Medium sized insects, usually between 3/8 to 5/8 inch long. Usually slender bodied with a pronotum narrower than the head or the base of the wing covers. The wing covers are soft and flexible.

Biology

Most blister beetles are found on plants where they eat leaves and flowers. Some feed on nectar. The bodies of blister beetles contain a chemical known as cantharidin which they secrete to protect themselves. This substance can cause blisters to human skin and can be poisonous if eaten by people or animals. Many blister beetles exhibit a rather unusual and complex life cycle known as hypermetamorphosis. The larva is alligator-like when it first hatches. This stage, called a triungulin, is very active. The following stages are grub-like and inactive. Many are associated with bee nests and some feed on grasshopper eggs.

Ash-gray Blister Beetle *Epicauta fabricii*

This widespread species of eastern North America is found in meadows and fields from late May to early July. The larvae feed on grasshopper eggs, but adults only feed mainly on peas and lupines. Color varies from light to dark gray, and males have distinctively bent antennae. Young female blister beetles lack the blistering compound cantharidin, but acquire it from a male during mating.

Black Blister Beetle *Epicauta pennsylvanica*

Epicauta is our largest genus with 173 species north of Mexico. The Black Blister Beetle occurs through most of the U.S. and southern Canada. Adults are active July to September and can be abundant on flowers of goldenrod and aster. The Margined Blister Beetle (*Epicauta funebris*) is closely related and occurs through the east in the same time and habitat. Color forms lacking the margin are identified by the enlarged palpi and thin antennae.

Striped Blister Beetle   *Epicauta vittata*

Sometimes considered a pest, adults feed on a variety of garden plants, especially potatoes and tomatoes, earning them the name "Old Fashioned Potato Bug." Found from Quebec to Texas, and are uncommon in New England. In the Northeast our most colorful blister beetle is active during July and August.

Bronzed Blister Beetle   *Lytta aenea*

Larvae of blister beetles in the genus *Lytta* are parasites in solitary bee nests while adults feed on fruits, leaves and pollen. The Bronzed Blister Beetle is active April and May in the Northeast. The very similar *Lytta sayi* (inset) is found only in the northeast and adjacent Canada during May and June.

Oil Beetle   *Meloe impressus*

Lacking wings and only having reduced elytra, these beetles are totally flightless. They get their name from cantharidin, an oily substance emitted from leg joints when disturbed. Some *Meloe* larva chemically attract a male bee that they attach to and after the bee mates, are transferred to the female and become parasitic in the bee nest. One of our 22 similar species.

Blister Beetle   *Nemognatha nemorensis*

This southeastern beetle is now becoming a regular sight in New England in June and July. Adults most often found on black-eyed susans, where they use their long beak to suck nectar from the flowers. First instar larvae (triungulins) attach themselves to bees visiting flowers and become kleptoparisites in the bee's nest.

Tumbling Flower Beetles Family Mordellidae

Appearance

Small insects, generally 1/8 to 1/4 inch long. They are humpbacked with the abdomen tapering to point. The head is pointed down and is difficult to see from above.

Look for tumbling flower beetles on umbelliferous flowers where they feed on pollen.

Biology

Commonly seen on composite flowers, especially parsley, goldenrod and aster. When threatened their escape method is to jump and tumble about wildly. Adults are flower feeders, while larvae can be stem and leaf miners, fungi and decaying wood eaters, predacious or parasitic in galls.

Northeast Species Notes

We have over 200 of these small wedge-shaped beetles. ***Falsomordellistena pubescens*** is a widespread nicely patterned eastern species. ***Mordella*** is made up of 25 species like this common eastern ***M. marginata***. ***Mordellaria serval*** is a rare northeastern species found on flowers. The large genus ***Mordellistena*** has 131 species including ***M. convicta*** which parasitizes the Goldenrod Gall Fly.

Eight-spotted Tumbling Flower Beetle
Hoshihananomia octopunctata

A large (8-9mm) and beautiful tumbling flower beetle, it's the only one of the 3 species in the genus occurring in the Northeast. During June and July it can be found especially on Queen Ann's Lace. Somewhat similar to *Glipa oculata* in size and color, but *oculata* is found south of New York.

Tumbling Flower Beetle *Yakuhananomia bidentata*

This is the largest tumbling flower beetle we have, reaching to 15mm. Widespread through the east, but not commonly encountered, possibly because most people don't look at dead hardwood tree trunks where these beetles are usually found. Adults are active May to August.

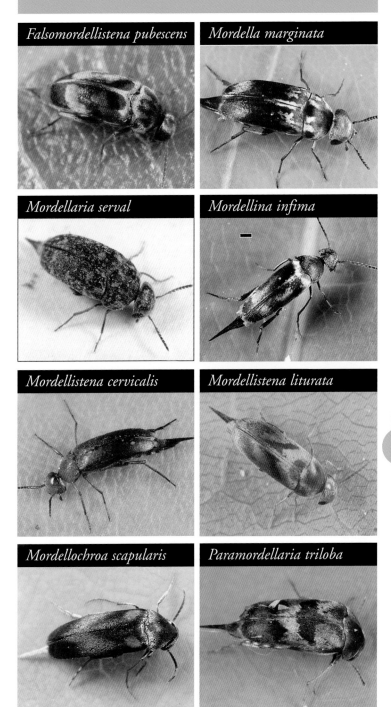

Falsomordellistena pubescens

Mordella marginata

Mordellaria serval

Mordellina infima

Mordellistena cervicalis

Mordellistena liturata

Mordellochroa scapularis

Paramordellaria triloba

Darkling Beetles
Family Tenebrionidae

Appearance

Usually between 1/8 to 1 inch long and ranging from elongate oval to oval in shape. They are typically black or brown, although there are few that are brightly marked red. The antennae are moderate in length and are inserted under an brow ridge on the head. Although this is one of the larger groups of beetles in North America, most occur in the west, while relatively few occur in the Northeast.

Biology

Darkling beetles are found under leaf litter, stones, on plants, in rotting wood, associated with fungus, animal nests and dry pet food. Some species are found on sand dunes. Darkling beetles are typically scavengers or fungus feeders. They are usually active at night.

Forked Fungus Beetle *Bolitotherus cornutus*

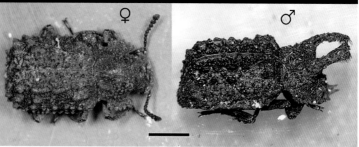

The prominent "horns" on the males are used for battling other males over females. Both adults and larvae live in bracket fungi growing on trees. Their warty cryptic appearance makes them difficult to see, and when threatened, they play dead. Found throughout the east, this is the sole member of the genus. Larvae overwinter inside bracket fungi and emerge in spring and summer.

Yellow Mealworm Beetle *Tenebrio molitor*

The yellow mealworms sold in pet stores are often this species. Though not native, this beetle has been here for almost two centuries, and occurs worldwide, except in the tropics. Considered stored grain pests, they also feed on dead insects and meat. Found outdoors during the spring and summer, but can occur year round indoors.

Alobates pennsylvanica
False Mealworm Beetle

Arthromacra aenea
Long-jointed Beetle

Corticeus parallelus

Diaperis maculata

Haplandrus fulvipes

Androchirus erythropus

Neomida bicornis

Upis ceramboides
Roughened Darkling Beetle

False Darkling Beetles
Family Melandryidae

False Darkling Beetles are forest dwellers that are active during the night. Their diet is composed of either fungi or rotting wood, depending on the species. The family is varied. Most are brown or black, but ones with bright red, orange or yellow markings also occur. Antennae are usually thread-like, but some are slightly clubbed. Shape varies from long and narrow to oval, and size ranges from 2-15mm.

False Darkling Beetle   *Dircaea liturata*

There's no mistaking this torpedo-shaped beetle with distinctive pale markings. Looking at dead trees during the night is one way to find these beetles, but watching for them at night lights is a lot easier. These beetles are xylophagous—they feed on rotting wood. May to August.

4-spotted False Darkling Beetle   *Spilotus quadripustulatus*

This is a rarely found beetle, even though it has a wide distribution (Quebec to Louisiana). Its small size (3.5mm) and habitat may be responsible for more people not finding it. I've found a few by using a sweep net in woods through low leafy branches during May and June.

Ironclad Beetles
Family Zopheridae

The family Zopheridae is made up of 3 subfamilies; Zopherinae, the Ironclad Beetles, Monommatinae, the Opossum Beetles and Colydiinae, the Cylindrical Bark Beetles. Named for their thick armor-like exoskeleton that has bent more than one collector's pin, Ironclad Beetles (Zopherinae) live in rotting wood and polypore fungi. Formerly considered part of the Darkling Beetle family Tenebrionidae, 30 species occur in North America, with only one species occurring in the east.

Eastern Ironclad Beetle *Phellopsis obcordata*

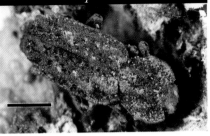

Found in the eastern U.S. and southeast Canada forests under hardwood bark, and polypore fungi that they feed on, especially birch polypore fungi. Larvae feed on fungi growing between the layers of wood in rotting logs. Adults are around spring through fall and play dead when threatened.

Fire-colored Beetles
Family Pyrochroidae

Medium-sized, often black with some red (the "fire" in Fire-colored). Elytra is wider than pronotum and often wider at rear. Head has a distinct neck. Antennae of males often branching. Larvae mostly in decaying wood where they eat fungi. Adult males prod blister beetles into exuding cantharidin, then store the chemical and use it to attract females. Most adults are nocturnal and come to lights on occasion. Also attracted to fermenting fruit and other vegetable matter.

Fire-colored Beetle *Dendroides concolor*

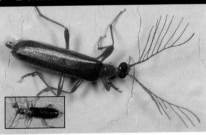

Two *Dendroides* species in the Northeast, *D. canadensis* (inset) with black body and red legs and pronotum, and the solid brown *D. concolor*. Males have elaborately comb-like antennae and enormous eyes that touch. Active in June and July, and often show up at lights.

Fire-colored Beetle *Pedilus lugubris*

Pedilus look like soldier beetles with a bulbous pronotum. Many of our 30 species are similar, and some like this *Pedilus lugubris* vary from all black to black with a red pronotum. These beetles acquire cantharidin from blister beetles to attract a mate. The cantharidin is transferred to the female in the sperm packet and is used as a protective coating for the eggs. May and June.

Narrow-waisted Bark Beetles
Family Salpingidae

Salpingidae is a family of small seldom seen beetles with a constricted waist, consisting of 20 North America species in 8 genera. The Northeast has 3 species in 2 genera, with the 2 species of *Sphaeriestes* being rare. Both adults and larvae are under bark dwellers that feed on inner bark.

Narrow-waisted Bark Beetle *Rhinosimus viridiaeneus*

This small 3mm beetle has a striking resemblance to a weevil. But it lives under bark and has been associated with birch, linden, alder and other hardwoods. On early warm sunny spring days, adults will come out from under the bark to sun themselves on tree trunks. Across Canada and the northern U.S. Spring to summer.

False Blister Beetles
Family Oedemeridae

False Blister Beetles resemble soldier beetles and blister beetles. Like true blister beetles they possess toxins that can cause blistering. We have 87 North American species which have larvae that live in rotting wood or in the soil. One species, the Warf Borer *Nacerdes melanura* (not pictured) native to Europe, bores into pilings and driftwood along the coast. Adults are pollen feeders that are active in spring to early summer.

Red-necked False Blister Beetle *Asclera ruficollis*

Don't wait too long in the spring to look for these beetles. Adults are active on flowers and on tree trunks starting in March and are gone by the end of May. The only other *Asclera* species in the Northeast, *A. puncticollis* is easily identified by the black central spot on the red pronotum.

Carpet Beetles
Family Dermestidae

Appearance

Small beetles, measuring between 1/16 to 1/4 inch long. They are usually convex oval to elongate oval beetles. Their elytra are often covered with hair or scales. They have short, clubbed antennae. Most are black and brown, although a few can have interestingly colored patterns.

Biology

Dermestid beetles are scavengers feeding on dried animal and plant material high in protein, including fur, hair, feathers, and similar materials. Sometimes they are associated with dead animals. Some dermestid beetle adults are found on flowers in the spring and summer, where they feed on pollen.

Larder Beetle *Dermestes lardarius*

Dog owners probably recognize this beetle. Larder Beetles feed on high protein foods like dry dog food. They also feed on dried grain, dead insects, wool carpets and furs. This introduced species is worldwide, wherever people live. With its indoor habitat, these beetles occur year round.

Varied Carpet Beetle *Anthrenus verbasci*

A nicely patterned little beetle, it's our most commonly found Dermestid in homes. The hairy larvae mostly feed on dead insects, and can decimate an insect collection if undetected. Adults visit outdoor flowers where they feed on pollen during the spring and summer. In the fall they return indoors to lay eggs. Found throughout North America and internationally.

Sapfeeding Beetles
Family Nitidulidae

Appearance

Small beetles, most under 1/2 inch long. Most have short wing covers leaving part of the abdomen exposed. Most black, some with orange, yellow or red spots.

Biology

Associated with decaying plant matter, such as rotting fruits and vegetables, fungi and oozing sap. Some associated with carrion or flowers.

Picnic Beetle *Glischrochilus fasciatus*

The 9 species of *Glischrochilus* are also called Beer Beetles because of their appetite for fermented foods like compost, tree sap and beer. Found in spring and fall under bark of trees that are oozing sap, in the sap flow or in rotting fruit. Adults probably overwinter, judging by New England sightings as early as March and as late as October.

4-spotted Sap Beetle *Glischrochilus quadrisignatus*

Very similar to the Picnic Beetle, but slimmer and has smaller spots that tend to be more tan than orange. They are often found together around sap flows and rotting compost, and have been known to fly into beer mugs. Widespread on our continent and also in Europe. Active spring through fall.

Glischrochilus sanguinolentus

Glischrochilus siepmanni

Lobiopa undulata   *Nitidula bipunctata*

Flat Bark Beetles
Family Cucujidae

Appearance

Small to medium very flat beetles, up to a little over 1/2 inch. They are elongate oval and are generally reddish or brownish.

Biology

Found under the loose bark of dead trees and logs. Thought to be predaceous on other insects while some may be fungivorous.

Red Flat Bark Beetle   *Cucujus clavipes*

There's no mistaking the Red Flat Bark Beetle when you find one under a piece of poplar or ash bark from a recently felled tree. Both larvae and adults are adapted for living under bark where they prey on other insects. Even in the coldest winters, larvae live under bark and avoid freezing because of antifreeze like substances in their blood. Widespread through most of the continent.

Handsome Fungus Beetles Family Endomychidae

Appearance

Many of our 45 species of Endomychidae are small black-and-orange beetles that can be mistaken for lady beetles. But a closer look reveals the dimpled pronotum that often gives a winged appearance, and multi segmented antennae ending with several clubs. In some species (like *Phymorpha pulchella* below) the male clubs are hugely exaggerated.

Biology

Usually found under bark or under logs associated with fungus. Adults of many species overwinter, sometimes in aggregations under bark.

Handsome Fungus Beetle — *Endomychus biguttatus*

This lady beetle mimic can be found spring through fall across the eastern half of the continent. Adults overwinter, sometimes in large groups under bark. Often feeds on Split Gill Fungus (*Schizophyllum commune*) and can be seen on birch trees with the fungi *Piptoporus betulina*.

Aphorista vittata

Lycoperdina ferruginea

Mycetina perpulchra

Phymaphora pulchella
♂

Lady Beetles
Family Coccinellidae

Appearance

Small, between 1/16 to 3/8 inch long. They are oval and convex beetles with the head mostly hidden underneath the pronotum when viewed from above. They have short, clubbed antennae and relatively short legs. Lady beetles typically have a black and white pronotum and have red or orange wing covers with black spots, although they are infrequently black with red or orange spots. But the vast majority of Coccinellids are tiny, non-descript and hairy beetles!

Biology

Lady beetles, also commonly called ladybugs, are typically found on leaves, stems, flowers, and other plant parts where they are predaceous on aphids and other soft-bodied insects, although they can supplement their diet with pollen when prey is lacking. A few lady beetles are plant feeders. Lady beetles overwinter as adults, sometimes in large aggregations. Lady beetles can protect themselves against potential enemies by secreting a noxious fluid from leg and body joints, called "reflex bleeding." These beetles can pass through several generations during a year.

Eye-spotted Lady Beetle   *Anatis mali*

A large distinctive lady beetle with a series of spots with a pale ring around them. As the beetle ages, it darkens to where the spots are barely noticeable. Usually found on conifers where they prefer to hunt for aphids. Occurs across southern Canada and the northern states, with adults active spring through fall.

The Eye-spotted's close cousin is the Fifteen-spotted Beetle (*Anatis labiculata*). It normally has seven spots on each elytron and a 15th spot spanning the middle. These spots lack the lighter ring and are easy to see on younger individuals but eventually the elytron darken so spots are difficult to distinguish (see photo).

Fifteen-spotted Lady Beetle
Anatis labiculata

Anisosticta bitriangularis

Brachiacantha felina

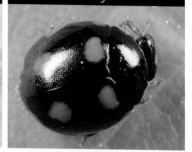

Brachiacantha quadripunctata

Brachiacantha ursina
Orange-spotted Lady Beetle

Twice-stabbed Lady Beetle *Chilocorus stigma*

I find these lady beetles on hardwood tree trunks looking for scale insects to eat. They appear from early spring to late fall, and are found throughout eastern North America. The larvae have six rows of long spines covering their entire body. Check the underside of this beetle to separate it from similar species.

Seven-spotted Lady Beetle *Coccinella septempunctata*

Named for its 7 black spots, this lady beetle was repeatedly introduced to North America starting in the mid 1950s to control aphids. Those attempts failed, but an accidental release in the 1970s has resulted in its spread all over the continent. Adults can be found in fields from spring through fall.

Three-banded Lady Beetle *Coccinella trifasciata*

Coccinella trifasciata perplexa is the subspecies of Three-banded Lady Beetle occurring through New England and north into Canada, and west past the Great Lakes. It varies from light yellow to dark orange with 3 transverse black bands.

Spotted Lady Beetle *Coleomegilla maculata*

Adults congregate in overwintering sites under leaf litter, logs or bark. They emerge early in spring when the aphids, insect eggs, larvae and mites they prey on aren't abundant. So unlike most lady beetles, this species feeds on pollen for about half its diet. Widespread in North America. Very common around farm fields in New England.

Cycloneda munda
Polished Lady Beetle

Epilachna varivestis
Mexican Bean Beetle

Exochomus marginipennis

Multicolored Asian Lady Beetle *Harmonia axyridis*

Introduced from Asia many times on both coasts for aphid control, it took almost 70 years for these beetles to become well established. Now they're the most common lady beetle in many parts of the country. In the fall adults start seeking shelter for the winter, and can invade homes in large numbers. Highly variable with over 20 different color and pattern forms (see inset).

Convergent Lady Beetle *Hippodamia convergens*

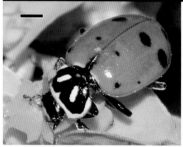

Convergent Lady Beetles are regularly collected from large aggregations in California to be sold as a biological aphid control. When released they quickly disperse before feeding. This native species is found throughout the Northeast, but is much more common in the west.

Hippodamia parenthesis
Parenthsis Lady Beetle

Hippodamia variegata
Variegated Lady Beetle

Hyperaspis bigeminata

Hyperaspis proba
Esteemed Lady Beetle

Mulsantina hudsonica
Hudsonian Lady Beetle

Mulsantina picta

Naemia seriata
Seaside Lady Beetle

Propylea quatuordecimpunctata
14-spotted Lady Beetle

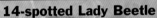

Psyllobora vigintimaculata
20-spotted Lady Beetle

Scymnus americanus group

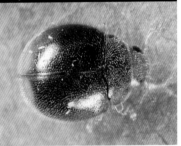

Mealybug Destroyer *Cryptolaemus montrouzieri*

Imported from Australia in the 1890s to control scale insects on citrus in California, they've become popular greenhouse additions. Mealybug Destroyers can't survive cold winters, so the ones found in the Northeast most likely escaped from a greenhouse. They're well established in southern states where both larvae and adults eat soft scales and mealybugs.

Leaf Beetles
Family Chrysomelidae

Appearance

Leaf beetles are brightly colored and spotted and are easily confused with ladybird beetles. Leaf beetles are the fourth largest group of beetles.

Biology

Leaf beetles are plant feeders feeding primarily on leaves and flowers and are found on nearly

Tortoise beetle larva with frass camo on its back.

all types of plants. Many leaf beetles are particular to specific plants. Adults typically spend the winter as adults.

Golden Tortoise Beetle *Charidotella sexpunctata*

Adults have the ability to change color from metallic gold to red when disturbed. Larvae have developed an unusual defensive system, hiding under a fecal shield that's held over their back. Food includes morning glory and related plants. Late spring to early fall in most of North America.

Mottled Tortoise Beetle *Deloyala guttata*

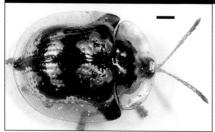

Plants in the morning glory family are the food for both larvae and adults. Larvae use masses of excrement as a shield. Adults overwinter beneath leaf litter and are active spring to early fall through most of North America. They're found in gardens, weedy fields and meadows.

Goldenrod Leaf Miner *Microrhopala vittata*

The larvae usually feed inside the layers of goldenrod leaves, leaving telltale mines. Adults are variable in color and striping, depending on what host plant they developed on. Occurring through most of North America, and usually found from May to September.

Cassida flaveola
Pale Tortoise Beetle

Chelymorpha cassidea
Argus Tortoise Beetle

Physonota helianthi
Sunflower Tortoise Beetle

Plagiometriona clavata
Clavate Tortoise Beetle

Chalepus walshii

Sumitrosis inaequalis

Odontota dorsalis
Locust Leaf Miner

Odontota scapularis

Broad-bodied Leaf Beetles Subfamily Chrysomelinae

We have 135 species of Chrysomelinae in 16 genera in North America. Called Broad-bodied Leaf Beetles because of their noticeable round or oval shape. Many are brightly colored with stripes, spots or blotches. Both larvae and adults feed on leaves and flowers of various plants.

Russet Alder Leaf Beetle *Calligrapha alni*

The 38 species of *Calligrapha* north of Mexico are well represented in New England by nearly half the species. Oval with various hieroglyphic style markings, and many species are host specific. This species feeds on alder. May to September.

Calligrapha californica

Calligrapha confluens

Calligrapha lunata

Moon-marked Leaf Beetle

Calligrapha multipunctata
Common Willow Calligrapha

Calligrapha philadelphica

Dogwood Leaf Beetle

Calligrapha vicina

Swamp Milkweed Leaf Beetle *Labidomera clivicollis*

Extremely variable in pattern
and can be yellow or orange.
Widespread east of the Rockies,
and the sole species of
Labidomera north of Mexico.
Both adults and larvae feed on
members of the milkweed family by first cutting the leaf vein
to reduce the amount of latex
on the leaf they're feeding on.

Colorado Potato Beetle *Leptinotarsa decemlineata*

Native to Mexico and originally
fed on nightshade (*Solonum*), but
spread through North America
with cultivated potatoes where it's
a crop pest. Note 10 black stripes
that separate from similar species.

Chrysolina quadrigemina/hyperici

Klamath Weed Beetle

Chrysomela knabi
Knab's Leaf Beetle

Chrysomela mainensis
Alder Leaf Beetle

Gonioctena americana
American Aspen Beetle

Prasocuris vittata

Zygogramma suturalis
Ragweed Leaf Beetle

Shining Leaf Beetles
Subfamily Criocerinae

Three-lined Potato Beetle *Lema daturaphila*

Widespread across the continent, it feeds on potato and other species of *Solonum*, plus occasionally on ground cherry (*Physalis*). Adults May to September. Some of our other 13 *Lema* species are similar, like *Lema trivittata* that also feeds on potato.

Lily Leaf Beetle *Lilioceris lilii*

Even the beauty of the Lily Leaf Beetle doesn't get it any fans with lily growers. The larvae of this Eurasian import feed on true lilies, and will devastate the plant while hiding behind piles of feces on the leaves they're eating. Only in the Northeast and adjacent Canada. May to August.

Asparagus Beetle *Crioceris asparagi*

Introduced from Europe in the mid 1800s the Asparagus Beetle is now widespread in North America. These beetles are a common sight to any asparagus grower. Even with all their variation, this is a very distinctive beetle.

12-spotted Asparagus Beetle *Crioceris duodecimpunctata*

Like its cousin above, the beautiful Twelve-spotted Asparagus Beetle was also accidently introduced from Europe. The larva feeds on asparagus leaves. This and the above species can emit a squeek to startle predators.

Casebearing Leaf Beetles Subfamily Cryptocephalinae

The approximately 350 North American species of Casebearing Leaf Beetles are named for the protective case over the eggs and larvae. Adults are typically barrel shaped with the head hidden by the thorax. When eggs are laid, the female covers them with a fecal shield, and the larvae continue to add more feces around them as they grow, creating a protective case. Many of the larvae consume dead leaves on the ground, while others eat green foliage.

Casebearer beetle larva bearing its barrel-shaped protective case.

Northeast Species Notes

Pachybrachis is the largest genus with 33 species occurring in the Northeast. ***Cryptocephalus*** is another abundant genus with 19 northeastern species. Larvae of this genus feed in leaf litter, while the adults eat foliage. The **Warty Leaf Beetles** fall to the ground when they feel threatened, remaining motionless with their legs pulled in, looking like a piece of caterpillar frass.

Anomoea laticlavia
Clay-colored Leaf Beetle

Bassareus clathratus

Bassareus literatus

Bassareus mammifer

Coleothorpa dominicana

Cryptocephalus calidus

Cryptocephalus mutabilis

Cryptocephalus quadruplex

Diachus auratus
Bronze Leaf Beetle

Neochlamisus species

Warty Leaf Beetle

Pachybrachis bivittatus

Saxinis saucia

Aquatic Leaf Beetles
Subfamily Donaciinae

All but 5 of the 53 North American species of Donaciinae belong in just 2 genera, *Donacia* and *Plateumaris*. And in the Northeast we have 29 species of *Donacia* and 15 *Plateumaris*. Adults of most species have a metallic sheen, are long-horned with thickened hind femurs, and are found near water where they feed on vegetation. Larvae feed on submerged aquatic stems and roots where they insert specialized tubes on their hind quarters into the stem for oxygen.

The easiest way to tell these 2 genera apart is the posterior elytral suture is rounded and slightly separated in *Plateumaris* and *Donacia* has normal looking elytrae tips that stay together and don't have a rounded suture (see photos below).

Donacia species

Plateumaris species

Donacia sp. elytrae tips

Plateumaris sp. elytrae tips

Oval Leaf Beetles
Subfamily Eumolpinae

Most members of the Oval Leaf Beetles are as the name implies, oval. Many are dull brown little beetles, but a fair number of them are shiny gems. Not much is known about the larval history on our 145 species, except that they seem to be mostly root feeders. Adults of some species probably overwinter, judging by the ***Graphops curtipennis*** I found under a log in Massachusetts during February.

Dogbane Beetle *Chrysochus auratus*

This beautiful beetle has a blue, green and coppery metallic sheen that changes with the angle of the light. They feed exclusively on dogbane, with adults feeding on foliage and larvae on the roots. Widespread east of the Rockies, and common in any dogbane patch through the summer months.

Bromius obscurus
Western Grape Rootworm

Colaspis brunnea
Grape Colaspis

Graphops curtipennis

Paria frosti

Skeletonizing Leaf Beetles Subfamily Galerucinae

Roughly 700 North American Galerucinae species. Many larvae feed between the veins on the upper surface of leaves, leaving a skeletonized appearance, but many *Diabrotica* larvae feed on roots (rootworm beetles). Flea Beetles (Alticini) hop like a flea when threatened, and make up about 400 species in this subfamily.

Northeast Species Notes

Adults like the **Striped Cucumber Beetle** feed on leaves and pollen. *Disonycha pensylvanica* is a widespread eastern species usually found near water. The **Water Lily Beetle** can also feed on Purple Loosestrife. *Capraita subvittata* is a widespread northeastern species that feeds on viburnum. *Kuschelina thoracica* is a beautiful iridescent flea beetle found in dry sandy habitats. The **Striped Flea Beetle** is a cabbage feeder. The pale colored **Cypress Leaf Beetle** is one 20 species in the genus that mostly have stripes. *Ophraella communa* is a Common Ragweed feeder. *Trirhabda borealis* feeds on goldenrod.

Sumac Flea Beetle *Blepharida rhois*

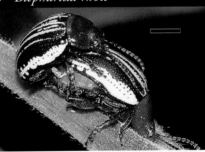

Larvae protect themselves while feeding on sumac leaves by placing excrement across their back. Adults have a rusty base color with the markings varying from white stripes to blotches. Only one species in the genus north of Mexico. Widespread in the U.S. and southern Canada, except on the west coast.

Bean Leaf Beetle *Cerotoma trifurcata*

Leaves of beans, peas and other legumes make up the diet of the Bean Leaf Beetle. Background color varies greatly —shades of yellow, red and orange. Widespread east of the Rockies, where they can be a crop pest. Adults probably overwinter, based on one I found under bark during March in Massachusetts.

Spotted Cucumber Beetle *Diabrotica undecimpunctata*

Widespread through the U.S. and southern Canada, larvae feed on roots of corn, grasses and legumes. Also called the Southern Corn Rootworm, they can be a serious pest of corn. Have been recorded on over 200 species of plants. Color varies from yellow to green, but easily recognized by the 11 black spots. Western Corn Rootworm Beetle *Diabrotica virgifera* (inset photo).

Purple Loosestrife Beetle *Neogalerucella calmariensis*

Introduced into the NE and NW states from Eurasia in 1992 to combat the invasive Purple Loosestrife. This beetle works in conjunction with another imported loosestrife beetle the similar looking *N. pusilla* to weaken and kill off the plant. These beetles have become very common and Purple Loosestrife hasn't gone away, but is now under control.

Capraita subvittata

Disonycha caroliniana

Disonycha pensylvanica

Kuschelina thoracica

Phyllotreta striolata

Striped Flea Beetle

Systena marginalis

Cypress Leaf Beetle

Acalymma vittatum

Striped Cucumber Beetle

Diabrotica barberi

Northern Corn Rootworm

Galerucella nymphaeae

Water Lily Beetle

Ophraella communa

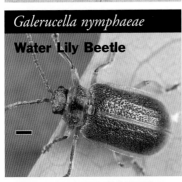

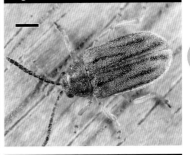

Pyrrhalta viburni

Viburnum Leaf Beetle

Trirhabda borealis

Family *Chrysomelidae* LEAF BEETLES | **197**

Long-horned Beetles
Family Cerambycidae

Appearance

Small to large insects, ranging in size from 1/8 up to almost 2 1/2 inches long. They are elongate, some are almost triangular, and cylindrical. They have long antennae, at least half the length of the body, many as long as the body or longer. The antennae are typically at least partly surround by the compound eyes. They vary widely in color ranging from black, brown, grayish, red, yellow, and/or orange.

Biology

Most long-horned beetles are wood borers attacking dying or recently dead trees. Some species are stem borers. Adults are commonly found on trees and under loose bark. Many are also found on flowers. Long-horned beetles may feed on leaves, pollen or wood. Longhorn beetles typically spend the winter as larvae, maturing into adults in the spring.

Round-necked Longhorns
Subfamily Cerambycinae

Longhorn Beetle   *Clytus ruricola*

Just like the Locust Borer this beetle is a wasp mimic often found on flowers or low tree leaves. Larvae develop in rotting hardwoods, especially maples. By far the more common of the 2 *Clytus* from New England. I've found them in New England from June to August.

Phymatodes amoenus

Psyrassa unicolor

Branch Pruner

Sugar Maple Borer *Glycobius speciosus*

One of our most beautiful beetles, and one that mimics wasps. The larvae have a 2 year life cycle feeding only on Sugar Maple, with adults emerging June or July. The beetles can be found anywhere sugar maple grows. A pest of Sugar Maples, but rarely kills the trees.

Locust Borer *Megacyllene robiniae*

This wasp mimic feeds exclusively on Black Locust, and an infestation can kill weakened trees. Native to the Northeast, the beetles have spread with the planting of Black Locust for reclamation across the U.S. Adults emerge in August and September and are commonly seen feeding on goldenrod.

Callimoxys sanguinicollis
Blood-necked Longhorn Beetle

Euderces picipes

Purpuricenus humeralis

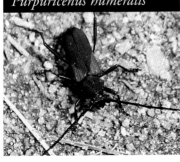

Xylotrechus colonus
Rustic Borer

Flat-faced Longhorns *Subfamily Lamiinae*

Northeastern Pine Sawyer *Monochamus notatus*

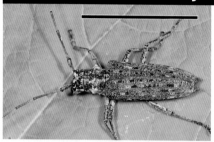

Found throughout the Northeast, these longhorn beetles have antennae nearly twice the length of their body. They feed on dying conifers and dead logs, with a preference for pine. Adults start emerging in June and last until September, and are often attracted to lights.

Whitespotted Sawyer *Monochamus scutellatus*

This most common of the 5 northeast species of *Monochamus* is variable in the amount of spotting, but the white scutellum is constant. Females have shorter antennae than the long "horned" males. They develop in dead or dying fir, pine and sometimes spruce. Across Canada and northern U.S. from May to September.

Round-headed Apple Tree Borer *Saperda candida*

An attractive pest of apple, hawthorn, mountain ash, pear and other related trees that have been weakened. During its 3 year life cycle an infestation can kill the host tree. Adults start showing up in May and are around until August. Found throughout New England and most of eastern North America.

Red Milkweed Beetle *Tetraopes tetrophthalmus*

Wherever you find Common Milkweed, you're sure to see this beetle. Eggs are laid on vegetation near the milkweed, and the larvae drop to the ground and find their way to the milkweed roots and start feeding. The most common of the 2 *Tetraopes* in the Northeast (*T. melanurus* inset). June to August.

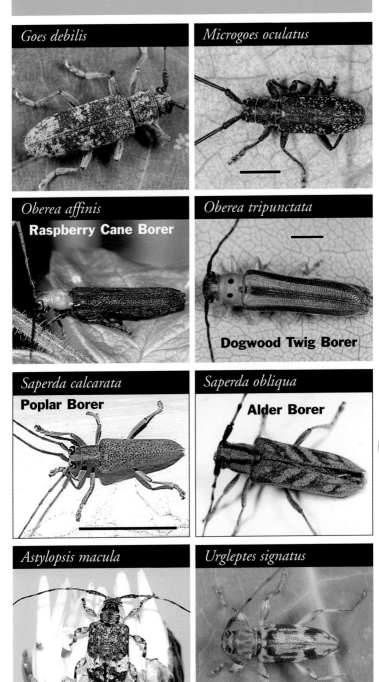

Goes debilis

Microgoes oculatus

Oberea affinis
Raspberry Cane Borer

Oberea tripunctata
Dogwood Twig Borer

Saperda calcarata
Poplar Borer

Saperda obliqua
Alder Borer

Astylopsis macula

Urgleptes signatus

Flower Longhorns *Subfamily Lepturinae*

Elderberry Borer *Desmocerus palliatus*

These large and distinctive bee-tles can be found on flowers in the spring and summer, with elderberry being their favorite. Eggs are laid on elderberry, where the larvae feed in the stem and migrate down into the roots before completing their 2 year life cycle. Widespread in the east.

Flower Longhorn *Judolia montivagans*

This black and cream colored beetle is an important pollina-tor. Occurring in the west as well as the east. One subspecies in the east—*J. montivagans barberi*—is solid black. Eggs are laid in dying pine and spruce as well as some hardwoods, like poplar and willow. Adults are found in June and July.

Flower Longhorn *Leptura subhamata*

This flower longhorn is one of 14 species of *Leptura* in North America. They're found in mixed hardwood and conifer-ous forests, where the larvae develop in damp rotting pine and hemlock logs. Adults are active in June and July, and are found in the Northeast and adjacent Canada.

Flower Longhorn *Strangalepta abbreviata*

During June and July this is a common beetle on flowers along forest trails and woodland edges. A variable species typical-ly black with a tan stripe on each elytra, but occasionally all black or all tan. Larvae develop in decaying hardwood and coniferous logs. Widespread through eastern North America.

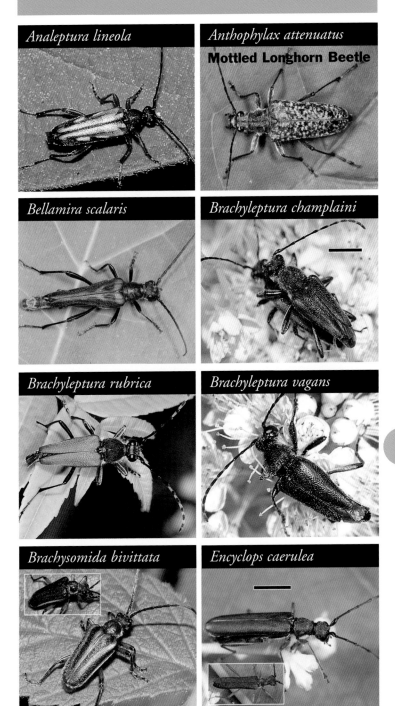

Analeptura lineola

Anthophylax attenuatus

Mottled Longhorn Beetle

Bellamira scalaris

Brachyleptura champlaini

Brachyleptura rubrica

Brachyleptura vagans

Brachysomida bivittata

Encyclops caerulea

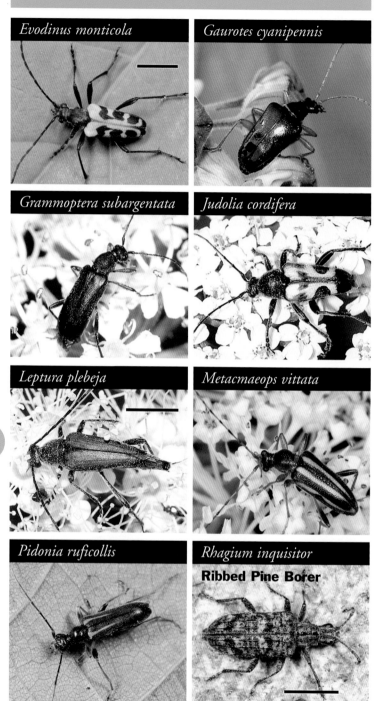

Evodinus monticola

Gaurotes cyanipennis

Grammoptera subargentata

Judolia cordifera

Leptura plebeja

Metacmaeops vittata

Pidonia ruficollis

Rhagium inquisitor
Ribbed Pine Borer

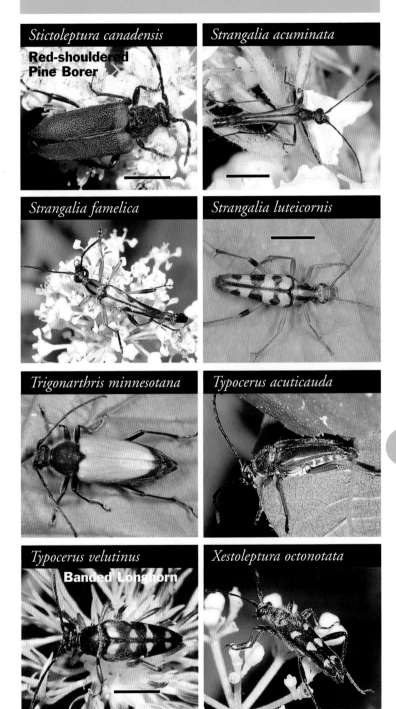

Stictoleptura canadensis

Red-shouldered Pine Borer

Strangalia acuminata

Strangalia famelica

Strangalia luteicornis

Trigonarthris minnesotana

Typocerus acuticauda

Typocerus velutinus

Banded Longhorn

Xestoleptura octonotata

Weevils & Bark Beetles
Family Curculionidae

Appearance

Small to medium size beetles that are generally elongate oval and cylindrical. Weevils are conspicuous as the head is prolonged into a snout or beak. This snout can be relatively short and blunt or can be slender and long (sometimes longer than the entire body length of the weevil). They have short, elbowed antennae. Many species are drab colored with some resembling bark. Some species are brightly colored. Weevils are the second largest family of beetles.

Biology

Weevils are plant feeders, feeding on a wide variety of plants, attacking leaves, trunks, branches, stems, fruits, seeds, and roots. Some species have a wide host range while others have a much narrower list of preferred plants. Many weevils will play dead when they feel threatened.

Oak Leafrolling Weevil *Attelabus bipustulatus*

I see these weevils often in May and June on oak and hornbeam sapling leaves along powerlines making a circular cut in a leaf (photo bottom right), starting on one side of the mid vein, and ending on the opposite side of the vein. The weevil then rolls the cut portion into a cylinder (photo bottom left) that serves as an incubation chamber for its egg. They occur across the eastern U.S. and southeast Canada.

Oak Timberworm *Arrhenodes minutus*

These primitive weevils live under bark of recently dead or dying oak, poplar or beech. They're sexually dimorphic; females are smaller and have a weevil-like beak. The larger males have sizable jaws that the use to guard a female from other suitor males. May to August.

Neapion frosti

Ceutorhynchus erysimi

Microplontus campestris

Rhinoncus castor

Iris Weevil *Mononychus vulpeculus*

At just 5mm this is the largest of the Minute Seed Weevils (Subfamily Ceutorhynchinae). This chunky little weevil is found in damp areas with Blue Flag Iris (*Iris versicolor*), where larvae develop in the seed heads. Often found right on the iris flowers. A widespread eastern species.

Weevil *Lechriops oculatus*

The large alien-looking eyes touching each other are characteristic of Subfamily Conoderinae. I commonly find this small (3mm) weevil from early spring to late fall on trunks of white pines, and less often on hardwood trunks. The beak is neatly tucked away and not easily seen. Widespread in the eastern half of the continent.

Apple Curculio   *Anthonomus quadrigibbus*

Related to the infamous Boll Weevil of the south, the Apple Curculio develops in crabapple or hawthorn fruit, and dropped apples early in the season. It's wide ranging in North America, and is not considered a serious crop pest. Look for the adults near their host trees from May to July.

Anthonomus lecontei

Anthonomus signatus
Strawberry Clipper

Cionus scrophulariae

Myrmex chevrolatii
Antlike Weevil

Orchestes alni
European Elm Flea Weevil

Tachyerges ephippiata

Cryptorhynchus lapathi

Tyloderma foveolatum

Eubulus bisignatus

Listronotus sparsus

Hunting Billbug *Sphenophorus venatus*

Billbugs have a unique oval shape that's easily recognizable. Over 30 species of *Sphenophorus* in the Northeast. Eggs are laid on grass where the larva feeds on shoots and on to the roots. Considered a pest in the lawn industry, where infestations can kill the roots. Skunks and moles can then damage lawns further by digging for the grubs.

Green Immigrant Leaf Weevil *Polydrusus sericeus*

Accidentally introduced to New York in the early 1900s from Europe, these beetles are now a common sight throughout the Northeast and out past the Great Lakes. Adults feed on foliage of birch, apple, oak, poplar plus others, and the larvae feed on roots. Adults active from May to August.

Hypera nigrirostris
Black-beaked Green Weevil

Hypera zoilus
Clover Leaf Weevil

Cylindrical Weevil *Lixus rubellus*

This medium sized (10mm) weevil lives in damp areas where its host plant, smartweed grows. Adults feed on the leaves, while the larvae feed inside the stem. Widespread through North America, but not commonly found. Adults are active from May to September.

Plum Curculio *Conotrachelus nenuphar*

The name is deceiving; this isn't a curculio like the Acorn Weevils. Plums and apricots are their primary food. The legless larvae feed inside the fruit, causing the spoiled fruit to fall from the tree. They occur through most of the continent, with adults found May to July in the north, longer in southern regions.

Piazorhinus scutellaris

Pissodes similis

Rhyssomatus palmacollis

Pissodes nemorensis
Northern Pine Weevil

Rose Curculio   *Merhynchites bicolor*

Rose Curculios are associated with both wild and cultivated roses, where the female lays eggs on the flowers. Larvae develop in the rose hip and drop to the ground to pupate. Adults are active May to July across southern Canada and the northern states, feeding on roses, blackberries, raspberries and nectar.

Bark & Ambrosia Beetles Subfamily Scolytinae

Once classified as the family Scolytidae, they've been reclassified as a subfamily, which contains about 525 North American species that live under bark. Also called "engraver beetles" because their tunnel galleries under bark look as though an artist was at work. The main channel is made by the adult, and all the radiating arms are the work of the larvae. As the larvae grow, the mine widens. Some Scolytinae are referred to as ambrosia beetles because they introduce and cultivate fungi into their tunnels.

Red Turpentine Beetle   *Dendroctonus valens*

Our largest bark beetle is considered a pest of pine and spruce, attacking weak trees. Adults drill a hole through the bark to mate and lay up to 100 eggs. A telltale sign of these beetles is a reddish ball of pitch on the tree where the hole was bored. The larval gallery can be up to one square foot under the bark. Most of the continent except the southeast.

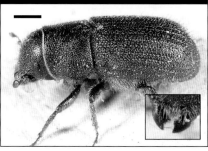

Nerve-winged Insects
Order Neuroptera

Diversity

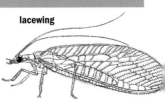
lacewing

There are 15 families and 401 species in
North America. Nerve-winged insects are
fairly common in the Northeast.

Appearance

Adults: Nerve-winged insects are small to large, ranging from 1/8 to 2
inches long. They have elongate, cylindrical, soft-bodies with a long,
slender abdomen and well-developed legs. They have chewing mouthparts and long, slender antennae that occasionally is clubbed. They
have four, similarly sized membranous wings that are usually longer
than the abdomen with a characteristic net-like arrangement of veins.
These wings are held over their body, typically tent-like when at rest.
Nerve-winged insects are not very strong flyers.

Larvae: Nerve-winged larvae are typically cylindrical or somewhat flattened with a conspicuous head. They possess either chewing or sickle-
like sucking mouthparts which face forward. Nerve-winged larvae have
conspicuous legs and lack prolegs. The abdomens of aquatic species
possess filaments sticking out to the side.

Habitats

Nerve-winged insects are common in a variety of terrestrial sites, such
as deciduous or conifer forests and nearby areas and sites adjacent to
rivers, lakes, ponds and other water. The larvae are either terrestrial in
the same sites or are aquatic.

Biology

Adult nerve-winged insects are usually predacious on aphids and other
insects or feed on nectar and pollen. Some adults are short-lived and do
not feed. The larvae are nearly always predacious on other insects. Eggs
are generally laid in the soil, on the tips of stalks on plants, or objects
near water. Look for nerve-winged insects May to September.

Don't confuse them with...

...dragonflies and damselflies. You can distinguish between them as dragonflies and damselflies have very short, straight antennae (never clubbed). Stoneflies also look similar but are more flattened and possess legs that are more widely spaced out. Sometimes caddisflies are confused but they have hairy wings and very long antennae (as long or longer than their bodies). Mantids could be confused with certain nerve-winged insects but mantids have leathery wings and longer antennae.

Spongillaflies
Family Sisyridae

Spongillafly larvae live inside freshwater sponges and feed on them with their long hair-like jaws. Larvae come out of the water to spin a double walled cocoon on vegetation. The outer layer of the cocoon is a fine lace-like structure. Adults resemble Brown Lacewings. There are 6 North American species in 2 genera, *Sisrya* (uniformly brown), and *Climacia*. In the Northeast we have 2 species of *Sisrya* (*nigra* and *vicaria*) and 1 species of *Climacia*.

Spongillifly   *Climacia areolaris*

A nicely patterned spongillifly, *C. areolaris* can be found throughout eastern North America where freshwater sponges occur, and is the only member of its genus in the Northeast. Look for adults from June to September resting on vegetation near water, and at night attracted to lights.

Alderflies
Family Sialidae

Appearance

Alderflies have a 3/16 to 1/2 inch long black body with a smoky wings; the hind wings are broad at the base.

Larval "gills" are the long filaments on the sides of the abdomen, and the single tail filament is distinctive to alderflies.

Biology

Eggs are laid on emergent vegetation along slow moving streams and lakes. The larvae are aquatic insect predators. They pupate on shore in soil or wet plant litter. Alderflies are found on foliage and other nearby objects close to water, although they are attracted to lights and can be further away. They are present May and June.

Alderfly   *Sialis species*

Sialis is the only genus in North America, with 24 species. Larvae can tolerate poor water quality, and are found under stones in slow moving streams, rivers and lake edges. Adults are not strong fliers, and are usually found on vegetation near water.

Dobsonflies & Fishflies
Family Corydalidae

Appearance

These are often large insects ranging in size up to 1/2 to 2 inch long. They have large mandibles and have hind wings that are broad at the base. They are typically brown.

Biology

Dobsonflies and fishflies lay eggs on branches hanging over streams or lakes. Once the larvae hatch they drop into the water. Eventually they pupate on the shore in soil or wet plant litter. Adults are found on foliage and stones near streams and lakes, although they are attracted to lights and can range away from water. They are active from May to August.

Spring Fishfly *Chauliodes rastricornis*

Adults active in spring into early summer. The Summer Fishfly (*Chauliodes pectinicornis*) is very similar but come out in the summer and fall. Males have feathery antennae, while females have thin beaded antennae. During the day they rest on trees and bushes near water. Active at night and attracted to lights. Larvae found in still water of rivers, ponds and swamps.

Eastern Dobsonfly *Corydalus cornutus*

This is a huge insect with a wingspan of about 5 inches. Males have extraordinarily large mandibles, which are used to fend off other males. Despite its ferocious looks, males can't bite, but females and the larvae can give a good nip. The larvae know as hellgrammites live in fast moving rivers and streams, and prey on aquatic insects and small fish. They're found throughout the United States and southern Canada. Adults can be found hiding under leaves near their larval rivers during the day, and can be attracted to lights in July and August.

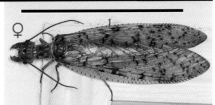

larva a.k.a. hellgrammite

Dark Fishfly *Nigronia fasciata*

This is one of a few dark Fishflies in our area. The amount and pattern of white on the blackish wings is different in each species. The larvae live in fast moving streams and rivers, and in June and July the adults can be seen flying like a large slow moth near these streams. The antennae have a comb-like appearance.

Mantidflies
Family Mantispidae

Appearance

Mantidflies are 3/8 to 5/8 inch long. They have a prolonged prothorax, the area directly behind the head, and have large front legs modified for grabbing prey. Mantidflies are reddish brown or dark brown; wings are either partly brown or are entirely clear.

Biology

As larvae, Mantidflies parasitize the egg sacs of spiders or live in the soil where the larvae prey on scarab beetle grubs, noctuid moth larvae, or social wasps. The larvae go through a type of development known as hypermetamorphosis where the first instar (stage) of the larva is very active and the subsequent instars become grub-like. Mantidfly adults prey on small insects they capture. They are active during June through September.

The raptorial front legs of the Brown Mantidfly are used to capture and hold insect prey.

Wasp Mantidfly *Climaciella brunnea*

Our most ornate mantidfly occurs throughout most of North America. Adults are a convincing mimic of paper wasps (*Polistes* sp.), and fre-quent flowers where they catch prey with their powerful front legs. Larvae are parasites of wolf spider eggs.

Say's Mantidfly *Dicromantispa sayi*

Of the 13 species of mantidflies north of Mexico, 4 species occur in the Northeast includ-ing the small brownish-yellow *Dicromantispa sayi* (pictured left) and the similar *Leptomantispa pulchella*, the Green Mantisfly (*Zeugomantispa minuta*).

Brown Lacewings
Family Hemerobiidae

Appearance
Brown lacewings are 1/8 to 1/4 inch long. They have a brown body with somewhat smoky wings and brown veins.

Biology
Brown lacewings prefer to live in wooded areas where they lay their eggs on plants. They feed on soft-bodied insects, including aphids; they will also feed on pollen and scavenge on dead insects. The lar-

Larva are called "aphid wolves" as they prey on aphids.

vae—known as "aphid wolves"—are predacious on aphids. Brown lacewings usually spend the winter as pupae, although they can overwinter as adults. Brown lacewings are present May to September (or later). Look for adults at lights at night.

Brown Lacewing *Hemerobius humulinus*

Found across eastern North America, this is our most common of the 14 species of *Hemerobius*, which are characterized by oval wings. It's distinguished from the similar *H. stigma* by the wide dark stripe on the thorax. Since they can overwinter as adults, look for these brown lacewings early in the season until fall.

Brown Lacewing *Micromus angulatus*

A boreal species found through the Northeast and in montane areas further south. This small (7-8mm) brown lacewing is one of 8 *Micromus* species. Not just native to North America, but Europe and northern Asia, they have a good appetite for aphids, mealybugs and other plant pests, making them beneficial to agriculture.

Green Lacewings
Family Chrysopidae

Appearance

Green lacewings are 3/8 to 7/16 inch long, generally greenish with coppery colored eyes and have clear wings with greenish veins.

Biology

Green lacewings are found on herbaceous plants as well as trees and shrubs. They are predacious on soft-bodied insects, especially aphids, or they feed on pollen or honeydew. They attach their eggs on stalks anchored to plants. The larvae—known as "aphid lions"— are predacious on aphids and similar soft-bodied insects; some larvae may cover themselves with debris to better ambush prey and avoid detection by ants, the chief protectors of aphids. Eventually they pupate on the underside of leaves. Green lacewings are active at dusk or a night and are often attracted to lights. They are present May to September.

eggs

larva ("aphid lion")

adult

Green Lacewing *Chrysopa oculata*

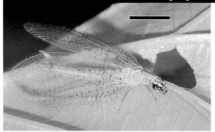

This green lacewing is easily identified by the color and pattern of the face and head. Found through most of North America, this is the most common of our 9 species of *Chrysopa*. Look for these weak fliers in fields and meadows during the summer months, and also at lights.

Green Lacewing *Leucochrysa insularis*

Larvae of the 8 species of *Leucochrysa* are "trash carriers," camouflaging themselves from predators by attaching plant material to their backs. Adults are large for lacewings (13mm), and have distinctive yellow markings. Meadows and woodlands. Frequently attracted to lights.

Antlions
Family Myrmeleontidae

Appearance

Antlions are up to 1 1/2 inches long. Their abdomen is long and slender, often longer than the wings, resembling a damselfly. Antennae are not quite as long compared to other nerve-winged insects and are clubbed. They have wings that are clear or with dark color spots.

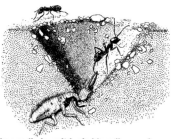

Larvae lie in wait buried in soil, or make pits in dry dusty soil in protected areas. They actually flip sand or dirt on to potential victims to cause them to slide down.

Biology

Adults can be scavengers on plant and animal material or predacious. Larvae (also known as "doodle-bugs") are predacious and either hunt prey or construct conical pits (illustration right) and wait concealed at the bottom for prey to fall in. They overwinter as larvae in the soil. Adults are active in the evening and some are attracted to lights at night. June to August.

Common Antlion *Myrmeleon immaculatus*

Myrmeleon is our only genus of antlion with larvae that build funnel shaped pits in loose sand where they trap ants and other small insects. Although the pits are a common sight, the weak flying adults are rarely seen.
Adult Common Antlions lay on twigs and plant stems motionless where they blend in. They're nondescript gray to brown with a white stigma on the wings, and most commonly seen at lights.

Spotted-winged Antlion *Dendroleon obsoletus*

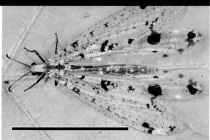

The wing spots are distinctive on this adult antlion, which occurs through eastern North America, and is the only one of the 2 species of *Dendroleon* found in the Northeast. Adults are often attracted to lights from June to September. Larvae live in tree holes and in rotting wood, and are rarely seen.

Bees, Wasps, Sawflies & Ants
Order Hymenoptera

Diversity
There are 74 families and about 20,000 species in North America, making this group one of the largest insect orders. The sawflies, wasps, bees, and ants are very common in New England and New York.

Appearance
Adults: Sawflies, wasps, bees, and ants are generally cylindrical-shaped insects that range from slender to robust. Sawflies and horntails have the abdomen broadly joined to the body, while all other Hymenoptera have a narrowed or waist-like attachment to the body. They possess conspicuous mandibles. Their antennae are variable in form but are generally slender, ranging from short to very long. They have four membranous wings which varies from few to a moderate number of veins. The first pair of wings are longer than the hind wings and sometimes held straight over their body. Some species lack wings. The females of many species have conspicuous ovipositors while others possess short, sting-like ovipositors. The remaining ants, wasps, and bees usually have stingers which are modified ovipositors.

Larvae: Sawfly larvae are caterpillar-like possessing a conspicuous head and mandibles. They also have conspicuous true legs and six to ten prolegs on the abdomen. Other Hymenoptera larvae are grub-like with an inconspicuous head and lacking legs.

Habitats
Hymenoptera are found in essentially all terrestrial habitats in the Northeast. They particularly seek out warmth and are found in woodlands, forest edges, fields, and prairies where they are found on foliage, flowers, on trunks and branches, and in the ground.

Life Cycle
Sawflies, wasps, bees, and ants are holometabolous insects, using complete metamorphosis to develop. They typically produce one generation during the year. In the Hymenoptera, fertilized eggs develop into females while males are produced from unfertilized eggs. Certain bees

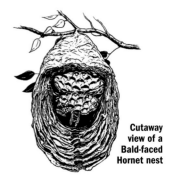

Cutaway view of a Bald-faced Hornet nest

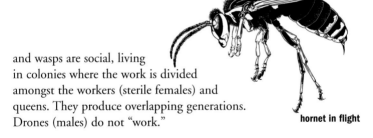

and wasps are social, living
in colonies where the work is divided
amongst the workers (sterile females) and
queens. They produce overlapping generations.
Drones (males) do not "work."

hornet in flight

Food
Adult Hymenoptera generally feed on nectar, honeydew, and plant
secretions. Sawfly larvae are plant feeders, feeding on leaves, needles and
boring into trees. Many wasps are parasitic on other insects, i.e. they lay
eggs on or in prey which the hatching larvae slowly consuming after
they hatch, eventually killing the host. The larvae of social and solitary
wasps eat paralyzed insects or spiders which are provided to them. Bee
larvae are provided nectar and pollen.

Don't confuse them with...
...lacewings and other nerve-winged insects. You can distinguish
between them as nerve-winged insects have more numerous and complex net-like system of veins in the wings, both pairs of wings are similar in size and held roof-like over their bodies. Some Hymenoptera may
also be confused with Diptera. However the true flies have only two
wings and sucking mouthparts, and usually inconspicuously small
antennae. Some moths are similar to some Hymenoptera. However
moths have scales on at least part of the wings and have long, slender,
coiling, sucking mouthparts.

Cimbicid Sawflies
Family Cimbicidae

There are 12 North American species in 3 genera; ***Abia***, ***Cimbex*** and ***Trichiosoma***. All 3 genera occur in the Northeast, with *Cimbex* being the most common. ***Trichiosoma triangulum*** is the only member of its genus occurring in the Northeast.

When the larvae are disturbed, they fall to the ground and stay curled up in a ball. They can emit a defensive fluid from glands along their abdomen.

Elm Sawflies do resemble large flies.

Elm Sawfly   *Cimbex americana*

larva

A HUGE sawfly. Found throughout North America, the Elm Sawfly is not only the most common Cimbicid, but the only species in the genus occurring in the Northeast. It also has the largest sawfly larva, reaching 2 inches, white or yellow with a dark line down its back. Adults usually have black abdomens, but some have varying amounts of white spotting or stripes, while others may have red abdomens. Despite the name, larvae also feed on birch, maple, basswood, willow and poplar.

Argid Sawflies
Family Argidae

medium-sized stout wasps, having 3 segmented antennae with the third segment being the largest. *Arge humeralis* with its brilliant red and black coloration, larvae feeds on poison ivy. *Arge pectoralis* larvae feed on birch, hazelnut, alder and willow, but not on oak like the similar looking *Arge quidia*.

Arge coccinea

Arge humeralis
Poison Ivy Sawfly

Conifer Sawflies
Family Diprionidae

All these chunky sawflies with 13 or more segments in their antennae feed on conifer needles. Males have large bushy antennae, like this non native **Introduced Pine Sawfly** *(Diprion similis)*, that was introduced from Europe, are now common throughout the east. The **Red-headed Pine Sawfly** *(Neodiprion lecontei)* larvae are gregarious when young, and can cause shoot damage.

Diprion similis
Introduced Pine Sawfly

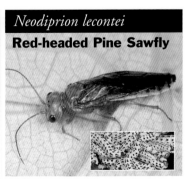

Neodiprion lecontei
Red-headed Pine Sawfly

Webspinning & Leafrolling Sawflies
Family Pamphiliidae

Larvae spin webs in various plants and trees where they feed on the foliage. The **Cherry Webspinning Sawfly** *(Neurotoma fasciata)* larvae have a nest that looks like a tent caterpillar nest, in cherry leaves.

Onycholyda luteicornis

Neurotoma fasciata

Cherry Webspinning Sawfly

Xiphydriid Wood Wasps
Family Xiphydriidae

Wood wasps look like smaller versions of horntails, and share a similar lifestyle. All 10 species north of Mexico are in the genus *Xiphydria*, and the larvae bore into decaying hardwood trees.

Xiphydriid Wood Wasp *Xiphydria mellipes*

The males of this uncommon wasp are small (8mm) while the females get up to 15mm, and have a short stout ovipositor. They're widespread, ranging across the northern U.S. and southern Canada. Females lay their eggs in dead hardwood, usually maple, that's been softened by a fungus. Adults can emerge in the winter from firewood that's been taken indoors.

Horntails
Family Siricidae

Appearance

Large, thick-bodied insects, measuring from ¾ to 1⅜ inch long. They get their name from a hornlike plate on the upper tip of the abdomen which on males is relatively short while it is longer and somewhat spearlike in females. Females also possess a conspicuous ovipositor. Horntails are generally dark-colored metallic blue, black, or brown with red or yellow on their legs and abdomens.

Biology

Horntails are usually associated with conifer trees, although at least one species attacks hardwood trees. They lay eggs into trees that have either recently died or are in a greatly weakened condition. The larvae are parasitized by *Megarhyssa* wasps. They are typically found July to September.

Pigeon Tremex (Pigeon Horntail) *Tremex columba*

Both male and female Pigeon Tremex have horn tails, but the female also has a rigid ovipositor. She lays eggs in hardwood trees, along with a wood rotting fungus to soften the wood for the larvae. The larval stage can last up to two years, with adults active during the summer and early fall. This is our most common and widespread horntail, occurring through most of North America.

Common Sawflies
Family Tenthredinidae

Appearance

They are small to medium insects, generally slender to medium bodied, usually from 3/16 to 3/4 inch long. Their thorax is broadly joined to the abdomen and they usually have short, slender antennae. Common sawflies are dark-colored insects, some species with bright colors, white, yellow, orange, patches or bands on the legs or body.

Biology

Common sawflies are common on foliage and sometimes on flowers. They lay eggs on various trees and

Sawfly larvae resemble caterpillars. These are Birch Sawfly (*Arge pectoralis*) larvae.

shrubs where the larvae often feed externally on the leaves or needles, although a few are leafminers, stem borers, or gall formers. They typically overwinter as pupae in the ground or in cocoons in exposed areas. Common sawflies are found throughout the spring and summer.

Northeast Species Notes

Our most common and diverse group of sawflies includes *Strongylogaster* species like this **S. tacita** that feeds on ferns. Others like the **Butternut Woolly Worm** *(Eriocampa juglandis)* larvae feed on walnut, and have fur-like wax covering them. Our 46 *Macrophya* species are slender like this colorful **M. Formosa**, while others like **M. trisyllaba** are all black. ***Rhogogaster californica*** with its green coloration blends in well with vegetation. ***Tenthredo*** is our largest genus with at least 118 species. **Dusky Birch Sawflies** *(Craesus latitarsus)* larvae raise their abdomens in a defensive posture when threatened.

Sawfly larva rival the most beautiful moth caterpillars (*Macremphytus tarsatus*).

The distinctive white larva of the Butternut Woolly Worm, *Eriocampa juglandis*.

The defensive posture of a Dusky Birch Sawfly larva (*Craesus latitarsus*).

Ametastegia glabrata
Dock Sawfly

Macrophya formosa

Macrophya trisyllaba

Rhogogaster californica

Strongylogaster tacita

Tenthredo fernaldii

Tenthredo rufopecta

Tenthredo verticalis

Leafcutter Bees
Family Megachilidae

Appearance
moderate-sized, stout bodied, wide-headed, hairy insects, ¼ to ¾ inches long. Generally dark-colored, sometimes metallic blue and occasionally with striped abdomens. Unlike other bees, leaf-cutting bees collect pollen on the underside of the abdomen. Long tongues.

Biology
Leafcutter bees are solitary insects that live in nests they line with pieces of leaves they cut. Nests are in natural cavities they find in wood or in the ground. They provision the nest with pollen that is carried under their abdomen. Look for them on foliage or flowers in spring and summer.

A leaf-cutting bee emerges from its ground nest. Some nest in wood.

A cut-away view of the leaf-lined nest of a leaf-cutter bee. Larva will develop inside individual cells.

Note the pollen-collecting hairs under the abdomen.

European Wool Carder Bee *Anthidium manicatum*

A recently introduced bee from Europe that's spread through most of the country. Females line their cavity nests with fuzzy plant material ("wool"). Males aggressively defend territories and nectar sources. If you see a bee in your garden attacking other flower visitors, it's probably a male European Wool Carder Bee.

Parasitic Leafcutter Bee *Coelioxys modesta*

Coelioxys modesta lacks pollen baskets under their abdomen or on their legs, and so do not collect their own food. Instead, the female is a kleptoparasite, taking eggs out of other Megachilid bee nests, and replacing them with her eggs. Look for these pointy tailed bees consuming flower nectar during the summer.

Giant Resin Bee *Megachile sculpturalis*

Our largest Megachilid bee is an alien that was first discovered in North Carolina in the mid 1990s. These East Asian bees use existing cavities where the female will make up to 10 cells using resin, sap, mud and pieces of wood. Larvae feed on pollen in the cells. Aggressive to other bees, reportedly killing honey bees.

Plasterer Bees & Yellow-faced Bees
Family Colletidae

Plasterer Bees are an early spring ground nesting solitary bee. Colonies build large congregations of nest holes in sandy soil. The nests are lined with a polymer made from secretions from the female. Nearly 100 species.

Yellow-faced Bees are small, slender and black. Males have more extensive yellow markings on the face than females. Having very little hair and no pollen scoops, they resemble small wasps. Nests are built in hollow stems.

Colletes inaequlis entering nest hole.

Cellophane Bee *Colletes inaequalis*

As soon as the snow is gone in March, look for aggregations of nest holes in sandy soil near woods. This boldly banded bee is very hairy, and the size of a honey bee. Females line their burrow with a waterproof cellophane-like material, keeping the store of liquid food fungus-free. She suspends an egg from each cell.

Yellow-faced Bee *Hylaeus modestus/affinis*

H. modestus male has black at the base of the antennae, and narrow yellow bands at the top of its face. *H. affinis* males have a yellow scape (base of the antennae) and thick yellow at the top of the face. Both species occur throughout the Northeast during the summer months, and are common on flowers.

Halictid Bees (Sweat Bees) Family Halictidae

Appearance

Fuzzy bees, 1/8 to 3/8 inch long, that are often metallic green or blue or black or brown. Hind legs are flattened and hairy to carry pollen.

Biology

Solitary bees that nest in clay, sandy stream banks, and even in bare patches in lawns, sometimes forming congregations. They get their name because some species are attracted to the perspiration of people. Common on flowers.

Northeast Species Notes

Over 500 species in 21 genera, with many brightly colored, like *Agapostemon virescens*. Any eastern female *Agapostemon* with a black abdomen with white bands is *A. virescens*. Males have yellow banding. *Augochloropsis metallica* is one of the brilliant metallic green Halictids, and is active from spring until fall. *Lasioglossum* consists of nearly 300 species ranging from the mostly black *L. coriaceum* to the golden *L. pilosum*. Female *Sphecodes* are easily recognized by their black head and thorax and red abdomens, but in most of our 80 species, the males are entirely black.

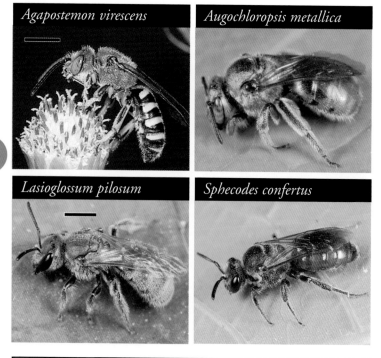

Agapostemon virescens

Augochloropsis metallica

Lasioglossum pilosum

Sphecodes confertus

Andrenid Bees
Family Andrenidae

Appearance
Often hairy bees, 3/16 to 1/2 inch long, generally dark-colored. Their back legs are hairy and flattened, like halictids, to carry pollen. About 3,000 species of these usually black or brown, usually hairy bees.

Biology
Although solitary bees that make burrows along dirt paths, fields and other areas of sparse vegetation, many nests are often close to each other. Females dig a hole with about 8 side tunnels ending in a brood chamber, where she places a pollen ball for the larva to feed. Many species are plant specific for their nectar source.

Northeast Species Notes
The largest genus in the Northeast is *Andrena* with about 500 species north of Mexico. *A. nubecula* has little hair and looks like a Halictid. *A. dunningi* is the other extreme, abdomen and legs covered in orange hairs. The largest North American genus is *Perdita* (about 700 species) but the Northeast has few, with *Perdita octomaculata* the most common.

Andrena dunningi

Andrena erythrogaster
Red-tailed Andrena

Andrena nubecula

Perdita octomaculata

Honey Bees & Bumble Bees, etc. Family Apidae

Appearance

These common bees vary in size from ¼ to 1 inch long. They are black and brown, black and yellow, or dark bluish green. They have back legs modified for carrying pollen and have long tongues for obtaining nectar.

Biology

Honey bees and bumble bees are social insects, establishing colonies while carpenter bees and digger bees are solitary bees. They are common around flowers spring and summer.

Honey Bee   *Apis mellifera*

Honey bees are very important in pollination and honey production, but in recent years populations have been declining. Introductions of a parasitic mite in hives and a virus originating from Australia may be major contributors to the decline. None of the many subspecies of *Apis mellifera* are native to the Americas. One subspecies that gets plenty of attention in the warmest parts of the country are the African "Killer" Bees *(Apis mellifera scutellata)*. Their nomadic behavior doesn't allow enough food storage to survive cold winters. Our local honey bees, either in boxes or tree cavities, store large amounts of honey to make it year after year through the winter.

Golden Northern Bumble Bee   *Bombus fervidus*

Queen
Male

The Golden Northern Bumble Bee is common on flowers, and recognized as mostly covered with yellow hair, except for a black band across the thorax and a black rear end. Found across the U.S. except the southern states, and most common in the Northeast. May to October.

Common Eastern Bumble Bee *Bombus impatiens*

B. impatiens is our most common bumble bee in the Northeast, and is distinguished by only having yellow on the first abdominal segment behind the thorax. Occurs across eastern North America from April to October.

Confusing Bumble Bee *Bombus perplexus*

The Confusing Bumble Bee is covered with yellow hair, except the last 2 abdominal segments that have sparse yellow hair, or are black. Also the shades of yellow are variable. Found across the northern states April to September.

Tricolored Bumble Bee *Bombus ternarius*

The Tricolored Bumble Bee is the only eastern species with the second and third abdominal segments orange. Also known as Orange-belted Bumble Bee. Found across Canada and the northern U.S. states April to October.

Yellowbanded Bumble Bee *Bombus terricola*

Yellowbanded Bumble Bees have a bands of yellow on the front of the thorax, second and third abdominal segments and yellow on the tip of the rear end. April to October across the northern states and Canada.

Cuckoo Bees
Subfamily Nomadinae

Northeast Species Notes

Cuckoo bees resemble wasps, are nearly hairless and are attractively colored in yellow, black or red. Females lay eggs in the nest cells of Andrenidae and Halictidae bees, where the larvae eat the host egg and pollen supply. Most are active in the spring like this ***Nomada maculata***, a red bee in the ***ruficornis*** species group. ***Nomada*** is the largest genus in the cuckoo bees, with over 300 species. ***Nomada luteoloides*** is another of the *ruficornis* species group, with brilliant yellow stripes, that has adults active in April and May. Cuckoo bees found later in the season tend to be more uncommon species, like this ***Epeolus bifasciatus***, active during the summer months. It's a nest parasite of plasterer bees, like the uncommon ***Colletes latitarsus***. Some species are even found in the fall, like this rarely seen ***Epeolus autumnalis***.

Epeolus autumnalis

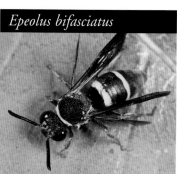

Epeolus bifasciatus

Nomada luteoloides

Nomada maculata

Carpenter Bees
Subfamily Xylocopinae

Northeast Species Notes

Xylocopa virginica looks just like a large bumble bee but with a shiny hairless abdomen. Commonly seen getting nectar from flowers, which they store in nest holes drilled into wood. Females chew a dime-sized nest hole in wood, either standing dead trees or house siding, decking or fence posts. Males will hover outside the nest hole, keeping other males away from the female inside. Adults overwinter and are active in the spring, then again in the fall.

Ceratina calcarata/dupla
Small Carpenter Bee

Xylocopa virginica
Eastern Carpenter Bee

Digger Wasps
Family Crabronidae

Members of the Crabronidae were formerly treated as several subfamilies of the Sphecidae (thread-waisted wasps) but were recently raised to family status.

Appearance

More compact and robust than their thread-waisted wasp cousins.

Biology

Most digger wasps dig their own nests in the ground and stock them with insect or spiders. Typically, each species specializes on a specific type of prey including aphids, beetles, bees, true bugs, butterflies, moths, cicadas, cockroaches, flies, grasshoppers, crickets, mantids or spiders. The larvae feed on the cached prey. A few species are kleptoparasitic, feeding their larvae prey that was caught by other wasp species.

American Sand Wasp *Bembix americana spinolae*

American sand wasps are gregarious solitary nesters in areas of loose sand like beaches, sand boxes and sand pits. Flies are often caught in flight, and are used to provision their nests. Females add provisions as the larva grows, and always covers the entrance after each visit, concealing its existence. Adults are active in the summer and occur through the U. S. and southern Canada.

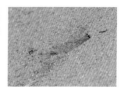

Eastern Cicada Killer *Sphecius speciosus*

Females capture adult cicadas (see photo below) and fly back to the nest hole with their paralyzed victim. The nest hole is up to four feet deep in sandy soil. Colonies of these solitary wasps can number over 100, and with many flying around, Cicada Killers look very intimidating. But they rarely sting, and don't pay any attention to people unless provoked.

Sand Wasp *Bicyrtes quadrifasciatus*

Stink bugs and leaf-footed bugs are hunted by *Bicyrtes quadrifasciatus* to provision their nests. Adults actively feed on nectar during the summer and fall months, and are more easily approached than most other wasps. They're widely distributed east of the Rockies.

Square-headed Wasp *Ectemnius cephalotes*

Nests are made in twigs or holes in dead wood, which the female provisions with flies. During summer months, look for these small wasps nectarring on Queen Anne's Lace. Of the 31 species of Ectemnius north of Mexico, this is one of the more boldly colored.

Cricket Wasp *Liris argentatus*

Crickets (Gryllidae) usually larger than the small wasps are the prey target. The paralyzed cricket is the food supply of the wasp larva. The only other species of *Liris* in the Northeast is larger with dark pubescence, and other closely related genus prey on mole crickets and camel crickets.

Square-headed Wasp *Rhopalum clavipes*

The 7 North American species of *Rhopalum* are mostly stem nesters, and provision their nests with flies. A small black square-headed wasp, *Rhopalum* is distinguished by the bump on the petiole, just like an ant would have. Look for adults to be active during the summer and fall in vegetation along forest edges.

Square-headed Wasp *Anacrabro ocellatus*

The only member of the genus, these small stout wasps can be confused with cuckoo bees *(Nomada sp.)*. Tarnished Plant Bugs *(Lygus lineolaris)* are captured to feed their larvae inside burrows in the ground. Look for *A. ocellatus* visiting flowers during the summer months, where they occur across the eastern U. S.

Aphid Wasp *Psen erythropoda*

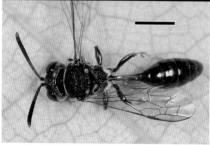

Unlike its family name, this wasp preys on spittlebugs. Its favorite seems to be the four-spotted spittlebug *(Aphrophora quadrinotata)*. One of the larger aphid wasps (10-12mm) it's easily recognizable as the only eastern species of *Psen* with a red petiole and a black gaster.

Jewel Beetle Wasp *Cerceris fumipennis*

Researchers tracking the progression of the invasive Emerald Ash Borer *(Agrilus planipennis)* often watch *C. fumipennis* colonies because this is one of the wasp's prey items. Burrows are dug in hard packed soil in dirt roads, fields and even ballparks, where females bring Buprestidae beetles ("jewel beetles"...including Emeralds) to provision their young.

Weevil Wasp *Cerceris halone*

A weevil specialist, *Cerceris halone* only preys on acorn weevils *(Curculio sp.)*. Look for aggregations of burrows along old dirt roads and other hard packed soil areas near forests with oak trees. During August and September if you're patient at one of their colonies, you'll see a number of wasps flying back to their burrows carrying acorn weevils. Nearly 90 species of Weevil Wasps *(Cerceris)* north of Mexico, and despite the name, many different beetles are used by the many wasps in this genus.

Bee Wolf *Philanthus gibbosus*

Females like to dig their burrows on a slope or even a steep bank with relatively firm soil, where she provisions it with several Halictid bees in each nest cell for her larva to consume. From June to September it's common to see these wasps visiting flowers. Of our 31 North American species of *Philanthus*, this is the most common and widespread, occurring through most of the continent.

Thread-waisted Wasps
Family Sphecidae

Appearance

Most have a smooth body with few hairs and possess short to moderate length antennae. Common colors are black or metallic blue and black with orange or yellow on the legs and abdomen.

Biology

Sphecid wasps are solitary, living in individual nests, although in some species many individuals can live in a small area. Most sphecid wasps nest in the ground, while some nest in cavities, such as in hollow plant stems or cavities in wood, while a few construct nests made of mud. They prey on insects or spiders which they paralyze and feed to their young. They either drag immobilized prey to their nest or they carry them back while they fly. A particular sphecid wasp usually attacks a specific type of insect.

Thread-waisted Wasp — *Ammophila nigricans*

Most of the 61 species of *Ammophila* are medium-sized (15-20mm) and this is one of the largest, up to 38mm. In the east, this wasp can be identified by the large size combined with the black wings and unmarked black thorax. Adults feed on nectar, and the larvae are supplied with up to a dozen hairless caterpillars and sawfly larvae. After provisioning the nest, the female covers the burrow entrance with a small pebble to keep kleptoparasites out.

The closely related *Ammophila procera* is distinguished from *A. nigricans* by the pair of bold silver dashes on the thorax and the lighter colored wings. Smooth bodied caterpillars and sawfly larvae are paralyzed and carried into the single cell burrow for her young to feed on. Early morning before they're active, you might find one in their characteristic sleeping position, holding a small stem with their jaws.

The wasp first drags the captured and immobilized caterpillar back to the underground nest. It then drops the caterpillar so it can remove the pebble from the entrance. (The pebble camouflages the entrance so kleptoparasitic flies can't find it.) The caterpillar is then pulled down into the nest where its young will feed on it.

Blue Mud Dauber *Chalybion californicum*

Females have the amazing ability to land on a spider web, shake it to lure the spider out and paralyze it, all without getting entangled! Spiders are used to provision their nests which are built under eaves, etc. Occasionally females will transport water and simply reshape the nest of a Black and Yellow Mud Dauber.

Grass-carrying Wasp *Isodontia apicalis/mexicana*

Crickets and katydids are paralyzed and stored in hollow stems, or other suitable cavities for their larvae. The female seals off the nest hole with a grass plug to protect her brood from predation. Adults are commonly seen taking nectar during the summer months where they occur through most of North America.

Thread-waisted Wasp *Prionyx parkeri*

Like the other 6 species of *Prionyx* north of Mexico, *P. parkeri* preys on grasshoppers to provision her nest. They have a more compact look than other Sphecid wasps, and can be found in dry regions through most of the country.

Black & Yellow Mud Dauber *Sceliphron caementarium*

Female often seen gathering mud balls to build her vertical nests consisting of up to 2 dozen tubes under bridges or eaves of buildings. Each cell is provisioned with a dozen or more spiders, and then an egg is laid on the last spider. A mud door is placed on the stocked cell to protect it from parasites. Long yellow legs conspicuously dangle below these slow flying wasps.

Great Golden Digger Wasp *Sphex ichneumoneus*

A common visitor to flowers, the Great Golden Digger Wasp is easily recognized by its large size and distinctive coloration. Females dig a vertical burrow with several radiating cells that she provisions with crickets, grasshoppers or katydids. Adults active through the summer, and occur from southern Canada to South America.

Great Black Wasp *Sphex pensylvanicus*

From July through September, watch for these very large blue black wasps visiting flowers. Katydids are placed in an underground burrow for the larvae to feed upon. Females larger than males. They're common and widespread, occurring throughout eastern North America.

In these two photographs we can see how the Great Black Wasp is able to capture, grasp and fly off with prey much larger than itself. In this case it is a *Neoconcephalus* species of katydid.

Cuckoo Wasps
Family Chrysididae

Appearance
Bright metallic green or blue with sculptured bodies. Underside of abdomens concave which allows them to curl their bodies into balls.

Biology
Common around flowers. They parasitize various bee and wasp larvae, especially solitary species. June to August.

Cuckoo Wasp   *Chrysis species*

It's difficult to identify individual species of the nearly 80 *Chrysis* species we have north of Mexico. Look for these green/blue multi punctured small wasps on flowers and moving around on the ground and in the foliage.
Females lay eggs in the nest cells of other wasps and bees, where their larvae develop by consuming the host plus the stored food supply.

Caenochrysis doriae

Elampus species

Hedychrum species

Holopyga ventralis

Velvet Ants
Family Mutillidae

Appearance

Females resemble stout ants. Males possess wings and are sometimes larger than females. Often red or orange.

Biology

Found in dry, sandy areas where vegetation is sparse. Parasitize various ground nesting wasps or bees. Females search the ground; males visit flowers. The females can administer a painful sting.

Northeast Species Notes

Due to the extreme sexual dimorphisms, many species of velvet ants are only known by females or males. We have almost 500 described species of velvet ants north of Mexico, and with more research, such as DNA coding, some species described only from females may be matched up with male species thought to be distinct.

Our largest genus of Mutillidae is ***Dasymutilla*** with 140 species that range in size from 12 to 25mm, like these typical females of ***D. bioculata*** and ***D. vesta***. Males are often black with an orange patch, but this ***D. gibbosa*** lacks any orange. ***Pseudomethoca*** consisting of 43 species is smaller (4-10mm) with females having a blocky head and thorax like the diminutive (4mm) ***P. frigida***, and the larger (8-10mm) and more slender ***P. simillima***. Our 30 species of ***Timulla*** all have a convex shaped thorax, viewed from above.

Cow Killer · *Dasymutilla occidentalis*

A southeastern species, the Cow Killer just makes it into southern Connecticut and New York. Be careful not to handle the females of this largest eastern species—they pack a powerful sting. Larvae are parasites in bumble bee brood chambers. Females can be found running around in open sandy areas during the summer months.

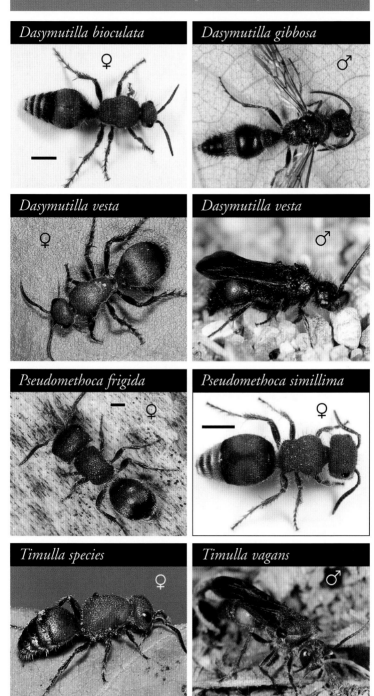

Dasymutilla bioculata ♀

Dasymutilla gibbosa ♂

Dasymutilla vesta ♀

Dasymutilla vesta ♂

Pseudomethoca frigida ♀

Pseudomethoca simillima ♀

Timulla species ♀

Timulla vagans ♂

Ants
Family Formicidae

Appearance
Very small to moderate in size, measuring about ¹⁄₂₀ to ¹⁄₂ inch long. The anterior part of the abdomen is narrowed to form one or two nodes or bumps. Many ants are brown or black while some are yellow and some species are black and red. Workers are wingless while reproductive females and males are winged when they emerge from pupae.

Biology
Ants are social insects forming colonies that are typically found in the ground either exposed or under objects, like stones or logs while others can be found in rotted wood. Colonies can number from dozens to thousands. Ants feed on a variety of foods including insects, nectar, honeydew, and human food. Newly mated females found new nests after mating swarms of flying males and females leave their nests. The males die shortly afterwards. Females remove their wings after mating and landing. Ants are common from spring into fall. Some species can even be found during the winter when they nest inside buildings.

New York Carpenter Ant *Camponotus novaeboracensis*

New York Carpenter Ants are a common northeastern species that nests in dead trees and logs, where the wood is chewed to make nest chambers, and is not eaten. Insects, sap and honeydew make up their diet. We have 51 species of *Camponotus*, with swarms of winged *C. noveboracensis* occurring in the spring.

This cross-section of a tree trunk show the vertical burrows of the carpenter ants. It also shows the chiseled cavity of a Pileated Woodpecker trying to get at the ants.

Allegheny Mound Ant *Formica exsectoides*

Look at grassy fields in the Northeast for the large mounded nests of these ants. Colonies can have over a quarter million workers and more than 1,000 queens. The enlarged venom reservoirs are filled with formic acid that is sprayed at intruders. Birds have been known to land on a mound and intentionally be sprayed by the ants to rid themselves of parasites. This is one of the 97 species of *Formica* in North America.

Odorous Ant *Dolichoderus plagiatus*

An arboreal species consisting of small colonies that nest on dry twigs of willow, poplar or elm, where it feeds on sap or honeydew from aphids. This is the only one of the 4 North American species with a bold color pattern on its abdomen. Widespread, with small patchy populations, and not commonly found.

European Fire Ant *Myrmica rubra*

European Fire Ants will swarm to attack with painful stings if their nest is disturbed. First discovered near Boston in 1908, they've spread to other New England states and adjacent Canada. Most sightings have been near water and not far inland. Ground nesters found under logs and piles of hay.

Dracula Ant *Amblyopone pallipes*

Aptly named, Dracula Ants use those large toothed jaws for capturing Soil Centepedes *(Geophilomorpha)*, which they subdue with a powerful sting. They inhabit small subterranean colonies in forests and are rarely seen. Winged adults emerge late summer to early fall.

Spider Wasps
Family Pompilidae

Appearance

Medium to large slender wasps, most ranging in size from ½ to 1 inch long. Spider wasps have long spiny legs and medium length antennae that is held curled by the females. They are typically black or dark blue often with dark-colored wings,

A spider wasp frenetically searches for spiders on a sandy patch.

which are sometimes spotted. As they move about on flowers or on the ground they constantly flick their wings in a seemingly nervous fashion.

Biology

Spider wasps are solitary wasps that typically live in nests in the ground while others make nests in cells of mud or rotted wood. Spider wasps

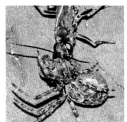

feed their young spiders they capture, paralyze, and bring to their nests. There is one egg per spider. Spider wasps are common throughout the summer. Spider wasps can inflict a painful sting to people.

This captured and paralyzed orbweaver spider will become a meal for the developing spider wasp larva.

Blue-Black Spider Wasp *Anoplius americanus*

Anoplius with 48 species is our largest genus of spider wasps. Wolf spiders and funnel-web spiders are paralyzed and deposited in a hole in soft soil for the wasp larva to develop on. Adults are active during the summer months, and frequently visit flowers.

Spider Wasp *Ceropales maculata fraterna*

All 14 species of *Ceropales* are kleptoparasites. While another spider wasp is dragging its prey back to the nest, the female *C. maculata* will deposit an egg on the spider. Hatching first, it will eat the host egg and spider. Visits flowers. Northeast, and west to the Great Lakes.

Spider Wasp   *Episyron biguttatus*

A common wasp in sandy areas of the Northeast, frequently visiting flowers from mid summer to early fall. After an orbweaver spider is paralyzed, the wasp will temporarily place the spider on vegetation while she prepares a nest hole. When hole is complete, the wasp retrieves the spider and places it in the hole.

Spider Wasp   *Poecilopompilus algidus*

Look in sandy areas along roadsides and woods for this very large wasp. Large orbweaver spiders are its prey. *P. algidus* is the most widespread of the 3 species we have, occurring through most of the country. Adults active July and August in the north, occasionally visiting flowers.

Gasteruptiid Wasps
Family Gasteruptiidae

Appearance

Slender-necked insects with a distinctive abdomen that is attached to the top of the thorax.

Biology

Common on flowers (wild parsnip, wild carrots) and also near logs, stumps, and twigs where certain solitary wasps and bees nest. Gasteruptiid wasp larvae either parasitize the larvae of these solitary wasps or bees or feed on food that has been provisioned for their hosts' larvae.

Gasteruptiid Wasp   *Gasteruption species*

The long thin abdomen held up high and the swollen "ankles" make this wasp rather distinctive. In the north, look for them visiting flowers in July and August. Our 15 species of Gasteruptiids are all in one genus. Females are kleptoparasites of wood nesting bees and wasps; their larva consuming the host egg and food supply.

Yellowjackets, Hornets, Paper Wasps, Mason Wasps & Potter Wasps
Family Vespidae

Appearance
Relatively smooth insects with few hairs and narrow wings folded over their back when at rest. Vespid wasps have elbowed antennae.

Biology
Many vespid wasps are social, insects constructing nests that survive one season. Only newly mated queens survive the winter and start new nests in the spring. Other species are solitary. Typically vespids make their nests from chewed wood fibers, while others construct their nests from mud or clay. Vespid wasps prey on a variety of insects (sometimes spiders) to feed their young. They often possess a stinger which can be used repeatedly. Vespid wasps are commonly seen from spring into the fall.

European Paper Wasp *Polistes dominula*

As the name suggests, this is an introduced Eurasian wasp that was first discovered near Boston in 1978, and has quickly expanded throughout most of North America. The multi-celled paper nests are placed in sheltered locations, usually under eaves on houses and sheds. In most urban and suburban areas it's become more common than the native *Polistes fuscatus*, and in some areas may be replacing native species. Adults feed on nectar and other sugary fluids. Larvae are fed chewed up caterpillars along with many other insect orders.

Northern Paper Wasp *Polistes fuscatus*

A native wasp has long been considered a northeastern North America species, but is now reported from most of the U. S. and Canada. This thin wasp is variably colored from black to light brown, with differing amounts of yellow on the abdominal bands (sometimes lacking bands). Commonly nest around houses, but can be found in woods and open fields in sheltered spots. New queens overwinter and in spring start a nest that will grow to 15-200 workers. In fall, they all die except the new crop of queens that repeat the cycle.

Parasitic Yellowjacket *Dolichovespula adulterina*

Parasitic Yellowjackets do not make a nest. Rather, a queen will invade the nest of *D. arenaria*, kill the host queen, taking her place and having the host workers rear her young. Found throughout the Northeast, Northwest and southern mountains from June through August. look for the workers collecting pollen from flowers.

Common Aerial Yellowjacket *Dolichovespula arenaria*

This is one of our most common wasps, occurring throughout most of North America. Their conspicuous paper hives are constructed in trees, bushes, on houses and sheds and on rare occasions, under the ground. Look for the overwintered queen visiting lowbush blueberry flowers in May, when she will begin forming her new colony.

Bald-faced Hornet *Dolichovespula maculata*

These wasps are not true hornets, but are large yellowjackets. The queens over-winter in leaf litter or under logs, and in the spring start constructing large oval paper nests in trees and shrubs, which can grow to several hundred workers. Nectar and sap are part of the Bald-faced Hornet's diet, along with many types of insects, including other yellowjackets. Despite their intimidating size, they aren't aggressive like most of the *Vespula* species are around the nest, unless they're disturbed.

N. Aerial Yellowjacket *Dolichovespula norvegicoides*

Like the name suggests, this is a northern wasp that can also be found in the central U.S. up in the mountains. Small paper nests are aerial, and mostly built in low shrubs. Not much is known about their biology, but males seem to be found visiting flowers more commonly than females.

Forest Yellowjacket *Vespula acadica*

An inhabitant of boreal forests of Canada and the northern U.S. with more southern populations restricted to mountains. Nests are usually built in rotten logs or underground. Most queens have a pair of tan spots on the second abdominal segment, but are only on about half the workers and males. They have a reputation of being very aggressive around their nest, but are not considered a nuisance, since their habitat is boreal and montane.

Blackjacket   *Vespula consobrina*

Frequently uses abandoned rodent burrows to nest, but will sometimes use cracks in trees, where a colony contains under 100 workers. Human contact is limited because of their forest habitat preference in its northern range. More southern populations occur at higher elevations. They feed on nectar and live arthropods.

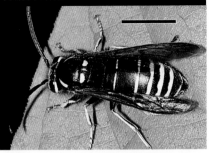

Downy Yellowjacket   *Vespula flavopilosa*

Just discovered in 1978, the biology isn't completely known yet. But it's believed these ground nesters are parasitic, where a queen will take over a colony of either *V. maculifrons* or *V. alascensis* by killing the existing queen and take her place. Food includes nectar, sap, live arthropods and carion.

Eastern Yellowjacket   *Vespula maculifrons*

The most abundant yellowjacket in the east. Nests are normally subterranean, but in urban areas, hollow walls and attics are used. When nest is threatened, they will aggressively and repeatedly sting the invader. Only the mated queens survive winter by hibernating under leaf litter and logs to start a new colony in spring. Nectar, rotting fruit, carrion.

Ground Hornet   *Vespula vidua*

This ground dwelling wasp normally builds subterranean nests, and less frequently in logs. After the queen has built up her colony of workers, males are raised from unfertilized eggs in the summer. An eastern species that feeds on live arthropods and visits flowers for nectar.

Mason Wasps & Potter Wasps Subfamily Eumeninae

Appearance

Eumenines are typically black or brown with yellow, white orange or red markings.

Biology

These wasps frequently visit flowers. Caterpillars are the most common prey, along with sawfly and beetle larvae. Nests types vary by species.

Northeast Species Notes

The common ***Eumenes fraternus*** uses a single pot-shaped mud cell, laying a single egg, and then provisioning the cell with a caterpillar. ***Eumenes crucifera*** is similar, but much less common in the east.

Ancistrocerus catskill usually uses holes in wood for its nest, but will occasionally make mud nests with several cells. ***Ancistrocerus unifasciatus*** takes advantage of someone else's work, and uses mud dauber nests.

The large ***Monobia quadridens*** will use a variety of nests. Usually borings in wood, but will also dig a hole in the dirt, use abandoned nests of ground bees, carpenter bees and mud daubers.

Euodynerus foraminatus most often nests in holes in wood and occasionally old paper wasp nests, using mud to partition cells, while ***Euodynerus hidalgo*** nests in holes in wood and dirt banks.

Our 26 species of ***Parancistrocerus*** are hosts to a specific species of mite, like this ***Parancistrocerus pennsylvanicus*** that nests in twig borings, and ***Parancistrocerus perennis*** that nests in hollow twigs, preferably sumac. This is just a small sampling of the more than 260 North American species.

Ancistrocerus adiabatus

Ancistrocerus catskill

Ancistrocerus unifasciatus

Eumenes crucifera

Eumenes fraternus

Euodynerus foraminatus

Euodynerus hidalgo

Monobia quadridens

Parancistrocerus pensylvanicus

Parancistrocerus perennis

Ichneumon Wasps
Family Ichneumonidae

Appearance

Antennae usually as long or longer than the body. The ovipositors of some are longer than the body, and cannot be withdrawn into the body. Diverse in size and color. This is one of the largest groups of all insects.

A few ichneumons are wingless like this *Gelis species.*

Biology

Ichneumonid wasps are solitary wasps that are parasitic on other insects: larvae and pupae of butterflies and moths, flies, sawflies, beetles, lacewings and caddisflies, as well as spiders, scorpionflies, and even other Hymenoptera. Sometimes an individual species attacks a wide variety of hosts, while others are quite specific. Some ichneumonid wasps are hyperparasitic, that is they attack other wasp and fly parasitoids (parasites). Most ichneumonids are endoparastic, i.e. feeding inside the body of their host. Those

The striking cocoon of a Ichneumon in the subfamily Campopleginae.

parastizing wood boring hosts are ectoparasitic, i.e. feeding on the outside of the body. Ichneumonid wasps are seen during spring and summer on flowers and foliage.

Northeast Species Notes

With about 5,000 described North American species in 33 subfamilies, Ichneumons represents the largest single family of insects, even larger than Carabidae with about 2,700 North American species. Some experts believe that only 35 percent of ichneumon species have been described so far. CAUTION: Very few of this diverse group can be identified from photographs, so after photographing these wasps, I had an ichneumon specialist identify the specimens.

Arotes amoenus is a very distinctive wasp in the subfamily Acaenitinae of only 18 species that has a specific host to parasitize, a false darkling beetle, *Melandrya striata*. **Therion morio** is a member of subfamily Anomaloninae of about 200 species that parasitizes moth caterpillars, including the Fall Webworm *(Hyphantria cunea)*.

Exetastes suaveolens is one of about 600 species in subfamily Banchinae that parasitizes caterpillars of the Goldenrod Hooded Owlet

(Cucullia asteroides). Cryptinae is our largest subfamily with 765 species, including **Pleolophus basizonus**, introduced from Eurasia to control conifer sawflies in the genus *Neodiprion*.

Ichneumoninae with about 700 species is our second largest subfamily of ichneumons. **Coelichneumon eximius** is know to parasitize Noctuidae caterpillars. Mesochorinae are represented by 105 species of small wasps that are often attracted to lights like **Mesochorus discitergus**.

We have about 150 species of Metopiinae, like the yellow jacket mimic **Colpotrochia crassipes**. Ophioninae consists of 37 species like the large slow flying **Thyreodon atricolor**, which parasitizes sphinx moth caterpillars. Of the 180 species of Pimplinae, **Acrotaphus wiltii** is very distinctive. **A. wiltii** temporarily paralyzes orb weaver spiders to lay an egg that becomes an external parasite.

A small subfamily with only 9 species, Poemeniinae, like **Podoschistus vittifrons** are parasites of wood boring beetle larvae. Xoridinae consists of 50 species that parasitize wood boring beetles, and are large, robust and mostly black like **Odontocolon ochropus** with a long upcurved ovipositor. But **Xorides calidus** is an exception, being small and brown.

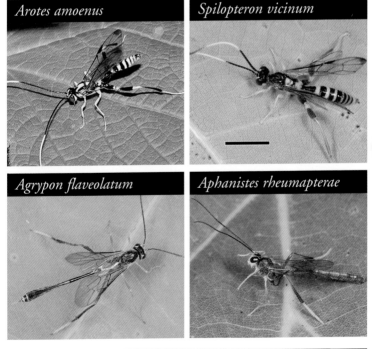

Arotes amoenus

Spilopteron vicinum

Agrypon flaveolatum

Aphanistes rheumapterae

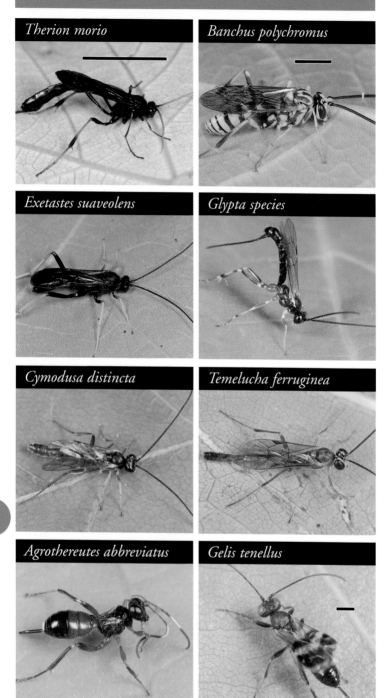

Therion morio

Banchus polychromus

Exetastes suaveolens

Glypta species

Cymodusa distincta

Temelucha ferruginea

Agrothereutes abbreviatus

Gelis tenellus

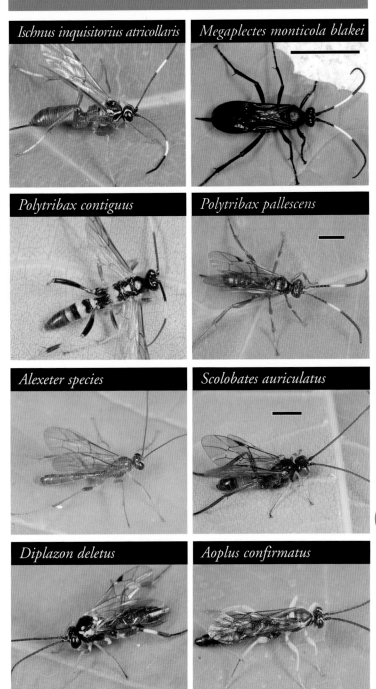

Ischnus inquisitorius atricollaris

Megaplectes monticola blakei

Polytribax contiguus

Polytribax pallescens

Alexeter species

Scolobates auriculatus

Diplazon deletus

Aoplus confirmatus

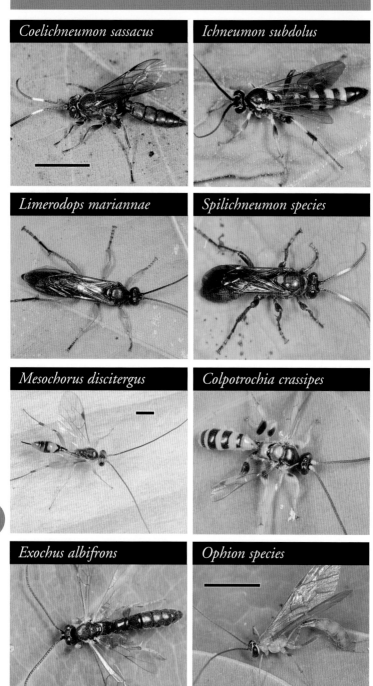

Coelichneumon sassacus

Ichneumon subdolus

Limerodops mariannae

Spilichneumon species

Mesochorus discitergus

Colpotrochia crassipes

Exochus albifrons

Ophion species

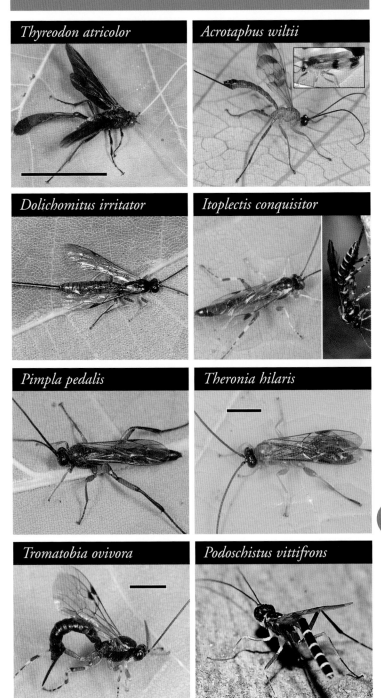

Thyreodon atricolor

Acrotaphus wiltii

Dolichomitus irritator

Itoplectis conquisitor

Pimpla pedalis

Theronia hilaris

Tromatobia ovivora

Podoschistus vittifrons

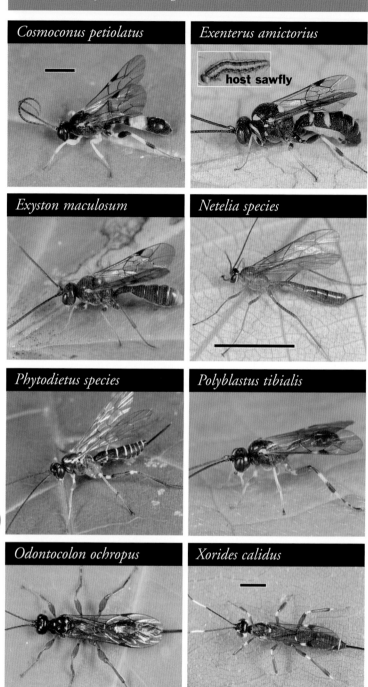

Cosmoconus petiolatus

Exenterus amictorius

host sawfly

Exyston maculosum

Netelia species

Phytodietus species

Polyblastus tibialis

Odontocolon ochropus

Xorides calidus

Giant Ichneumons
Subfamily Rhyssinae

"Stumpstabbers" as they're called by foresters, are our most impressive Ichneumons with a body length reaching 3 inches and an ovipositor up to 5.5 inches. Females detect horntail larvae deep in hardwood with their antennae, smelling a fungus associat-

The female *Megarhyssa atrata*'s ovipositor is up to 4-times her body length! It is used to lay eggs in horntail larva deep in the wood of a tree.

ed with the larvae. She then inserts her ovipositor into the wood with the help of a chemical that breaks down the wood fibers. The ovipositor permanently paralyzes the larva so the egg won't be damaged from any movement. The egg quickly hatches as an external parasite, and consumes the horntail larva. Found throughout North America, we have 14 species in 4 genera.

Giant Ichneumon *Megarhyssa atrata*

These giants are widespread east of the Rockies in hardwood forests, where the females search out horntail larvae inside the trees. The female's ovipositor can lay eggs on a horntail larva up to 5.5 inches deep in the wood. Look for these impressive wasps from May through the summer months.

Giant Ichneumon *Megarhyssa macrurus*

Female *Megarhyssa macrurus* use their long ovipositors to parasitize Pigeon Horntail larvae. Once the larva is located, the wasp's 3 in. ovipositor penetrates the wood with the help of a chemical that breaks down wood fiber. Males are smaller, mostly black and lack the ovipositor.

Giant Ichneumon *Rhyssella nitida*

Of our 3 species in the genus *Rhyssella*, only *R. nitida* has a black abdomen and thorax without any white markings. They occur in the Northeast from Maine and Quebec, south to the Carolinas and west to Minnesota.

Pelecinid Wasp
Family Pelecinidae

Appearance

There is only one species of this family in North America. The female is very large, measuring about two to three inches long with a very long, slender abdomen. The rarely seen male is about half as long as the female with a shorter club-like abdomen. Both are black with moderately long antennae.

Biology

A pelecinid wasp is a parasite of June beetle white grubs found in the soil. It uses its long abdomen to probe into the soil until it reaches the larvae to lay its eggs. They also appear to parasitize other insect larvae found in rotted wood. Despite its fearsome size and long abdomen, it does not possess a stinger and is harmless to people. It is active from July to September.

Pelecinid Wasp *Pelecinus polyturator*

♀

Females are unmistakable, with an extremely long curving abdomen over 2 inches long and wings that look too short for the body. Males are much smaller and rarely seen. An egg is laid in beetle larvae in rotting wood, or a scarab grub. This is our only species in the family, and is widespread east of the Rockies. Adults are said to nectar, but most often are seen resting on leaves or on the ground, looking for grubs.

━━━━━━━━━━━━━━━━━━━━━━━━━━━ **body length**

Braconid Wasps
Family Braconidae

Braconids parasitize many different insects, including caterpillars, beetles, aphids, plant bugs and fly larvae. Most are small, about 3-6mm, but some can get to 15mm, and they look like Ichneumonidae, with a difference in the recurrent wing vein. We have almost 2,000 species of Braconids, occurring throughout North America. Females lay their eggs inside the host, where the larvae feed. In most species, mature larvae bore exit holes through the doomed host to form external cocoons attached to the larva. **Mummy wasps** *(Aleiodes sp.)* pupate inside the empty caterpillar husk.

Aleiodes species
Mummy Wasp

Microplitis species

Chalcid Wasps
Superfamily Chalcidoidea

We have 18 families of chalcid wasps with over 2,000 species. Most are under 3mm, but some species can reach 20mm. Many are parasitic on other insects, but some like this ***Hemadas nubilipennis*** make galls on blueberry bushes. The distinctive ***Conura nigricornis*** uses hairstreak butterflies as its host. ***Leucospis affinis*** is one of the largest chalcids, and is parasitic on Leaf-cutting Bees. This 2mm ***Tetrastichus sp.*** parasitizes the Round Bullet Gall Wasp *(Disholcaspis quercusglobulus)*. Some of the Pteromalidae are hyperparisitoids, as are most of the Perilampidae.

Conura nigricornis

Leucospis affinis

Tetrastichus species

Hemadas nubilipennis

Tetrastichus on
Round Bullet Gall

Blueberry Gall of
Hemadas

Gall Wasps
Family Cynipidae

Dryocosmus decidua

Cynipids make galls on a variety of leaves, stems and branches, with oak being the most prevalent host. Not all galls are made by gall wasps, some aphids, midges, flies, moths, sawflies and mites can also make galls. Many cynipid galls are parasitized, so other insects can emerge, such as chalcid wasps. With more than 750 species in North America, the galls come in all sizes, shapes and colors. The **Oak Pea Gall** *(Acraspis pezomachoides)* is small and found on the underside of oak leaves. Often knowing the species of oak is important, as with *Disholcaspis bassetti*, forming on bur and swamp white oak. The **Banded Bullet Gall Wasp** *(Dryocosmus imbricariae)* uses red oaks, and makes the galls on twigs. *Amphibolips quercusspongifica* is a large gall up to 2 inches that is filled with spongy material surrounding a central cell area.

Amphibolips quercusspongifica

Disholcaspis bassetti

Acraspis erinacei
Hedgehog Gall

Acraspis pezomachoides
Oak Pea Gall

Dryocosmus imbricariae
Banded Bullet Gall

Andricus quercuspetiolicola
Oak Petiole Gall

Caddisflies
Order Trichoptera

Diversity
There are 26 families and 1556 species in North America. Caddisflies are very common in New England and New York.

Appearance
Adults: Small to medium-sized moth-like insects with very long antennae, commonly as long or longer than their bodies. Their four wings, covered with short, fine hairs, are held tent-like over their abdomens. These wings are similarly-sized and shaped to each other. Caddisflies possess mouthparts with conspicuous palps; the mandibles are absent or highly reduced. Most have a short, stubby proboscis. Many caddisflies are brownish or otherwise dull-colored.

Larvae: Small to medium-sized caterpillar-like insects with cylindrical-shaped bodies. Caddisfly larvae have conspicuous heads with chewing mouthparts and possess short peg-like antennae. They possess

adult caddisfly

conspicuous legs behind their heads on their thoraxes but lack prolegs, i.e. false legs, on their abdomens, except for the pair at the very end. The abdomen often bears filament-like gills.

Habitats
Immature caddisflies are found in essentially all fresh water environments, including streams, ponds, lakes and even temporary pools of water. They prefer cool, running water, although some species take advantage of warm, still aquatic environments. Adults are weak flyers and are generally found near water. Adults are active at night and can be commonly found around lights.

Life Cycle
Caddisfly larvae are holometabolous insects, using complete metamorphosis to develop. Adults lay eggs in the water often on objects, like stones, or on nearby sites, such as overhanging branches. Caddisfly larvae can generally be divided into one of three groups: case-makers, net-makers and free living. All caddisfly larvae have the ability to make silk using modified glands on their heads which they use for building cases, nets, retreats and cocoons.

Case-makers make little shelters our of objects on hand (see following pages). Net-making caddisflies employ a different strategy. Found in swift moving water, they construct silken nets which collects food the currents bring to them. The larvae stay nearby in retreats while waiting for food. Free-living caddisfly larvae do not make cases, nets, or retreats. Instead they actively search for food among rocks or other objects in moving water. They make a dome-like silken case only when they pupate.

Larvae pupate in the water, often under stones or logs. As they complete metamorphosis, the pupae swim to the surface and crawl to shore where the adults emerge. Caddisflies in New England typically take one year to develop.

caddisfly larva without its case

Food
Many larval caddisflies are scavengers, feeding on decaying organic debris that they encounter in the water. Others are plant feeders, consuming algae and diatoms while some caddisfly larvae are predacious, eating small aquatic invertebrate animals, like black fly larvae. Some adult caddisflies may feed on liquids but most probably do not feed.

Water Quality
Although some species are tolerant of polluted water, most require clean water, making this insect group important in determining water quality.

Don't confuse them with...
...moths and butterflies. Moths and butterflies possess scales on their wings which they hold flat or straight up and down when at rest. They possess coiled, tube-like mouthparts and their antennae are much shorter than their bodies. Moth and butterfly larvae possess prolegs, i.e. fleshy false legs on their abdomens. Moth and butterfly larvae are rarely aquatic.

Caddisfly Families

Netspinning Caddisflies: Family Hydropsychidae
The larvae live in fast moving streams and rivers where they build a silken net attached to a small stone or debris. The net billows out in the current to trap small aquatic insects, but if it's taken out of the water it falls apart. The larvae build a pebble and silk shelter beside their net where they stay hidden until prey is caught in their net. With about 150 species of Hydropsychidae, expect to find them in every suitable stream and river in North America. **Zebra Caddisflies** (*Macrostemum zebratum*) emerge from large fast moving rivers in the east during late spring and early summer. Adults can be seen on rocks, foliage and bridges near the river.

Microcaddisflies: Family Hydroptilidae

Microcaddisflies at about 3mm are our smallest caddisflies, but the family with the second most species in North America with over 300 described, found in virtually every type of freshwater habitat. Larvae feed on algae, and do not build a protective case until the fifth and final instar. Most cases are made up of fine sand grains cemented together with oral secretions. Adults look like small moths, and are attracted to lights like the nicely colored **Salt and Pepper Microcaddis** (*Agraylea multipunctata*).

Bizarre Caddisflies: Family Lepidostomidae

Usually found in springs and streams, larval cases can be 4 sided and made from bark pieces, or a round conical tube made from plant material or grains of sand. The larvae are similar to Limnephilidae, but lack the dorsal hump on the first abdominal segment. Lepidostomidae is made up of 2 genera with about 70 species, with *Lepidostoma* species being the most common. Adults like *L. vernale* are 8-10mm with oval shaped wings, and are common at lights from May through September.

Longhorned Caddisflies: Family Leptoceridae

Longhorned Caddisflies adults have antennae up to 3 times their length, and typically the wings are long and thin, like our most common genus, *Triaenodes*. **Black Dancers** (*Mystacides sepulchralis*) are more triangular shaped with large maxillary palps that look like a mustache. This diverse group has 115 species in 8 different genera, with many different food and water preferences. Cases (usually about 10mm) also come in a variety of shapes and materials used to make them. Some species have large mating swarms, and most are attracted to lights.

Northern Caddisflies: Family Limnephilidae

Northern Caddisflies are our most abundant family with over 300 species. Larvae inhabit marshes, ponds and slow moving streams, where they live in cases built of grass, bark, branches, pine needles, wood, sand or any combination of materials. The **Chocolate and Cream Sedge** (*Platycentropus radiatus*) builds a case out of plant material, bark and sticks, while the **Giant Red Sedge** (*Pycnopsyche scabripenni*) uses rough pieces of wood and bark. *Pycnopsyche* start with a wood and bark shelter, but as the larva grows, sand and small pebbles are used. During the day adults are found on vegetation near water, but at night many are attracted to lights like this distinctively marked *Limnephilus sericeus*, and the very large *Hydatophylax argus* that can release a foul smell when handled.

Mortarjoint Casemakers: Family Odontoceridae

This is a small family of caddisflies with 13 North American species. The larvae build sturdy curved cases made up of grains of sand cemented together, and they live under the sand and sediment in streams. The only time they expose themselves is when they're ready to pupate, groups will gather on rock surfaces. Adults are typically brown to black with few markings. We have 1 genus in the Northeast with 4 species present. *Psilotreta labida* and *P. frontalis* are the most common, and are very similar in appearance.

Fingernet Caddisflies: Family Philopotamidae

The bright orange-yellow larvae group together and build small finger shaped fine lace nets on submerged rocks in streams, where they feed on algae, and small bits of plant and animal material that gets caught in their nets. Adults are typically a uniform dark brown or black, and small. ***Dolophilodes distinctus*** is different than most Fingernet Caddisflies with adults active most of the year. Female *D. distinctus* are always wingless, except for some that emerge in the summer, and males are spotted and are not a uniform brown. All 3 genera of Philopotamidae occur in the Northeast, with 6 species represented out of the 47 species in North America.

Giant Casemaker Caddisflies: Family Phryganeidae

Giant Casemakers construct tubular shelters made of bits of leaves and bark usually arranged in a spiral fashion. The young larvae feed on plant material, but as they reach about 40mm in length, they become efficient predators in swamps, lakes and slow moving rivers. Larvae typically have yellow heads with black markings, and will occasionally wander out of their shelters. Adult ***Banksiola*** are one of the smaller of the Phryganeidae, with most about 15-18mm, and there are 7 species in the Northeast. Both species of North American ***Phryganea*** occur in the Northeast. During the day adults blend in well with tree bark and rocks, while at night they will sometimes come to lights. Four of the 5 species of ***Ptilostomis*** can be found in the Northeast. Adults are about 22mm, and have warm coloration with a distinct faint spotted pattern. Two species of ***Oligostomis*** occur in the Northeast, like this orange spotted *O. pardalis*.

Tube Maker Caddisflies: Family Polycentropodidae

The larvae build trumpet-like or tube-like shelters attached to submerged roots and rocks, where they dart out from to catch prey. We have about 70 species and they can be found in both fast running and slow water. Adults are small, usually under 10mm, and mostly brown. with or without light colored spotting. ***Polycentropus crassicornis*** is one of two dozen species of the genus found in the Northeast.

Free-living Caddisflies: Family Rhyacophilidae

Rhyacophilidae larvae do not build cases, and most are green. They're predators freely wandering about in fast streams, feeding on small aquatic insects, including other species of caddisfly larvae. The cocoons are translucent enclosing the pupa in a tight woven silk housing. Eggs are laid on rock surfaces of fast moving streams and rivers, with some species laying on exposed rocks, but in many species the female will go underwater to deposit her eggs. In the Northeast we have about 20 species of Free-living Caddisflies, all in the genus ***Rhyacophila***. Adults are about 10mm with a wedge shaped tail of the wing, and are called ***Green Sedges***.

Stonecase Caddisflies: Family Uenoidae

Until 1985 Uenoidae were part of Limnephilidae. Larvae build heavy cases with small stones, and live in clean brooks and small streams. ***Neophylax oligius*** are found in sandy-gravely bottom streams where the larvae feed on rock surfaces for diatoms and other small organic material. Larvae feed during the winter, and by spring are mature. They cement their case closed and stay that way until adults emerge in the fall. There are 50 North American species in 5 genera with 25 belonging to ***Neophylax***. In the Northeast we just have 6 species of ***Neophylax***.

Caddisfly Larval Cases

The case-making caddisflies are renown as architects for the distinctive and unique cases they construct. Caddisflies use an array of different types of materials to construct these shelters, especially sand, leaves and small pieces of wood. These cases take on a wide array of shapes, such as tube-like, saddle-like, snail shell-like and turtle shell-like. These cases are portable, allowing the larvae to move about as they look for food.

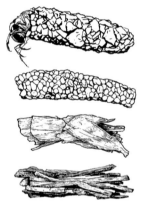

examples of larval cases

Top: *Psilotreta labida*; Middle two: *Phryganea* species; bottom: possibly *Limnephilus* species.

Zebra Caddisfly *Macrostemum zebratum*

A striking member of the Netspinning Caddisflies (Family Hydropsychidae) is the boldly marked Zebra Caddisfly. Adults emerge from large, fast flowing rivers in the east during late spring and early summer. Adults can be seen on rocks, foliage and bridges near the river.

Black Dancer · *Mystacides sepulchralis*

Black Dancers belong to the Longhorned Caddisflies (Leptoceridae). Adults have antennae up to 3 times their body length, and typically the wings are long and thin. Black Dancers are more triangular shaped with large maxillary palps that look like a mustache.

Giant Red Sedge · *Pycnopsyche scabripennis*

The Giant Red Sedge belongs to the Limnephilidae, the Northern Caddisflies—our largest family with over 300 species. Their larva uses rough pieces of wood and bark to construct their case (inset photo), but as the larva grows, sand and small pebbles are used. Adults foundon vegetation near water.

Chocolate & Cream Sedge · *Platycentropus radiatus*

Another of our Northern Caddisflies of the family Limnephilidae, the wonderfully-named Chocolate and Cream Sedge builds a case out of plant material, bark and sticks (inset photo). Larvae inhabit marshes, ponds and slow moving streams

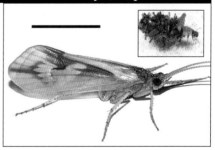

Giant Casemaker Caddisfly · *Oligostomis pardalis*

Two species of *Oligostomis* occur in the Northeast including this boldly-marked orange-spotted *O. pardalis*. They belont to the Giant Casemaker Caddisfly family (Phryganeidae). Larvae construct tubular shelters made of bits of leaves and bark usually arranged in a spiral fashion.

Butterflies & Moths
Order Lepidoptera

Diversity
There are 80 families and over 11,000 species in North America, making this group one of the largest insect orders. Butterflies and moths are very common in New England and New York.

Appearance
Adults: Lepidoptera have four wings, often large, nearly always completely covered with scales, although there are a few cases where scales are lacking. Butterflies and moths have slender, sucking mouthparts that are coiled underneath their head when not in use.

Larvae: Typically, cylindrical-shaped with a conspicuous head, chewing mouthparts, six true legs, and two to five pairs of prolegs on the abdomen. Leaf miners and aquatic larvae are modified for their unusual lifestyles. Their bodies may appear smooth or covered with many hairs or spines.

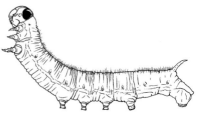

caterpillar

Habitats
Adult butterflies and moths are found in all terrestrial habitats in New England and New York. Butterflies are typically daytime flyers and are commonly found on flowers and foliage. Most moths are nocturnal and attracted to lights. However, clearwing moths, hawkmoths and others are both nocturnal and daytime flyers. The Virginia Ctenucha moth is often found nectaring alongside Monarchs at milkweeds in mid-late summer.

Larvae (caterpillars) can be found in many different terrestrial micro-habitats. Some species hide in leaf litter or under bark during the day. Others create temporary feeding and hiding shelters by gluing leaf parts together with silk.

Life Cycle
Butterflies and moths are holometabolous insects, using complete metamorphosis to develop. Butterflies and moths typically have one or two generations in a year. Butterflies form a chrysalis, a pupa without an outside covering; whereas moths form a cocoon, a pupa surrounded by an outside silken covering.

Food

Butterflies and moths typically feed on nectar, although they are also known to feed on sap and other liquids. Puddling is a behavior where butterflies (and some moths) congregate and appear to feed on damp soil at the edges of a shallow water body to obtain salts concentrated through evaporation. Coprophagy (feeding at feces) can also be observed. Butterflies are obtaining protein and salts by regurgitating saliva onto the feces and then reimbibing. The larvae of many species typically feed on living plants, primarily leaves,.

Some are borers in twigs, stems or wood or leaf miners. Others (lichen moths, ermines and some noctuids) specialize on fungus or lichens as larvae.

Don't confuse them with...

...adult wasps. You can distinguish between clearwing moths (Sesiidae) and stinging wasps as the wasps have a clearly constricted "wasp waist." Sessiids have thicker bodies and different coloration than yellow jackets or paper wasps.

...larval sawflies. You can distinguish between them as sawflies have prolegs on nearly all abdominal segments.

...hummingbirds. Hawkmoths feeding at hummingbird feeders or large hibiscus flowers confuse some bird watchers. Hawkmoths have antennae whereas hummingbirds do not.

Swallowtails
Family Papilionidae

Appearance

Medium to large sized butterflies with wingspan varying from 2 5/8 to 5 inches. Typically have dark-colored wings with yellow markings or yellow wings with black markings with a long conspicuous tail on each hind wing.

Puddling Canadian Tiger Swallowtails are taking up moisture and minerals from wet soil. Often witnessed in June.

Biology

Swallowtails lay their eggs on a variety of herbaceous and hardwood trees and shrubs. They overwinter as a chrysalis. Look for swallowtails adults and from May to August.

Black Swallowtail *Papilio polyxenes*

Our common dark swallowtail. Males search for mates while "hilltopping." Often found in gardens, caterpillars feed on members of the carrot family. Many times I've seen them on my dill plants, and outside the garden on Queen Anne's Lace. Two broods. Spring through fall.

Canadian Tiger Swallowtail *Papilio canadensis*

Eastern Tiger Swallowtail

Split off from the Eastern Tiger Swallowtail (right photo) in the early 1990s, the Canadian Tiger Swallowtail is single brooded and found throughout Canada and the Northeast from late spring to mid summer. Caterpillars of both species feed on the same wide variety of tree leaves, except Tuliptree which is toxic to Canadians. To differentiate from the Eastern Tiger Swallowtail, look for the solid yellow band on the trailing edge of the forewing's undersides. Wingspan to 3 ½ inches.

Whites & Sulphurs Family Pieridae

Appearance

Small to moderate sized butterflies with wingspans of 1 1/8 to 2 inches. They usually have white, yellow, or orange wings, often with black markings.

Large groups of sulphurs congregate at wet soil to drink and take in minerals.

Biology

Whites and sulphurs lay their eggs on a variety of herbaceous plants, especially in the mustard and legume families. Whites and sulphurs overwinter as a chrysalis and are seen May into October.

Clouded Sulphur   *Colias philodice*

Originally restricted to the north and east, but with spread of agriculture now occur over most of the continent. Unlike Orange Sulphurs, males do not reflect UV light and rely on pheromones to find mates. Caterpillars feed on legumes, especially White Clover. Spring through late fall.

Cabbage White   *Pieris rapae*

Accidentally introduced in Quebec from Europe in the 1860s, and now found throughout North America. A crop pest, caterpillars feed on mustards, cabbage and related plants. Unlike the native Mustard White and West Virginia White, the invasive Garlic Mustard isn't toxic to Cabbage Whites. Early spring to the first hard frost.

Mustard White   *Pieris oleracea*

Formerly considered to be the same species that occurs in Europe, *Pieris napi*. Transcontinental in Canada and the northern U.S. We have 2 flight periods, early and late summer. Caterpillars feed on various mustards.

Coppers, Hairstreaks & Blues
Family Lycaenidae

Appearance

Small, fragile butterflies with a slender body 1/4 to 1/2 inch long and a wingspan of 5/8 to 1 3/8 inch wide. Their wings are typically orange and black, brown, or blue, sometimes with small tails on their hind wings. Their antennae often have small white rings on them and their eyes are usually encircled by white scales.

Biology

Gossamer-winged butterflies are associated with a wide variety of herbaceous and deciduous trees and shrubs. Some species have a wide host range while are others are much narrower in their preferences. The larvae of many these butterflies are attractive to ants as they secrete a sugary substance the ants feed on. Gossamer-winged butterflies are common spring and summer.

Lucia Azure *Celastrina lucia*

The complex of Azures includes 4 New England species and 5 in New York, each with a different flight time. In the Northeast the flight phenology begins with the Lucia Azure (*C. lucia*), followed by the Spring Azure (*C. ladon*), Cherry Gall Azure (*C. serotina*) and Summer Azure (*C. neglecta*). The Appalachian Azure (*C. neglectamajor*) is restricted to the mountains from New York to Georgia.

Eastern Tailed-Blue *Cupido comyntas*

A small butterfly that resembles azures with tails. Unlike azures, dorsal basking is common. The way to tell males from females is the dorsal color, boys are blue and girls are gray. Occurs throughout the east with at least 3 broods a year from April through October. Caterpillars feed on legumes. I've found many in flower heads of bush clover.

Harvester *Feniseca tarquinius*

Harvesters are distributed throughout the east, but are uncommon and local. The larva is our only fully carnivorous caterpillar, feeding on wooly aphids on alders. Adults do not nectar, they feed on aphid honeydew, dung and puddle. Two broods in the Northeast from May to September.

American Copper *Lycaena phlaeas*

American Coppers are a locally abundant butterfly in the Northeast with sedentary populations. Adults fly from May to October, sipping flower nectar. Habitats include disturbed areas, power lines, fields and pastures where caterpillars feed on Docks and Sorrels.

Bog Copper *Lycaena epixanthe*

Bog Coppers live exclusively in native or abandoned commercial cranberry bogs. Eggs laid on cranberry leaves where they overwinter. In spring the young larvae feed on old leaves and later newer ones as the plant grows. Adults stay in the bog where they drink dew on the plants and nectar from the cranberry flowers. Mid June to early July.

Bronze Copper *Lycaena hyllus*

Bronze Coppers are widespread but local across the northern U.S. east of the Rockies, becoming increasingly rare in the Northeast. Found in damp meadows and marsh edges where the caterpillars feed on Water Dock and Curly Dock and adults feed on flower nectar. Two broods produce adults from June to October.

Hairstreaks

19 species in the Northeast. The **Gray Hairstreak** flies April to October and often perches with wings spread. In May and June watch for the rare **Early Hairstreak** in mature beech forests. The **"Olive" Juniper Hairstreak** is associated with Red Cedar May to July. Shake juniper trees to find resting butterflies. **Acadian Hairstreak** is associated with willows. **Edwards' Hairstreak** uses scrub oaks as larval food. **Banded Hairstreak** caterpillars feed on oak and hickory catkins, leaves. **Coral Hairstreak** caterpillars are tended by ants. Most on the wing in June-July.

Coral Hairstreak
Satyrium titus

Acadian Hairstreak
Satyrium acadica

Edwards's Hairstreak
Satyrium edwardsii

Banded Hairstreak
Satyrium calanus

Striped Hairstreak
Satyrium liparops

Juniper Hairstreak
Callophrys (Mitoura) gryneus

Gray Hairstreak
Strymon melinus

Early Hairstreak
Erora laeta

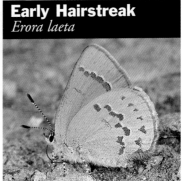

Elfins

6 species in the Northeast. **Brown Elfin** caterpillars feed on various heaths; fly early April to mid June. **Hoary Elfins** are locally rare to common, preferring pine barrens, wetland and forest edges where they feed on Bearberry. Adults mid April to early June. **Eastern Pine Elfin** is widespread and our most common Elfin. Late March to early July. Caterpillars feed on both hard and soft pines. The **Bog Elfin** is our smallest and one of the rarest butterflies in the Northeast. It's found in Black Spruce bogs where it feeds on spruce needles. Mid May to early June.

Brown Elfin
Callophrys augustinus

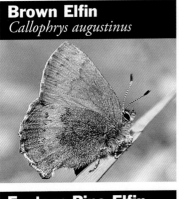

Hoary Elfin
Callophrys polios

Eastern Pine Elfin
Callophrys niphon

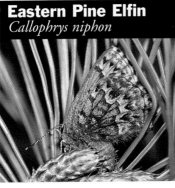

Bog Elfin
Callophrys lanoraieensis

Brush-footed Butterflies
Family Nymphalidae

Appearance
Moderate to large butterflies with wingspans ranging from 1 to 4 inches. The front legs of brush-footed butterflies are reduced; these butterflies use just their second and third pair of legs to walk.

Biology
Brush-footed butterflies lay their eggs on a wide variety of woody tree and shrubs and herbaceous plants. They overwinter either as larvae or adults. You can see brush-footed butterflies from early spring into the fall.

Great Spangled Fritillary *Speyeria cybele*

largest and most widespread of the 3 northeastern greater fritillaries (3 ½ in. span). Flies June to October. Males are the first to emerge, preceding females by weeks. Adults nectar on milkweed, coneflowers, butterfly bush, etc., occasionally feeding on the same flower for extended periods. Caterpillars feed at night on violets.

Atlantis Fritillary *Speyeria atlantis*

The smallest (wingspan to 2 ¾ in.) and most northerly (boreal) of our greater fritillaries, not occurring in southernmost New England. Often confused with Aphrodite Fritillary which has amber eyes; Atlantis has blue-gray eyes. Single brooded, adults fly from mid June to mid August. Caterpillars feed on violets.

Meadow Fritillary *Boloria bellona*

One of our 4 northeastern species of lesser fritillaries, this damp meadow-dweller is most easily identified by the lack of white spots under the wings and purple/brown tinge. Locally common with adults flying early May through September. Caterpillars feed on violets.

Pearl Crescent *Phyciodes tharos*

Two species of crescents in the Northeast. The Pearl Crescent is common and widespread throughout the Northeast except extreme northern New England and New York, where the slightly larger Northern Crescent (*P. cocyta*) occurs. Multi brooded. Fly early May through October. Caterpillars feed on asters.

Baltimore Checkerspot *Euphydryas phaeton*

The state insect of Maryland is named for the heraldic colors of Lord Baltimore. This single brooded beauty is found in wet meadows mid June through July. Caterpillars feed on Turtlehead, Smooth False Foxglove and plantains. Young caterpillars feed gregariously from inside a silk nest.

Question Mark *Polygonia interrogationis*

Our largest anglewing with two forms—The hind wing dorsal surface of the summer brood is nearly all black, while the fall/spring brood is bright orange with a frosty edge to the wings. Eastern North America, but rare in far northern New England. A migratory butterfly that flies from early spring to late fall. Caterpillar food is elm, hackberry and nettles.

Eastern Comma *Polygonia comma*

Like our 5 other northeastern anglewings, Eastern Commas overwinter as adults. Some migration is thought to occur. On a warm sunny winter day you might see one out basking on a tree trunk. Found in deciduous woods. Similar to Question Mark with two seasonal forms. Caterpillars feed on nettle, elms and hops.

Mourning Cloak · *Nymphalis antiopa*

Large (wingspan 3 to 4 inches). Found throughout our region and most of North America. Adults overwinter by crawling into sheltered places. They survive winter's cold because of "antifreeze" (glycerols) in their blood. Adults emerge on first warm days of spring to feed on sap. Summer broods occasionally will take nectar.

Milbert's Tortoiseshell · *Aglais (Nymphalis) milberti*

Formerly in the genus *Nymphalis*, this butterfly's closest relative is the Small Tortoiseshell (*Aglais urticae*) from Europe. A rare find in southern New England, but common in the boreal north. Flies from early spring to fall with 2 broods and overwinters as an adult. Caterpillars feed on nettles and false nettles.

Red Admiral · *Vanessa atalanta*

Red Admirals are a true migratory butterfly. Large northward spring flights are well documented along the East Coast, as well as southern fall flights, especially in peak years. It's suspected that some overwinter in northern ranges as pupa and emerge in the spring after a mild winter. Fly April through late fall.

American Lady · *Vanessa virginiensis*

American Ladies overwinter as adults in moderate zones and migrate north in spring to southern Canada. Painted Ladies (*V. cardui*) are less cold tolerant and rely on a more robust annual migration to colonize nearly the entire continent. Early April to November. Caterpillars feed on Pearly Everlasting and pussytoes.

Common Buckeye *Junonia coenia*

This southern butterfly shows up by late June in New England, has 2 broods before it migrates south in Oct–Nov. Found in open sunny areas with patches of bare ground. Caterpillars feed on plantain, gerardia, snapdragon where they acquire toxins that are not passed on to adults.

White Admiral *Limenitis arthemis arthemis*

White Admirals and Red-spotted Purples (*L. a. astyanax*) (inset) look very different, but are just sub-species of the same species. The White Admiral ranges across northern New England to Alaska; Red-spotted Purple from southeast New England to Florida. Overlap in southern NY and NE is mostly intergrades of the 2 forms. Late May through September.

Viceroy *Limenitis archippus*

The Viceroy avoids bird preda-tion by being a mimic of the distasteful Monarch. The cater-pillars mimic bird-droppings and feed on willow and poplar. To survive the cold, glycerols are produced before the caterpillar enters its hibernaculum (a rolled dead leaf shelter). Fly May to October in damp open areas.

Northern Pearly-eye *Lethe (Enodia) anthedon*

Mountain and boreal forests are home to this large brown but-terfly, often seen on tree trunks (Wingspan to 2 ½ inches). Adults don't take nectar, so they don't need to venture from the woods. They may feed along dirt roads and forest edges on sap, dung and mud. One flight period from mid June to mid August. Caterpillars feed on grasses.

Eyed Brown *Lethe (Satyrodes) eurydice*

Habitat preference for sedge meadows distinguishes it from the Appalachian Brown (*Lethe appalachia*)(woodland wetlands). The best way to distinguish these 2 species is to look for the inward facing "tooth" on the underside of the hind wing. Adults feed on sap and rotting matter. Flight slow and floppy. Mid June through August.

Common Wood-Nymph *Cercyonis pegala*

Our largest satyr comes in 2 color forms. The form with the large yellow patch on the forewing (photo) is seen in most of New England, except in northern and western areas. Males are short lived, emerging several days before females and dying soon after mating. Females fly in sunny open areas from July through September.

Monarch *Danaus plexippus*

A mass migration of Monarchs occurs in the fall to overwintering sites in the mountains of central Mexico. In spring, these overwintering butterflies start moving north. After a few generations they reach southern Canada by early summer. Caterpillars feed on milkweeds that arm them with toxins that are passed along to the adults. Wingspan up to 4 inches.

Dreamy Duskywing *Erynnis icelus*

Our smallest duskywing, and one of 2 that lack white spots near the tip of the forewing. Throughout our area and in boreal habitats across the continent. The Sleepy Duskywing (*E. brizo*) is more southern and not found in northern New England. The long palps are the easiest way to distinguish these 2 species. Late April through June.

Skippers—Family Hesperiidae

30 species in Northeast. Grass Skippers rest with hind wings held flat and the fore wings up at a 45degree angle, resembling a small jet. The **Arctic Skipper** is a holarctic boreal species that basks with wings held flat; late April-June. The introduced **European Skipper** is fast becoming one of our most abundant butterflies, 1000s flying in a single location. Male **Least Skippers** lack a black stigma. **Peck's Skippers** fly in meadows from May-October. The **Long Dash** flies in moist grassy areas; May-July. **Hobomok Skippers** fly mid May to mid July.

Arctic Skipper
Carterocephalus palaemon

European Skipper
Thymelicus lineola

Least Skipper
Ancyloxypha numitor

Peck's Skipper
Polites peckius

Long Dash
Polites mystic

Hobomok Skipper
Poanes hobomok

Sphinx Moths
Family Sphingidae

Appearance

Large heavy-bodied moths with long narrow forewings (some span 5 inches). Hind wings may be brightly colored. A few with clear wing patches.

Biology

While most sphinx moths fly at night, a few are active during the day, especially at dusk. Because of their size and the ability to hover, these species are sometimes confused with hummingbirds.

Small-eyed Sphinx *Paonias myops*

When these moths open up their wings, you can see the eye spots on each of the hind wings that it's named for. Common in a variety of habitats across the continent, and frequent visitors to lights from May to September in our area. Caterpillars feed on cherry, hawthorn, willow, poplar and wild grape.

Hummingbird Clearwing Moth *Hemaris thysbe*

Actively feeding on flowers during the day, these moths move from flower to flower like tiny hummingbirds. Widespread in the east and ranging into Alaska, adults fly in our area from June through August. Caterpillars feed on honeysuckle, snowberry and viburnum.

Azalea Sphinx Moth *Darapsa choerilus*

Nocturnal like most moths, adults feed on nectar and will visit lights and bait stations from May to August throughout the east. Usually found around hardwood forests, caterpillars feed on azalea, blueberry and viburnum leaves.

Giant Silk Moths
Family Saturniidae

Appearance
Medium to large stout-bodied moths with a body length of 3/4 to 1 7/8 inch long and a wingspan of 1 to 6 inches. They are often colorful and strikingly marked. Giant silk moths have feather-like antennae; in the males they are broad, while in females they are more narrow.

Biology
Giant silkworm moths lay their eggs on a variety of hardwood trees and shrubs. Different species may have a narrow or broad host range. Giant silkworm moths typically pass the winter as pupae. Watch for these moths from May to August.

Luna Moth   *Actias luna*

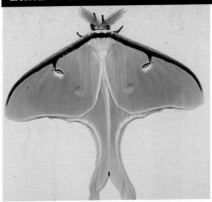

This stunningly distinctive moth is common throughout the east. Attracted to lights late at night, most people see them still clinging to the house in the morning. Caterpillars feed on many different hardwood leaves, but adults do not feed and live only about a week. Wingspan of 4 inches.

Pink-striped Oakworm Moth   *Anisota virginiensis*

Oakworm caterpillars have a pair of horns coming off their head and feed on oak leaves. There are three subspecies, with the Northern Pink-striped Oakworm A. virginiensis virginiensis in the Northeast. Flies from June into July, with females often attracted to lights.

Polyphemus Moth *Antheraea polyphemus*

Our most widespread silk moth, found in almost every state and province of North America. One of our largest nocturnal moths (wingspan up to 5 ¼ inches), it flies from May to July and often shows up at lights very late at night. Caterpillars feed on leaves of various trees and shrubs, but adults do not feed and have a short life span.

Promethea Moth *Callosamia promethean*

Promethea Moths are dimorphic, with males mostly black and females reddish brown. Occurs throughout the east with our single northern brood flying in June and July. Usually just the females are attracted to lights. Caterpillars feed on many species of trees and shrubs. Adults do not feed.

Rosy Maple Moth *Dryocampa rubicunda*

A beautiful pink and cream colored moth, it's widespread in the east. Adults fly from May to August in our area and are commonly attracted to lights. Young caterpillars are gregarious, feeding on maples and oaks, but become solitary when they mature. Adults do not feed. Wingspan to 2 inches.

New England Buck Moth *Hemileuca lucina*

Endemic to New England with very spotty distribution. Many adults can be found flying near wet meadows in September, which is an earlier flight period than its cousin the Buck Moth (*H. maia*). Caterpillars feed on spiraea and oaks, but don't handle the caterpillars, as they are covered with stinging hairs that can be rather irritating.

Inchworms & Geometers Family Geometridae

Appearance

Small to medium-sized moths with a wingspan of about 3/8 to 2 3/4 inch. The wings are broad, often with wavy lines on them. Males and females of the same species can vary in color. Some females are even wingless.

Biology

Eggs laid on a wide variety of trees and shrubs where the caterpillars feed on leaves or needles. Overwinter either as eggs or larvae. Active spring and summer and sometimes into fall.

Epelis (Macaria) truncataria
Variegated Orange Moth

Xanthotype species
Crocus Geometer group

Campaea perlata
Pale Beauty Moth

Plagodis serinaria
Lemon Plagodis

Haematopis grataria
Chickweed Geometer

Rheumaptera subhastata
White-banded Black Moth

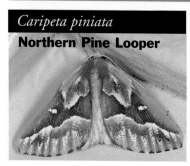

Caripeta piniata
Northern Pine Looper

Heliomata cycladata
Common Spring Moth

Prochoerodes lineola
Large Maple Spanworm

Euchlaena serrata
Saw-wing

Hooktip Moths
Family Drepanidae

Appearance

Medium-sized moths with a wingspan of 1 to 1 1/2 inch. The forewings are sickle-shaped and generally yellowish to brownish, sometimes with reddish brown.

Biology

Hooktip moths lay their eggs on a variety of trees and shrub where the larvae feed on the leaves from a loosely tied shelter. They overwinter as pupae in leaves on the ground. Watch for them from June to August.

Oreta rosea
Rose Hooktip

Pseudothyatira cymatophoroides
Tufted Thyatirin

Prominents
Family Notodontidae

Appearance

Medium-sized moths ranging in length from 3/8 to 1 1/4 inch. Their wings are usually brown or yellow with a wingspan of 3/4 to 2 3/8 inches. These moths often have a tuft of hair on their thorax projecting backwards.

Biology

Prominents and oakworms lay their eggs on a variety of hardwood trees and shrubs where the larvae feed on the leaves. They generally overwinter as pupae and are seen from June to August.

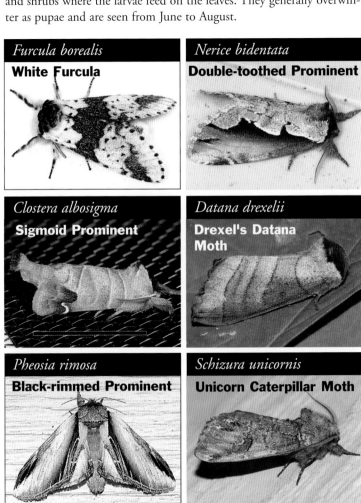

Furcula borealis
White Furcula

Nerice bidentata
Double-toothed Prominent

Clostera albosigma
Sigmoid Prominent

Datana drexelii
Drexel's Datana Moth

Pheosia rimosa
Black-rimmed Prominent

Schizura unicornis
Unicorn Caterpillar Moth

Tiger Moths
Subfamily Arctiinae

A couple common caterpillars are found in the Arctiinae. Top is the Spotted Tussock caterpillar and below is the Woolly Bear—larva of the Isabella Tiger Moth.

Appearance

Small to medium-sized moths with medium to stout bodies 1/4 to 7/8 inch long. They have a wingspan ranging from 1 to 2 3/4 inches. The forewings often are brightly colored white, red, or white and conspicuously striped or spotted. Tiger moths typically hold their wings tent-like over bodies.

Biology

Tiger moths are associated with a wide variety of herbaceous and hardwood trees and shrubs. In the Northeast, our species are typically generalists consuming a wide range of plants. Many tiger moths overwinter as partially developed larvae or as pupae. Adults are commonly found spring and summer.

Common names can be misleading. The Salt Marsh Moth (*Estigmene acrea*) is found in many habitats from Canada, across the U.S. and south to Central America.

Hypoprepia fucosa
Painted Lichen Moth

Lycomorpha pholus
Black-and-yellow Lichen Moth

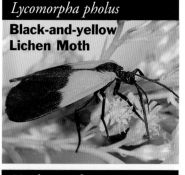

Haploa lecontei
Leconte's Haploa

Haploa confusa
Confused Haploa

Grammia virgo
Virgin Tiger Moth

Apantesis phalerata
Harnessed Tiger Moth

Phragmatobia fuliginosa
Ruby Tiger Moth

Hypercompe scribonia
Giant Leopard Moth

Utetheisa ornatrix
Bella Moth

Ctenucha virginica
Virginia Ctenucha

Lophocampa maculata
Spotted Tussock Moth

Pyrrharctia isabella
Isabella Tiger Moth

Tent Caterpillars & Lappet Moths
Family Lasiocampidae

Appearance
Medium-sized moths with stout hairy bodies. When resting, these moths often place their first pair of legs forward and its second pair of legs straight out at a 90 degree angle.

Biology
Associated with a variety of hardwood trees and shrubs where the caterpillars feed on leaves. These moths overwinter as eggs or larvae and are commonly seen spring and summer, and occasionally into fall.

The caterpillar of the Forest Tent Caterpillar is a common and unwelcome sight to homeowners during outbreaks.

Tolype velleda

Large Tolype Moth

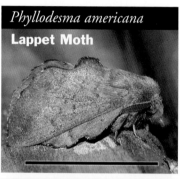

Phyllodesma americana

Lappet Moth

Malacosoma americanum

Eastern Tent Caterpillar

caterpillars

Malacosoma disstria

Forest Tent Caterpillar

caterpillar

Tussock Moths
Subfamily Lymantriinae

Appearance
Medium-sized moths with a body length of 1/4 to 5/8 inch and a
wingspan 1/2 to 2 inches. The wings are generally brownish, grayish, or
whitish. Some females are wingless.

Biology
Tussock moths lay eggs on a variety of hardwood trees and shrubs.
Many species feed on wide range of different plant hosts. Tussock
moths typically pupate late summer and emerge as adults during fall.
They quickly lay eggs which is the overwintering stage. Watch for tus-
sock moth caterpillars in spring and summer.

Lymantria dispar
Gypsy Moth ♀

Orgyia leucostigma
**White-marked Tussock
Moth**

caterpillar

caterpillar

Owlet Moths
Superfamily Noctuoidea

Appearance

Small to moderate moths, usually medium to stout-bodied between 1/2 to 1 1/4 inch long. They typically have a wingspan ranging from 1 to 3 3/4 inches. They have moderately narrowed forewings and broad hind wings.

Biology

The habits of noctuid moths vary considerably. Some are leaf feeders, others are borers, while some chew stems, i.e. cutworms. Noctuid moths generally pupate in the soil or leaf litter. Common spring and summer.

Hypena baltimoralis
Baltimore Bomolocha

Euclidia cuspidea
Toothed Somberwing

Euparthenos nubilis
Locust Underwing

Anomis privata
Hibiscus Leaf Caterpillar Moth

Zale horrida
Horrid Zale

Catocala epione
Epione Underwing

Catocala amica
Girlfriend Underwing

Catocala antinympha
Sweetfern Underwing

Catocala coccinata
Scarlet Underwing

Diachrysia balluca
Green-patched Looper

Chrysanympha formosa
Formosa Looper

Anagrapha falcifera
Celery Looper

Cerma cerintha
Tufted Bird Dropping Moth

Polygrammate hebraeicum
The Hebrew

Eudryas unio
Pearly Wood Nymph

Alypia octomaculata
Eight-spotted Forester

Harrisimemna trisignata
Harris's Three Spot

Agriopodes fallax
Green Marvel

Callopistria cordata
Silver-spotted Fern Moth

Papaipema lysimachiae
Loosestrife Borer Moth

Derrima stellata
Pink Star Moth

Schinia florida
Primrose Moth

Plume Moths
Family Pterophoridae

Appearance
Small, slender moths with a wingspan commonly between 2/3 to 7/8 inch wide. The forewings are divided into two lobes while the hind wings are divided into three.

Biology
They lay eggs on a variety of plants where the larvae are leaf rollers or borers.

Geina tenuidactlus

Himmelman's Plume Moth

Hellinsia species

Plume Moth

Clearwing Moths
Family Sesiidae

Appearance
Small to moderate in size with wings that either completely or mostly lack scales. The forewings are long and narrow; wasp-like in appearance.

Biology
Day-flying moths commonly on flowers or resting on foliage. They lay eggs on a variety of plants, trees and shrubs where the larvae are borers.

Alcathoe caudata

Clematis Clearwing

Synanthedon exitiosa

Peachtree Borer

Scorpionflies
Order Mecoptera

Diversity
There are five families and 83 species in North America. The scorpionflies are moderately common in New England and New York.

Appearance
Adults: Scorpionflies are medium-sized, slender, cylindrical, soft-bodied insects, ranging from 1/8 to 1/2 inch in length. They have a long looking face because of a prolonged beak; their chewing mouthparts are located at the end of this beak.

Scorpionflies have moderate to long slender antennae. They have four long, narrow membranous wings, often with bands or spots; one small group is wingless. The tip of the abdomen of common scorpionfly males is bulbous and held over their back, giving them the appearance of a scorpion. Scorpionflies are typically yellowish or reddish brown, rarely black.

"Hey, why the long face?" This head-on view of a scorpionfly highlights the elongated beak that gives them a long-faced look.

Larvae: Many scorpionfly larvae are caterpillar-like with small prolegs on eight abdominal segments. They have a couple of fleshy spines on the tail end of their abdomen, although a few have spines covering their entire body. Other scorpionfly larvae are grub-like lacking prolegs and spines. Scorpionfly larvae are rarely encountered.

Habitats
Scorpionflies are found in deciduous forests where they are found on low foliage or hanging from stems or the edge of leaves. One small group is associated with snow.

Life Cycle
Scorpionflies are holometabolous insects, using complete metamorphosis to develop. They typically have complex mating rituals where the males offer females food (dead insects) or secrete spittle to entice them to mate. Males lacking such a gift may try to forcefully mate with females. They lay eggs in soil, rotting wood, or moss where the larvae live. Larvae take about a month to mature. Eventually they pupate in the soil. There is typically one generation a year.

Food

Both adult and immature scorpionflies feed on dead insects; they may also feed on decaying animal matter. Some scorpionflies are predacious on other insects while a few feed on moss.

Don't confuse them with...

...wasps. You can distinguish between them as wasps lack a prolonged beak and they never have a scorpion-like abdomen. You may also confuse scorpionflies with true flies, especially crane flies, however true flies also lack a prolonged beak and only have two wings.

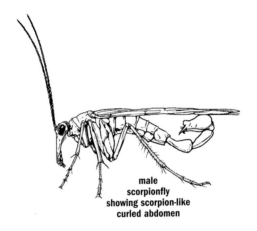

**male
scorpionfly
showing scorpion-like
curled abdomen**

Common Scorpionflies
Family Panorpidae

Appearance

Moderate sized scorpionflies about 3/8 inch in length. They are typically yellowish brown and black bands or spots on their wings. The tip of the abdomen of males is enlarged and usually held over their back giving them the appearance of a scorpion; despite their appearance, they are harmless to people.

Biology

Common scorpionflies are found in deciduous forests and forest edges where they are found on the leaves of low lying shrubs or herbaceous plants. They feed primarily on dead insects, although they have even been known to steal insects from spider webs. Scorpionflies are wary and are often difficult to approach closely. They are common June and July, although can be seen as early as May or later in August.

Scorpionfly *Panorpa species*

Panorpa mirabilis

Panorpa acuta

Common Scorpionflies are known by a single genus, *Panorpa*, containing 55 species, all of which are in eastern North America. In the Northeast we have about 12 species. Wing patterns can be used to determine most of the species, but experts prefer to examine the genitalia to be certain. Males have a large scorpion like tail while females have a simple tail process. Although called scorpionflies, they are not related to flies (Diptera). Clusters of eggs are laid in the soil where the caterpillar-like larvae come out of the burrow to feed on organic matter and small insects. After four molts, the larvae are ready to pupate. Depending on the species, adults will emerge in the summer, or the pupae will overwinter and emerge in the spring.

Snow Scorpionflies
Family Boreidae

Appearance
Small, 1/8 inch long insects that are dark brown or black. Females are wingless while males have short, slender, hard wings they use when mating.

Biology
Snow scorpionflies are active on the snow or moss during the winter, especially late winter or early spring as snow is melting. They can be active down to 21 degrees F. The larvae develop on moss. Both adults and larvae feed on moss. Although they can not fly, if they feel threatened, snow scorpionflies can jump straight up and land with their legs folded to try to resemble a bit of dirt.

Snow Scorpionfly *Boreus brumalis*

Adults are active through the winter months, and are commonly found on the snow surface. Of our 10 *Boreus* species, only 2 are found in the Northeast, with *B. brumalis* being the common species. Distributed through the Northeast and adjacent Canada, and as far south as Tennessee at high elevations.

Male wing stubs are used to hold a female on his back while mating occurs.

Snow Scorpionfly *Boreus nivoriundus*

Similar in range and habits as *B. brumalis*, but less common. Abdominal coloration can vary from brown to mostly black, but the cinnamon colored wings of the male, brown rostrum with a black tip and the yellow legs with thin black rings at each joint distinguish this other eastern species. Recent DNA studies have proven that these are the closest living relatives to fleas, which bear a close resemblance and share their hopping abilities.

True Flies
Order Diptera

Diversity
There are 105 families and over 19,000 species in North America, making this group one of the largest insect orders. The true flies are very common in New England and New York.

Appearance
Adults: Most true flies are small to medium-sized $\frac{1}{16}$ to $\frac{1}{2}$ inch long, although some species can measure over an inch in size. They are generally soft-bodied ranging from slender to robust. They are usually dark-colored, although some are black and yellow, green, and some are even metallic green or blue. True flies, unlike most insects, have just two thin, membranous wings while the second pair of wings are reduced to a pair of small knob-like organs called halteres. They have sucking mouthparts which vary considerably, e.g. sponging/lapping, piercing, and slashing. True flies typically have short antennae.

Larvae: True fly larvae, often referred to as maggots, are worm-like, legless, and often slender. They often lack a conspicuous head, although some species possess a well developed, prominent head. The mouthparts are variable, ranging from conspicuous mandibles to mouthparts reduced to rasping mouth hooks.

Habitats
True flies are found in essentially all habitats. Adults are commonly found on flowers and foliage. The larvae are found in all types of water, decaying plant and animal matter, as well as in living plants, such as leaves, stems, fruits and roots where they feed.

Life Cycle
True flies are holometabolous insects, using complete metamorphosis to develop. Individual true flies are generally short-lived. Eggs are inconspicuous and are laid close to a food source. Many species construct a protective covering around the pupa known as a puparium (pl. puparia). The puparium often consists of the last shed larval "skin," darkened and hardened into a capsule-like envelope. The pupae of many aquatic species can swim.

Food

Adult true flies feed on a variety of liquids including nectar, blood, sap, and honeydew as well as semi-liquid material, such as feces. Some true flies are predaceous on other insects. Blood feeders typically are able to find a blood meal through a combination of carbon dioxide, warmth, moisture, and chemical smells the hosts give off.

Don't confuse them with...

...bees and wasps. You can distinguish between them because bees and wasps have two pair of wings, chewing mouthparts, and often have longer antennae. It is also possible to confuse true flies with lacewings and other nerve-winged insects which also have four wings, chewing mouthparts, and moderately long antennae.

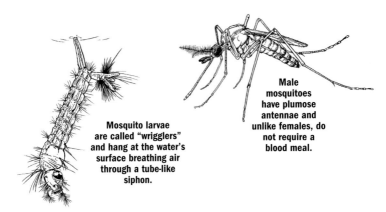

Mosquito larvae are called "wrigglers" and hang at the water's surface breathing air through a tube-like siphon.

Male mosquitoes have plumose antennae and unlike females, do not require a blood meal.

Large Crane Flies
Family Tipulidae

Appearance

Many folks mistakenly refer to these slender flies with long legs as "giant mosquitoes." They range in size from $3/8$ to 1 inch long. They have brown or gray bodies with wings that are often banded. Crane flies have a V-shaped groove on their thorax.

Some crane flies hang vertically.

Biology

Crane flies are usually associated with moist, damp environments with an abundance of vegetation, especially wooded areas near sources of moisture. They are typically found resting in shaded areas on foliage close to the ground. Despite their appearance to large mosquitoes, crane flies do not bite. They usually live for only a few days and typically don't feed. Crane flies are common spring and summer.

Northeast Species Notes

Crane flies in the genus ***Ctenophora*** are stout, shiny and bear a resemblance to Ichneumon wasps. Adults are most common in May and June at lights and in woodlands where the larvae live in rotting wood. We have 4 species north of Mexico with ***Ctenophora dorsalis*** being the most commonly found in the Northeast. ***C. dorsalis*** is highly variable in body color from black, yellow to red, while the wings can be black, clear or anywhere in between. Males have comb-like antennae and the females have a long up curved ovipositor.

Dolichopeza carolus is the only one of the 9 eastern species that has pure white tarsi. Most others in this genus can only be separated by examining the specimen. The typical posture of these long-legged crane flies is to hang by the front feet and let the hind legs dangle, making them look even longer and thinner than they are. ***D. carolus*** is found in forests and near marshes, hanging from vegetation. Other species can be found hanging from tree roots, rock surfaces or just about any shaded surface. Larvae of some ***Dolichopeza*** species feed on moss.

Tiger Crane Flies *(Nephrotoma sp.)* are medium to large and glossy. The abdominal color tends to be yellow or orange, often with black markings, almost tiger like. We have 40 species in North America, and most have larvae that inhabit the soil and feed on decaying plants and grass roots.

The widespread ***Nephrotoma alterna*** is commonly found in forests during June and July.

Nephrotoma ferruginea is the most common member of the genus in the eastern half of the continent. Look for adults from May through September along forest edges and open grassy areas. ***Nephrotoma pedunculata*** is most often found along forest edges in May and June. If you're lucky you might see a female bouncing up and down, jamming her ovipositor deep into damp sandy ground to lay her eggs.

Tipula is an extremely large genus with 480 Nearctic species. Some species have larvae that live in rivers and ponds, while others are terrestrial. The **Giant Crane Fly *(Tipula abdominalis)*** is the largest species in the Northeast, with females exceeding 40mm in body length. They have 2 generations a year, with adults occurring from May to October. Larvae are aquatic, feeding on decaying leaves. ***Tipula caloptera*** is another large crane fly reaching 25mm. Look for these distinctively marked flies in May and June. **Sooty Crane Flies *(Tipula fuliginosa)*** are dimorphic, and once were thought to be two separate species. Look for this species during May and June in grasses along streams and damp forests, plus they're often attracted to lights. ***Tipula longiventris*** females have an extremely long and pointed abdomen, nearly as long as the Giant Crane Fly, while males are half the body length. Adults fly from April to June, and larvae live in damp forest soil. ***Tipula sayi*** is one of the smaller species (15mm). It has clear wings with a dark leading edge. This is a late season flier, showing up in August in grassy forest edges.

Tipula trivittata is a large fly (up to 28mm) with patterned wings. Adults can be found around forests during May and June. Larvae live in the soil. ***Tipula tricolor*** inhabits grasses in swamps and along streams. Adults are most common in August, and larvae live in muddy soil.

Ctenophora dorsalis

Dolichopeza carolus

Nephrotoma alterna
Tiger Crane Fly

Nephrotoma ferruginea
Tiger Crane Fly

Nephrotoma pedunculata
Tiger Crane Fly

Tipula abdominalis
Giant Crane Fly

Tipula borealis

Tipula caloptera

Tipula fuliginosa

Sooty Crane Fly

Tipula longiventris

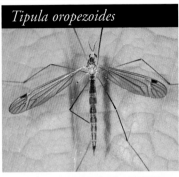

Tipula oropezoides

Tipula sayi

Tipula trivittata

Tipula tricolor

Limoniid Crane Flies
Family Limoniidae

Until recently Linoniinae was considered a subfamily of Tipulidae. This species rich family is mostly small to medium-sized, generally smaller than other families of crane flies. They can be brown, green, black, clear winged, patterned wings or no wings at all.

Band-winged Crane Fly *Epiphragma fasciapenne*

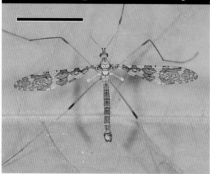

A beautifully patterned medium-sized crane fly of the Northeast that can be commonly found on low vegetation in moist forests in May and June. Males will form swarms before dark to attract females. After mating, females lay eggs in rotting wood, where the larvae develop. You can see the banded wings in the lower photo.

Crane Fly *Limnophila rufibasis*

Limnophila rufibasis is a medium-sized crane fly with a mix of brown and black markings. During May and early June, look in grasses and weeds near wetlands and slow moving water for this northeastern species. *Limnophila* is a rich genus with over 100 species, many having wing patterns.

Crane Fly *Gnophomyia tristissima*

Dark wings and bright yellow halteres make this small black crane fly unmistakable. A woodland species that can be seen resting on foliage near fallen hardwood. Larvae develop under bark of rotting hardwood logs, and adults are active from May to October.

Crane Fly *Erioptera chlorophylla complex*

The *Erioptera chlorophylla* complex consists of 8 species that can only be separated by genital differences. These mosquito-sized green crane flies can be numerous at lights during the summer. Otherwise they're normally found near water, where females lay eggs in moist soil.

Snow Fly *Chionea valga*

Resembling spindly-legged spiders, these wingless crane flies are active in winter, even out on the snow in temperatures as cold as the low 20s F. Male genetalia look like large hooked claspers, while females have a sword-like ovipositor. Of the 16 North American species, two are known from the Northeast, and both are uncommon.

Hairy-eyed Crane Flies
Family Pediciidae

Formerly a subfamily of Tipulidae, Pediciids include medium to very large crane flies that have slender bodies and spindly legs, making them look like thin daddy long legs *(Opiliones)*. **Pedicia** with 60 species is the most common and diverse genus in the family.

Giant Eastern Crane Fly *Pedicia albivitta*

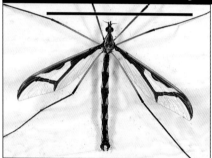

legspan

The Giant Eastern Crane Fly is one of the two largest in the Northeast, along with *Tipula abdominalis*. This spectacularly marked huge crane fly has two flight periods, one in June and the other in September. Adults inhabit damp to wet habitats in or near woods, and are commonly found at lights. Larvae are aquatic and predacious.

Crane Fly *Pedicia autumnalis*

About half the size of the Giant Eastern Crane Fly, adults inhabit weedy areas near swamps. The larvae are aquatic and have a disc with face-like markings and "tentacles" on its rear end. Adults fly from July through October, are pale tan, have black-tipped antennae, and females wings are much smaller than the males.

Phantom Crane Flies
Family Ptychopteridae

Appearance
Slender flies with long legs that resemble crane flies, they are about ¼ to ½ inch long. They are dark colored, sometimes with white bands on their legs. Some species have banded wings.

Biology
Phantom crane flies are found in wooded areas and near marshes and other damp sites. They are not particularly good flyers and are commonly carried by the wind. Look for phantom crane flies during spring and summer.

Phantom Crane Fly *Bittacomorpha clavipes*

It's memorable when you see one of these phantom crane flies in flight. They look like all legs just floating along without any wings. Obviously they do have wings which are small compared to the size of the fly. Found near swamps from April to September. Larvae are aquatic and have long breathing tubes on their rear end that act like a snorkel.

Phantom Crane Fly *Ptychoptera quadrifasciata*

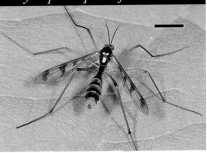

A small northeastern crane fly resembling a fungus gnat. Found around swamps and attracted to lights, adults have 2 flight periods, late spring and late summer. Larvae are semi-aquatic, living in the mud at the edge of forest streams. The larvae have retractable breathing tubes, their pupae form in the mud where they breathe with a pair of tubes, one long and one very short.

Winter Crane Flies
Family Trichoceridae

Slender insects, ⅕ to ⅖ inch long, very similar to crane flies but with ocelli, i.e. simple eyes, on top of their head which crane flies lack. Found during late winter and early spring walking on snow, often congregated in large numbers. Adults don't feed.

Winter Crane Fly *Trichocera species*

Mild days in early winter or late winter is when you may spy a winter crane fly of genus *Trichocera*. And like the photo shows, they will be on top of the snow. Attracted to lights on mild winter nights.

Midges
Family Chironomidae

Appearance

Delicate mosquito-like flies, from 1⁄16 to 3⁄8 inch long. The first pair of legs is usually the longest and is held up while at rest. Midges lack functioning mouthparts. Males have feather-like antennae.

Biology

Midges are weak flyers and are found near sources of water, typically resting on low foliage. Despite their resemblance to mosquitoes, they do not bite. In fact adult midges do not feed and are short lived. May occur in very large evening mating swarms. Particularly common during spring.

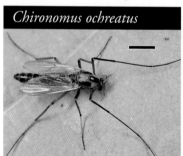

Chironomus ochreatus

Chasmatonotus unimaculatus

March Flies
Family Bibionidae

Appearance
Small to medium flies, from ¼ to ½ inch long. March flies are generally dark, sometimes with red and yellow, and are hairy or bristly. They have a large, bulging thorax and a generally flattened abdomen. Males have eyes where the facets in the upper two-thirds are larger than those in the lower third.

Biology
March flies are common around flowers in fields where decaying organic matter is common, such as decaying leaves, grass roots, and manure. Some species can occur in large mating swarms. Pairs have a tendency to remain coupled for hours, even days, due to the male's strong claspers. March flies are common in spring and early summer.

March Fly *Penthetria heteroptera*

A widespread fall species that commonly shows up at lights. This is our sole *Penthetria* species with both sexes solid black. Females are larger and males look like they have big heads because of their holoptic eyes. The parallel forks in the wing veins distinguish this from other northeastern species.

March Fly *Bibio longipes*

March fly can be a misnomer as in this fall occurring species. Males are black and very similar to the other fall species in the Northeast, *B. slossonae*. Females have a reddish thorax and easily distinguished from the black *B. slossonae* females. Males of the 53 North American species have holoptic eyes (enlarged eyes that touch at the top). Large swarms consisting of males are common in the fall throughout the eastern half of our continent.

Mosquitoes
Family Culicidae

Male mosquitoes have feathery antennae and do not bite.

Appearance

Slender, small flies with long legs that range from ⅛ to ⁵⁄₁₆ inch long. They have scales on their wings and conspicuous long mouthparts.

Biology

Mosquitoes are common around sources of standing water, like ponds and marshes, although they can be found essentially any-where. Peak activity occurs at dusk and dawn. Female mosquitoes feed on blood of a variety of

Females require a blood meal (be it human or otherwise) to produce eggs.

vertebrate animals, including humans, while males feed on flower nectar. Mosquitoes are generally less common during dry weather. Some mosquito species vector disease to humans, such as West Nile Virus.

Inland Floodwater Mosquito   *Aedes vexans*

The Inland Floodwater Mosquito is one of our most common species and is a known vector of EEE. Eggs are laid in lowland soil so when rains flood the area, the immersed eggs hatch. Small pools and puddles are the nursery for these mosquitoes. It's widespread east of the Rockies. May to October.

Mosquito   *Ochlerotatus canadensis*

This woodland mosquito breeds in vernal pools and other small temporary pools. Formerly classified in the genus *Aedes*, this and many others have been renamed to the *Ochlerotatus*, making this the largest genus with about 60 species. Adults target mammals, birds and herps to get a blood meal. Found throughout the east from May to September. They overwinter as an egg.

Golden Saltmarsh Mosquito *Ochlerotatus sollicitans*

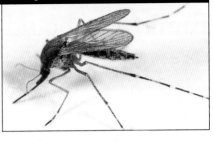

Hoards of these day active mosquitoes will drive all but the insane bug hunters out of a saltmarsh. Found along the east coast from New Brunswick to Texas. Also found in inland brine ponds. Golden hair and a white band on the proboscis, along with a coastal habitat, are all good clues pointing towards this species. In the northern range adults fly from June to October.

Black Flies
Family Simuliidae

Appearance
Small, stout flies from ¹⁄₁₆ to ¹⁄₄ inch long. They are black, dark brown, or grayish with short legs and broad wings. Black flies have a humpbacked appearance.

Biology
Black flies are particularly associated with rivers, streams and other types of moving water, especially in wooded areas. Female black flies bite vertebrate animals, including humans, while males feed on nectar.

Black Flies attraction to blue is a well known fact amongst wilderness travelers. Wear khaki!

Fortunately black flies are not known to transmit disease to people in the Northeast. Particularly common during spring and early summer.

Black Fly *Simulium species*

Over 100 species occur throughout North America, but fewer than 20 percent bite people and males do not bite. Most feed on birds and animals, and deliver a painless bite because of an anesthetic in their saliva. Males have large eyes and form mating swarms over fast moving water. Eggs are laid on rocks and vegetation in the water where large groups of larvae attach themselves and filter feed in the current. Most abundant and bothersome in the spring and early summer.

Moth Flies
Family Psychodidae

Appearance

Small 1.5 to 4mm flies that look like little moths. Hairs can be dense enough to make them look furry. More than 110 species occur in North America.

Biology

Larvae live in damp places where they feed on fungi, algae and bacteria. Also called Drain Flies, they often breed in shower drains, where the larvae feed on the organic film inside the drain pipe. Adults are often attracted to lights.

Filter Fly   *Clogmia albipunctata*

One of our most common a distinctive moth flies. It's found throughout most of the continent, breeding in stagnant water of drains, ponds and tree holes containing organic material. This one was found in an outdoor rest room, where the larvae were developing in the latrine pit.

Moth Fly   *Pericoma species*

Well marked and very hairy little flies. This one and a few of its siblings were found out in the middle of the woods, where standing water in a decaying stump, or inside a tree hole were probably where the larvae developed. Adults drink nectar from flowers, and fly with a jerky moth-like flight.

Wood Gnats
Family Anisopodidae

Appearance
Adults usually have patterned wings and will sometimes swarm.

Biology
Wood Gnat larvae are found in or near rotting wood, compost piles, manure and tree sap. They're commonly found at fresh tree sap and are attracted to lights. There's 9 North American species in 3 genera, and in the Northeast we have 5 species in 2 genera; *Sylvicola* and *Mycetobia*.

Wood Gnat *Sylvicola alternatus*

Larvae develop in decaying wood and vegetation, so they are common in compost piles. When the adult emerges from decaying wood, occasionally another inhabitant of the wood, a Pseudoscorpion will attach itself to the fly to be transported to a new piece of wood. This dispersal method is called phorecy and doesn't harm the fly. Of the 5 North American species, 4 are found in the Northeast.

Sylvicola flies develop as larvae in decaying wood and the emerging adults move to nearby pieces of wood for egg-laying. The pseudoscorpions (also common in decaying wood) are flightless and depend upon insects for dispersal. This type

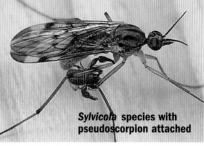

Sylvicola species with pseudoscorpion attached

of dispersal is called phoresy and it is typical for pseudoscorpions and mites.

Gall Midges
Family Cecidomyiidae

Gall midges are long legged, mostly clear winged with reduced venation and usually have long antennae. There's over 1,200 North American species in 3 subfamilies and only members of the **Cecidomyiinae** actually makes galls. **Lestremiinae** do not form galls, while **Porricondylinae** feed on decaying matter and fungus.

Midges may be less noticeable than the galls that result from their activities. This is *Asphondylia monacha*, one of our most ornate species.

Northeast Species Notes

If you see maple leaves in spring with brightly colored bulls-eyes, you've found **Maple Eyespot Galls**. Hickory leaves are host to a variety of galls, like the **Hickory Onion Gall** and the **Hickory Awl-shaped Gall**. **Willow Beaked-Gall Midges** form galls on willow twigs there they overwinter, and emerge in the spring. When you're at the coast in the summer, check out the Shadbush *(Amelanchier)* for *Blaesodiplosis sp.* that looks like little red mittens. Be aware that what emerges from galls may be the parasitoid as often as the gall-making midge itself!

Acericecis ocellaris

Maple Eyespot Galls

Apagodiplosis papyriferae

...forms on birch buds.

Blaesodiplosis species

...forms on Shadbush.

Contarinia cerasiserotinae

...forms on terminal buds of Black Cherry.

Caryomyia caryaecola
Hickory Onion Galls

Caryomyia subulata
Hickory Awl-shaped Galls

Dasineura serrulatae

...forms on alder buds.

Dasineura tumidosae

...forms on midrib of ash leaves.

Macrodiplosis majalis

...forms on oak leaves in fall.

Neolasioptera cornicola

...forms on dogwood stems.

Rabdophaga rigidae
Willow Beaked-Gall

Rabdophaga rigidae

Willow Beaked-Gall Midge

Horse Flies & Deer Flies Family Tabanidae

Appearance

Medium to large-sized, stout insects measuring from 1/4 to 1 inch long. They have very large eyes which are often brightly patterned iridescent green, turquoise or purple (see photos). The eyes of the males touch while are separate in the females. Horse flies and deer flies range in color from black to brown to yellow.

Deer Fly eyes can be iridescent blue, green or red.

The fearsome slashing-sucking mouthparts of a horse fly.

Biology

Horse flies and deer flies are found in woodlands and open areas along the edges of wooded areas. The females use slashing-sucking mouthparts to feed on the blood of mammals, including humans, as well as birds while males feed on nectar and pollen. The life cycle of most Tabanids start with eggs laid in clusters on grasses or leaves over water. Larvae are aquatic predators, and pupation occurs in the soil. Horse flies and deer flies are common throughout the summer.

Deer Flies Subfamily Chrysopsinae

Deer flies in the Northeast are all in the genus ***Chrysops***, with over 100 species occurring in North America. They're smaller than horse flies, have dark parches on the wings and colorfully patterned eyes. Most deer flies are found in damp woodlands, where they can be a major nuisance from June through August. Females will swarm around your head, and for the hair impaired like me, a hat is a must. An interesting interaction I discovered with swarming deer flies is when I walk out of the shaded woods into a sunny area, dragonflies, especially Eastern Pondhawks buzz past my head picking off a few flies, and the dozens of surviving flies disappear until I get back in the shade.

Chrysops ater

Chrysops callidus

Chrysops calvus

Chrysops frigidus

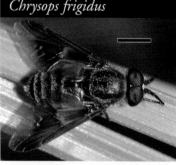

Chrysops geminatus

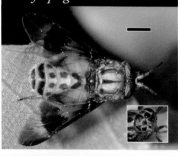

Chrysops lateralis

Chrysops sackeni

Chrysops vittatus

Family *Tabanidae* HORSE FLIES & DEER FLIES **325**

Horse Flies
Subfamily Tabaninae

Horse flies typically are larger and more robust than deer flies. Color patterns on the eyes if present, are usually horizontal bands, opposed to irregular patterns of deer flies. Males have large eyes that touch, while female eyes have a space between them. Female Tabaninae drink vertebrate blood for egg production and feed on flowers for energy, while males only feed on nectar and sugary plant fluids. Eggs are deposited in clusters on plants in wet habitats and larvae are carnivorous.

Horse fly eggs are laid in a fan-shaped mass on vegetation growing in, or hanging over water.

Hybomitra has 55 species ranging in size from 8-24mm. *Tabanus* contains 107 species like the large (22-24mm) *T. stygius* to the striped medium-sized (10-16mm) *T. lineola* and *T. similis*. During the heat of the summer beach goers become familiar with pesky *Greenheads* like *T. nigrovittatus* that breed in salt marshes.

Yellow-eyed Horse Fly *Atylotus palus*

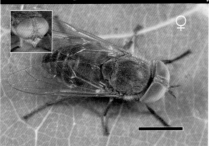

The first thing you may notice about this rarely seen horse fly is its yellow-green eyes with a single dark line; not a common trait in the Tabanidae. Yellowish brown abdomen and top of thorax. White hairs on face give a bearded appearance. 14 North American species of *Atylotus* with 12 east of the Rockies.

Horse Fly *Hybomitra lasiophthalma*

Spots of sunlight in dense woods is where you may see a hovering *Hybomitra* horse fly. Males aggressively dart at other males who are vying for the same female (or they may be guarding terrestrial larvae). On quiet mornings, the sound of many hovering males (especially along shrubby ditches) can be quite loud.

Hybomitra hinei

Hybomitra lasiophthalma

Tabanus catenatus

Tabanus lineola

Striped Horse Fly

Tabanus nigrovittatus

Greenhead

Tabanus similis

Tabanus stygius

Tabanus superjumentarius

Family *Tabanidae* HORSE FLIES & DEER FLIES | **327**

Snipe Flies
Family Rhagionidae

Appearance

medium-sized flies measuring ⁵⁄₁₆ to ¹⁄₄ with a fairly hairless body. They have a somewhat round head with a relatively long, tapering abdomen and long legs. They are typically brownish or grayish and often have spots on their wings.

Biology

Snipe flies live in wooded areas, especially near moist sites where they are common on foliage. Snipe flies are usually predaceous and are common from May to July.

Note the sexual dimorphism of this mating pair of *Chrysopilus ornatus* Ornate Snipe Flies. Females are bulkier and have a wider abdomen.

Ornate Snipe Fly *Chrysopilus ornatus*

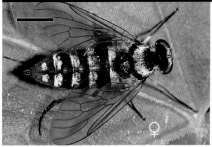

These striking snipe flies are found on low tree leaves and vegetation in damp woodlands with adults being most abundant in June with a few a little earlier and later. Distinguished from our other attractive *Chrysopilus* the Gold-backed Snipe Fly by the clear wings and slightly different markings. Eggs are laid in soil and damp leaf litter, where the larvae develop as predators of small insects. Range is most of eastern North America.

Snipe Fly *Chrysopilus quadratus*

One of our smaller species of the 32 *Chrysopilus* snipe flies that can vary from black, brown or oranges, but the dark patches on the wings are consistent. The head is almost entirely taken up by its huge eyes. Adults of this widespread species occur from June to September on low vegetation but are also attracted to lights.

Gold-backed Snipe Fly *Chrysopilus thoracicus*

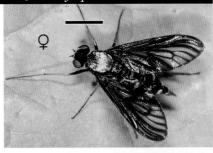

Gold-backed Snipe Flies are slow, easy to approach flies that rely on their smoky wings and bold color mimicking a wasp to fool predators. Commonly found on low vegetation near damp deciduous forests. Throughout eastern North America. Most often seen during June in the north and May and June in southern states.

Common Snipe Fly *Rhagio mystaceus*

Widespread throughout the east, Common Snipe Flies are among our earliest *Rhagios*, with adults active during May and June. They're also our most common species, and one of 25 species north of Mexico. Males are often found head down on tree trunks and on leaves, where they can be territorial.

Marsh Snipe Fly *Rhagio tringarius*

Introduced from Europe, the Marsh Snipe Fly is now the most common large *Rhagio* in the Northeast where it seems to have replaced the native *R. hirtus*. They're common on low vegetation around marshes and other damp areas during June and July. Of our 25 species of *Rhagio*, at least 7 occur in the Northeast. Note the fly's distinctive line of spots down the middle of the abdomen's top side (bottom photo).

Robber Flies
Family Asilidae

Appearance
Medium to large flies, measuring
between ⅜ to well over an inch in length.
They may be slender and smooth bodied
or stout, hairy and bumble bee-like.
Robber flies possess large, bulging eyes
creating a hollowed out space between
them at the top. Their face appears
bearded and they have a short, stout
beak-like mouthparts. Robber flies have
long, strong legs. Color varies.

If robber flies were the size of German
Shepherds we'd all be in trouble! They
are voracious predators, even taking
prey larger than themselves. This
Laphria species has taken a damselfly.

Biology
Robber flies live in a variety of habitats depending on the species. They
are predacious on many types of insects. Robber flies are strong flyers,
and usually capture prey on the wing. It is not unusual for them to
capture insects larger than themselves. Some have a flattened knife-like
beak which allows them to penetrate between the wing covers and
joints of the exoskeleton of beetles. Common spring and summer.

Northeast Species Notes
The genus **Asilus** has one North American species, **A. sericeus** a widespread eastern robber fly. Some of the best wasp mimics are another
eastern genus represented here by **Ceraturgus fasciatus**. Even the
antennae are wasp-like with an extra segment making them longer.
Cyrtopogon with 70 species is mostly a western genus, with at least 5
species of these robbers in the Northeast. Colorful markings on the legs
are used in courtship displays by some males.

The **Hanging Thieves** or **Diogmites** are more common in the south,
with 2 occurring in the Northeast **Diogmites discolor** and the larger
D. basilis.

Efferia is one of the most commonly seen robber flies with over 100
species, like this **E. aestuans** found throughout the east. **Pogoniefferia**
is a subgroup called the bearded **Efferia**, like this **P. pogonias** with a
pruinose section ahead of the curved up end of the abdomen. This
Eudioctria albius is two-toned, and others can be all dark morphs.

Bee-like Robber Flies as the **Laphria** species are known are usually
black with thick yellow hair. Most are bumble bee mimics like this

large ***Laphria thoracica*** which isn't being a cannibal, but eating a bumble bee (see photo below). A couple of exceptions are the ***laphria canis*** complex and ***Laphria sadales***, both lacking yellow hair. Coppertops like the ***Laphria index*** and ***L. sericea*** complexes are found in sunny patches of woods during June and July.

Leptogaster flavipes and ***Tipulogaster glabrata*** have a slow damselfly-like flight and prey on perched insects and sometimes spiders, unlike most other robbers that catch insects in flight.

The **Giant Robber Flies** in the genus ***Proctacanthus*** are huge and voracious predators, preying on many types of insects including bees, wasps and even large dragonflies.

The most common genus of robber flies in the Northeast is ***Machimus***, like this ***M. notatus*** that's found along woodland edges and the closely related ***Neoitamus flavofemoratus***.

The **Devon Red-legged Robber Fly**, ***Neomochtherus pallipes*** is a recent European import, so far only known from Massachusetts. The small **Three-banded Robberfly**, ***Stichopogon trifasciatus*** ranges throughout North America in bare sandy areas.

Asilus sericeus

Atomosia puella

Ceraturgus fasciatus

Cyrtopogon falto

Cyrtopogon marginalis

Diogmites discolor

Efferia aestuans ♀

Eudioctria albius

Laphria canis complex

Laphria flavicollis

Laphria grossa

Laphria index complex

Laphria posticata

Laphria sacrator

Laphria sadales

Laphria sericea/atkis complex

Laphria thoracica

Laphria virginica

Leptogaster flavipes

Machimus notatus

Neoitamus flavofemoratus

Neomochtherus pallipes
Devon Red-legged Robber Fly

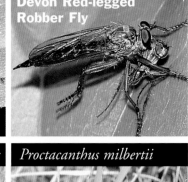

Pogoniefferia (Efferia) pogonias

♂

Proctacanthus milbertii

Proctacanthus nigriventris

Proctacanthus rufus

Stichopogon trifasciatus
Three-banded Robber Fly

Tipulogaster glabrata

Soldier Flies
Family Stratiomyidae

Appearance

medium-sized flies, ⅛ to ⅗ inch long. Soldier flies are variously colored, including green, yellow, black, and blue often with a patterned abdomen. The abdomen is often flat and broad. Many mimic wasps.

Biology

Found in a variety of habitats including forests, meadows, and near ponds, lakes, or moist areas. They visit flowers, such, feeding on nectar and pollen. Commonly encountered from May through August.

Soldier Fly *Odontomyia virgo group*

Check flowers near marshes in the spring and early summer for these small green flies feeding on nectar. Over 30 *Odontomyia* species in North America. All have aquatic larvae that feed on algae. They breathe at the surface through a tube on the end of their abdomen. Pupate in mud.

Soldier Fly *Stratiomys badia*

Stratiomys are distinguished by the shape of the antennae and a pair of spines on the scutellum. All are good mimics of bees, and *S. badia* is an especially good mimic. These northeastern flies are commonly found on flowers in summer. Larvae are aquatic, feeding on organic material.

Black Soldier Fly *Hermetia illucens*

Their large size, loud buzzing flight, purplish shiny wings and black body can fool predators into believing it's a wasp. Only reach as far north as Massachusetts in New England. Larvae breed in dung and compost where they can be numerous and effective at limiting house fly populations.

Stiletto Flies
Family Therevidae

Named for their narrow pointed abdomen, stiletto flies resemble medium-sized robber flies (Asilids) without the "beard" or a depression between the eyes. Adults are non predatory, while larvae feed on small invertebrates in the soil or in rotting wood. Although we have about 140 species in North America, they're not common. Most species live in open sandy areas and are wary, but a few live in forests and are easy to approach. Adults active late spring to early fall, and are occasionally attracted to lights.

Stiletto Fly   *Ozodiceromyia argentata*

Ozodiceromyia argentata is a distinct black fly with white rings found throughout eastern North America. It's one of our more common stiletto flies usually found on vegetation in sandy areas. Adults in the Northeast are active from June to August, and will occasionally come to lights.

Stiletto Fly   *Pandivirilia species*

Some members of *Pandivirilia* are snow white and fuzzy like this one. Not very common, they tend to be in sandy habitats with sparse vegetation. They're widespread through North America, Europe and Asia. Adults are active in the Northeast from June to August. Sometimes come to lights.

Stiletto Fly   *Thereva frontalis*

This is one of the species associated with woodlands. During summer look for it along forest trails and edges of fields. It's relatively common and can be distinguished from others in the genus by the black legs and a dark mark on the outer edges of the wings. Widespread through most of North America.

Mydas Flies
Family Mydidae

Mydas flies have clubbed antennae and are among our largest flies. The adults are wasp mimics that feed on nectar. Eggs are laid in either rotting wood or sand, where the larvae develop by feeding on beetle larvae. We have roughly 50 species, most of them in the southwest, and only one common species expected in the Northeast.

Mydas Fly   *Mydas clavatus*

The orange patch on these black bodied, smoky winged giant flies make them convincing mimics of spider wasps (Pompilidae). They even fly like a wasp, but unlike wasps the Mydas Fly doesn't pack a sting. Widespread through the east, look for easily approachable adults on foliage in meadows, gardens and on wood piles from June to September.

Xylophagid Flies
Family Xylophagidae

Slender medium to large flies that are usually found in woodlands. Some species are good wasp mimics. Adults are not commonly seen, but larvae are easily found under bark. Some species are predacious as larva and prey upon bark beetle larvae. Others feed on decaying wood or vegetation. 28 species occur in North America, with the greatest diversity in the northern ranges.

Xylophagid Fly   *Xylophagus reflectens*

Xylophagus reflectens is a small (8-9mm) wasp mimic fly with predacious larvae that live under bark of fallen logs or standing dead trees. It's the most common of the 7 *Xylophagus* species on our continent. It's widespread across the northern U.S. and southern Canada. Adults are active from April to June in forested areas.

Bee Flies
Family Bombyliidae

Appearance

Small to moderate, stout flies from ¹/₁₀ to ⅝ inch long. They are hairy and hold their wings straight out when at rest. The wings are often patterned. Range in color from black to brown, some with a dense mat of hairs, some banded. They have long, slender mouthparts.

Biology

Bee flies are commonly found in sunny areas particularly on flowers where they feed on nectar. They are good flyers and can hover and dart off suddenly. They generally lay eggs in the nests of ground-nesting solitary wasps and bees and grasshopper eggs where their larvae are ectoparasites. Look for bee flies spring and summer.

Bee Fly   *Anthrax georgicus (A. analis)*

Look for these flies hovering above the ground in sandy areas across most of North America. Females lay an egg at the burrow of tiger beetle larvae where it becomes an internal parasite of the beetle larvae. At high enough numbers they can significantly impact tiger beetle populations.

Bee Fly   *Anthrax irroratus*

The hairy abdomen and freckled wing pattern are distinctive for this species in the Northeast. Found from coast to coast, it's a parasite of wasp and bee larvae and pupae like most of the 27 North American species of *Anthrax*. Females will hover over sandy areas looking for a solitary bee or wasp hole to drop an egg into. Look on fences, telephone poles and other wooden structures for resting flies during the summer months.

Bee Fly *Bombylius incanus*

Easily recognizable by the clear wings and hairy white abdomen with black bands, and is the only northeastern *Bombylius* with a white face. Of the 61 North American *Bombylius* species, only 3 or 4 possible in the Northeast, with this being by far the least common. Look for this parasite of *Colletes* and other solitary bees in sandy areas.

Greater Bee Fly *Bombylius major*

In early spring look along woodland trails for these common bee flies. The dense hair varies from brown to yellow and the wings have a distinct dark leading edge. Adults feed on nectar from flowers and are a common site on the leaf litter. Greater bee flies parasitize ground nesting solitary bees, especially *Andrena* species.

Pygmy Bee Fly *Bombylius pygmaeus*

This is the smallest and most colorful of the northeastern *Bombylius*. Spots on the wings distinguish this from *B. pulchellus*. Widespread in the Northeast through Canada and into Alaska. Look for these wary little bee flies in April and May in sandy, brushy habitats. The long beak is used to sip nectar from spring flowers.

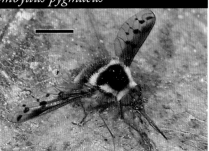

Progressive Bee Fly *Exoprosopa fascipennis*

Females drop an egg in a wasp burrow, where it becomes an ectoparasitoid (external parasites) of solitary wasp larvae. Found in arid habitats from coast to coast, they are commonly seen nectarring on flowers with their stiff but relatively short beak. June to September.

Hunch-backed Fly *Lepidophora lutea*

The humped back makes these flies easily identified to genus, and *L. lutea* is the only one of the 3 North American species occurring in the Northeast. Watch for the bouncy flight of these flies from July to September as they fly to Black-eyed Susans, asters and daisies to nectar. Larvae develop in solitary wasp nests.

Bee Fly *Paravilla separata*

Check the Black-eyed Susans from July to September in New England and southern Canada west to the Dakotas for these pollinators. It's the only species in the genus of 47 species found in the Northeast and is distinguished from other flies with half black wings by the black-banded abdomen.

Bee Fly *Poecilanthrax alcyon*

A large bee fly with a marbled pattern on the wings. *Poecilanthrax alcyon* larvae are parasitic on cutworms and armyworms in the soil. July and August.

Sinuous Bee Fly *Systropus macer*

Looking more like a thread-waisted wasp than a bee fly, these flies are most commonly seen feeding on goldenrod flowers in August and September. Of the 4 North American species of *Systropus*, this should be the only one found in the Northeast. Their larvae are parasites of slug caterpillars.

Bee Fly *Thevenetimyia funesta*

Forest trails are a great place to find these slender bee flies. Of our 27 species of *Thevenetimyia*, only 3 are known from the Northeast, where they're most commonly found nectarring on ground cover woodland flowers. They also hover around dead trees, looking for wood boring beetle larvae to parasitize.

Tawny-tailed Bee Fly *Villa fulviana*

From July to September look for these flies visiting flowers throughout most of North America. The lack of black hairs on the sides separates this from other northeastern *Villa* species. Two forms occur, one with clear wings, the other with a dark leading edge to the wings.

Bee Fly *Villa hypomelas*

Similar to *Villa nigropecta* whose fourth tergite is entirely black. Most common in August, look for these flies walking around on the ground and visiting flowers. The genus *Villa* has 37 of our most common species, but many more might exist. It's been over 100 years since this difficult to identify genus has been reviewed.

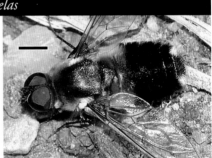

Tiger Bee Fly *Xenox tigrinus (Anthrax tigrinus)*

Being one of the larger bee flies, the larvae parasitize large carpenter bees. Widespread through eastern North America, look on vertical surfaces during July and August when they're most common. It's the only one of our 4 species of *Xenox* found in the Northeast. The large eyes and distinctive wing pattern make it easy to identify.

Long-legged Flies
Family Dolichopodidae

Appearance

Small to moderate-sized flies ranging $1/16$ to $1/4$ inch long. They are relatively slender with long legs. Long-legged flies are typically iridescent green, blue, or copper. Some males have conspicuous tufts of scales on their legs.

Biology

Long-legged flies are found in many types of habitats including woodland, prairies, meadows, especially when they are close to swamps and streams. They are typically found on foliage where they make short, darting movements. These flies are predaceous on small-sized insects. Long-legged flies are common from June through August.

Long-legged Fly *Argyra species*

Argyra species have spatula-like antennae and silvery-white pruinosity on the abdomen, easily distinguishing them from other Dolichopodidae. It's a widespread genus with about 50 North American species, yet it's uncommonly encountered. Larvae develop in damp habitats with adults active during the summer.

Long-legged Fly *Condylostylus patibulatus*

When watching these long-legged flies walk around on vegetation, their metallic color will change from green to blue to a coppery sheen depending on how the light hits them. Though tiny, they walk about on proportionately very long legs (hence, the common name). Look around moist woodlands on tree leaves for these shiny little flies. They can be abundant from May to September in the north, and year round in the southern U.S. Some of our 40 species have clear wings, while others like *C. patibulatus* have darkened wings.

Long-legged Fly *Dolichopus comatus*

Dolichopus is a large genus of over 500 North American species with males often having flattened front tarsi (feet) looking like small flags. Usually found near water on leaves and aquatic vegetation. This eastern species, *Dolichopus comatus,* has long bristles decreasing in size on the mid femur. May to August.

Long-legged Fly *Hydrophorus species*

These flies can walk on water! You need to take a close look to see that these are long-legged flies and not water striders. They skate along the surface of puddles searching for prey or mates, and make short quick flights to other nearby puddles. This is one of about 50 species found in North America.

Dance Flies Family Empididae

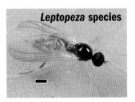

Leptopeza species

Mostly elongated small to medium-sized flies with a small round head on a distinctly thin neck. The proboscis is long and used to feed on small insects and in some species, flower nectar. Swarms with hundreds of individuals will fly in an up and down fashion. Common worldwide, with almost 500 North American species. In the Northeast adults fly April to September.

Dance Fly *Rhamphomyia species*

A large genus with over 150 described species and many yet to be described. 25 species in the Northeast. Females cannot hunt for themselves, and rely on males to bring them nuptial gifts of small insects. Some species specialize on mosquitoes and others on black flies, decimating local populations of these biting insects.

Flower Flies
Family Syrphidae

Appearance

Slender to robust flies, commonly ranging in length from ³/₈ to ³/₄ inch long. They are often black and yellow striped, sometimes black with orange or brown. Most are smooth-bodied, although some are fuzzy. Flower flies mimic bees or wasps.

Biology

Flower flies are very common in many different habitats and are frequently seen on flowers and foliage. They commonly hover around plants and can abruptly dart off in a different direction. After they land, their abdomens commonly bob up and down. Despite their menacing appearance, flower flies are harmless to people. The larvae of some species feed on aphids while others develop in aquatic environments and feed on organic debris. The well known "rat-tailed maggot" is the aquatic larva of the Drone Fly; its long breathing tube gives the larvae its common name.

Northeast Species Notes

Our 23 species of *Eristalis* start life off as aquatic or semi aquatic larvae called rat-tailed maggots, named after the retractable breathing tube it extends to the surface of the bacteria rich pools of water it inhabits. *Eristalis arbustorum* and the **Drone Fly *(Eristalis tenax)***, a good honey bee mimic, are both originally from Europe and now widespread in North America. The **Transverse Flower Fly *(Eristalis transversa)*** with a bicolored pronotum and a bright yellow scutellum, and *Eristalis dimidiata* are common in the eastern half of the continent. *Eristalis flavipes* is a good bumble bee mimic that occurs across southern Canada and the northern half of the U.S.

Helophilus has 34 North American species that have aquatic larvae. *H. fasciatus* is common in the Northeast on flowers from spring to fall.

Lejops curvipes is one of our 13 species of *Lejops*. It's most commonly found on flowers and vegetation in barren, sandy areas, such as beaches. *Blera* with its 17 species are represented in the Northeast by 5 such as *Blera analis* with its distinctive orange rear end, and *Blera confusa* with its yellow sides resembling a bee carrying pollen.

Spilomyia is represented with 11 species in North America, all of them large and fantastic wasp mimics. *Spilomyia fusca* is a dead ringer for a Bald-faced Hornet, with the most noticeable difference being the striped eyes. ***Spilomyia longicornis*** is a common eastern species in late summer and fall that resembles European paper wasps and yellow jackets. Look for ***Spilomyia sayi***, a good mason wasp mimic, during late summer and fall in the Northeast.

Of the 11 species of North American ***Sericomyia***, 7 occur in the Northeast with ***Sericomyia chrysotoxoides*** being the most common. ***Sericomyia militaris*** is found coast to coast in the northern U.S. and southern Canada from mid summer to fall.

Somula decora is one of only 2 species we have in the genus, and it occurs in the Northeast from May to July.

Chalcosyrphus plesia is one of the 29 North American species which mimic an assortment of different wasps. The larvae are found under bark of dead trees. The 12 species of ***Chrysotoxum*** north of Mexico are great wasp mimics and they all have long antennae. Larvae are thought to be predacious. The slender bodied ***Ocyptamus fascipennis*** is most common in August and September in its northern range. Its larva feed on aphids and scale insects.

The **American Hover Fly (*Eupeodes americanus*)** is one of the 28 members of the genus, with larvae that feed on aphids.

Syrphus torvus is distinguished from other similar species by the yellow hairs around the eyes and thorax. ***Epistrophe grossulariae*** had yellow hairs on the edges of the thorax plus down both sides of its abdomen. The small genus of ***Dasysyrphus*** is made up of 7 North American species like this ***D. osborni***, uncommon in the Northeast. The slender syrphids of our 16 species of ***Sphaerophoria*** are recognized by their black abdomens with yellow markings. The larvae feed on aphids as do the larvae of the 4 ***Allograpta*** species like the widespread ***A. obliqua***. ***Meliscaeva cinctella*** is the sole member of its genus on our continent, and is usually found near woods.

Toxomerus is made up of 17 small species north of Mexico, with the larvae being aphid eaters, welcome in any garden. ***Toxomerus geminatus*** is one of our most common syrphids during the summer in the Northeast. Also watch the flowers for the similar ***Toxomerus marginatus*** that is distinguished by the yellow margin *(marginatus)* on the abdomen.

Orthonevra nitida

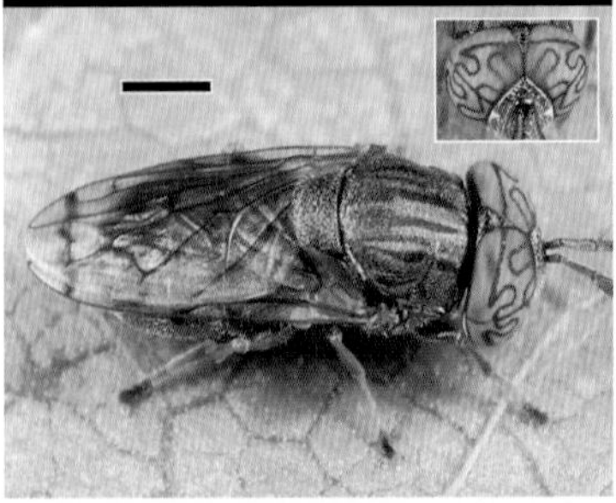

Sphegina species

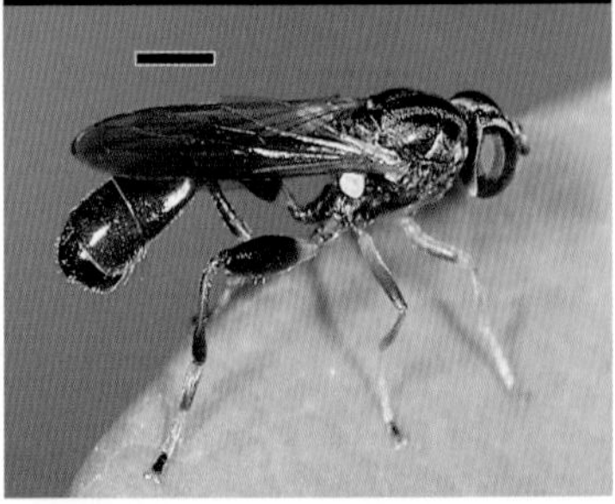

Eristalis arbustorum

Eristalis dimidiata

Eristalis flavipes

Eristalis tenax

Drone Fly

Eristalis transversa

Transverse Flower Fly

Helophilus fasciatus

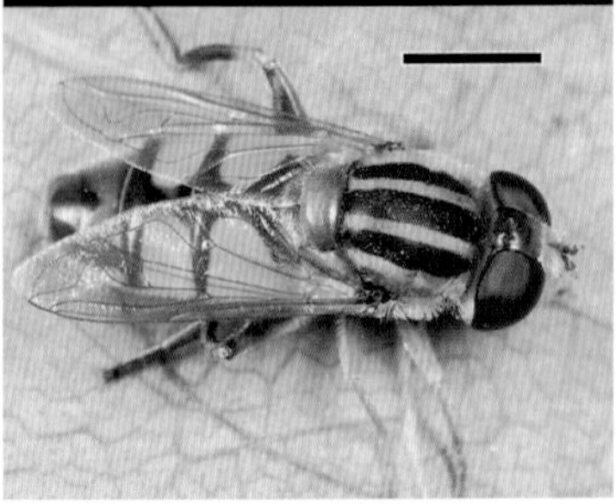

Lejops curvipes

Lejops species

Parhelophilus obsoletus

Merodon equestris

Narcissus Bulb Fly

Blera analis

Blera confusa

Milesia virginiensis

Sphecomyia vittata

Yellowjacket Hover Fly

Spilomyia fusca

Spilomyia longicornis

Spilomyia sayi

Temnostoma species

Tropidia quadrata

Rhingia nasica

Sericomyia chrysotoxoides

Sericomyia militaris

Somula decora

Chalcosyrphus plesia

Allograpta obliqua

Chrysotoxum species

Dasysyrphus osborni

Epistrophe species

Epistrophe grossulariae

Eupeodes americanus

American Hover Fly

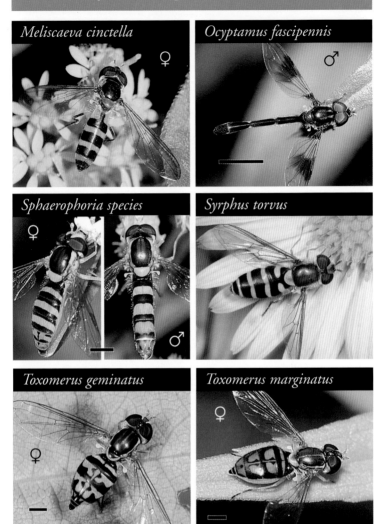

Meliscaeva cinctella ♀

Ocyptamus fascipennis ♂

Sphaerophoria species ♀ ♂

Syrphus torvus

Toxomerus geminatus ♀

Toxomerus marginatus ♀

Dung Flies
Family Scathophagidae

Appearance

Small to moderate-sized flies, ⅛ to ½ inch long moderately slender bodies. They are often yellowish and hairy, although some species are dark-colored.

Biology

Most dung flies are associated with fresh dung, the food of the larvae. Other species are associated with plants, either boring into stems or as leafminers. Adults prey on smaller insects.

Golden Dung Fly *Scathophaga stercoraria*

Fresh cow droppings are nurseries for Golden Dung Fly larvae where they feed on the dung. Males will guard egg laying females, and continue to be territorial over its dung pile. Adult flies are predacious, mostly on other flies. They're common throughout the continent and can be found all over the world. Active spring through fall with multiple generations. Adults are sometimes attracted to lights. Also called Pilose Yellow Dung Fly.

Leaf-mining Dung Fly *Cordilura scapularis*

A diverse group of slender elongate bodied flies without much hair. Many of our 50 widespread species are sexually dimorphic and are most common in the spring. Look for adults on logs and low vegetation in damp forests and around swamps where the larvae of most *Cordilura* develop as borers in the stems of sedge. At least 14 species occur in the Northeast.

Muscid Flies
Family Muscidae

Appearance

Small to medium-sized, moderate to robust-bodied flies, ranging in length from ⅛ to ½ inch long. They are blackish, brownish, or grayish, although some are yellow or metallic green or blue. They are more or less conspicuously bristled.

Biology

Muscid flies are found in many habitats. They are associated with decaying organic matter, including dung, although some species feed on blood from mammals (both females and males bite) while others are predaceous on insects. Muscid flies are found spring and summer.

Muscid Fly *Mesembrina latreillii*

With over 700 muscid flies around, most are difficult to identify. But the rusty-yellow base of the wings and red eyes are a dead giveaway that this distinctive fly is one of the *Mesembrina* sp. These wide-spread flies lay their eggs in dung, where the larvae develop. Look on leaves for these flies from late spring to early fall.

House Fly *Musca domestica*

Though not only found in houses, the House Fly can pass diseases on to humans. They are known vectors of over 100 diseases and parasites to humans and animals. They feed on garbage where pathogens can be picked up then later transferred to humans through the flies saliva or excrement. Found nearly everywhere, adults occur summer through fall. Adults only live about 3 weeks, but a single female can lay 500 eggs that mature in about a week during hot weather. Eggs are laid in manure and garbage piles, and they overwinter as larvae or pupae, sheltered under those piles.

Muscid Fly *Graphomya species*

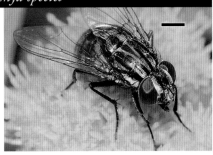

The 9 species of *Graphomya* bear a superficial resemblance to flesh flies (Sarcophagidae), and are a common sight on flowers during August and September. Unlike most of the muscids, they feed on nectar. The genus is distributed from coast to coast, and several species occur throughout the Northeast.

Root Maggot Flies
Family Anthomyiidae

Appearance

Small to medium-sized flies that are blackish, grayish, brownish with black bristles. They are similar to muscid flies but are usually more slender.

Biology

Commonly on foliage and are relatively slow to fly off when approached by people. Many are reported to be predacious. Common May into August.

Root Maggot Fly *Anthomyia oculifera*

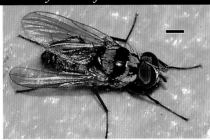

Unlike most root maggot fly larvae that feed primarily on plant material, these can be found on rotting vegetation, fungi, bird nests and carrion. Boldly patterned adults feed on sap and other sweet fluids and dung. Widespread through North America, look for them any month with moderate temps

Seaweed Fly *Fucellia species*

A very common and important fly in the wrack line along all our coasts (and the Great Lakes). Eggs laid on piles of seaweed, where the larvae help keep the beaches clean by breaking down the seaweed. Shorebirds benefit from this large supply of food, especially in migration. Adults active year-round on mild winter days.

Blow Flies
Family Calliphoridae

Appearance

Small to medium-sized, moderate-bodied flies, measuring between ¼ to ⅝ inch long. Many blow flies are metallic green or blue, although some species are blackish. Bristles are more or less conspicuous.

Blow flies are often seen on carcasses.

Biology

Blow flies are often associated with decaying organic matter, particularly carcasses and other sources of rotting meat and feces. In fact, they can figure prominently in forensic entomology, aiding in determining time of death. It is also common to find them on flowers. Blow flies are common spring and summer.

Common Green Bottle Fly *Lucilia (Phaenicia) sericata*

This might sound like the dark ages, but cultures of sterile maggots of green bottle flies are sometimes used in hospitals to clean up deep wounds and infections that otherwise are difficult to treat. They only eat dead tissue, and secrete an antibiotic, preventing further infection. In nature, the normal food source is carrion.

Common from coast to coast, these metallic flies vary from green, blue-green to coppery, and can be found from May to October.

Cluster Fly *Pollenia species*

All 6 of our *Pollenia* species are nearly identical, with a hairy thorax and crossed wingtips when resting. Two common northeastern species are *P. pediculata* and *P. rudis*, with the latter accidently introduced from Europe in plant soil, where it parasitizes worms. Adults can be found year-round in above-freezing temperatures.

Flesh Flies
Family Sarcophagidae

Appearance

Small to medium usually moderate to robust-bodied flies, measuring in size from ¹⁄₁₆ to ½ inch long with bristles on their body. Flesh flies are typically black or gray (never metallic) usually with dark colored stripes on the thorax.

Biology

Flesh flies are found in many habitats and are commonly associated with dead animals. The larvae of some species eat other insects, stealing the paralyzed prey from wasps. Unlike most insects, female flesh flies lay live young. They are found from spring to summer.

Friendly Fly *Sarcophaga aldrichi*

"Friendly" is a matter of opinion; called the Friendly Fly because of its tendency to land on people, and keep coming back after being shooed away. They don't bite and are most likely trying to drink salts off our skin. Forest Tent Caterpillars on the other hand have a lot to worry about. These flies are major parasites of the caterpillars, becoming abundant during peak years of Forest Tent Caterpillar outbreaks, during June and July. This is one of about 80 species of *Sarcophaga*, characterized by the red eyes and rear end.

Satellite Fly *Metopia species*

Females circle wasps and bees that are hunting—like a little satellite—waiting to deposit a larva at the entrance of the solitary bee's or wasp's burrow (not eggs, like most). Larva crawl down to the food source on their own. Larvae are kleptoparasites that feed on both the host egg and its food supply. Nine species in the genus. Found in sandy areas.

Parasitic Flies
Family Tachinidae

Appearance

medium-sized, generally stocky flies, typically ranging from ⅛ to ¾ inch long. They are conspicuously bristly and possess an enlarged postscutellum (a swelling on the posterior area of the thorax). Many parasitic flies are dark colored, and some resemble bees or wasps. Most are difficult to distinguish from muscid flies and root-maggot flies.

Biology

Parasitic flies (also known as tachinid flies) are common in many habitats and are often found visiting flowers. They commonly parasitize other insects, typically immature moth, butterflies, sawflies, beetles, true bugs and grasshoppers. Females have several strategies for delivering their young to hosts. They can lay eggs on or in hosts, lay eggs nearby and allow the maggots to hatch and find hosts, or lay eggs, which are particularly small, on leaves which are consumed by the hosts. Parasitic flies are found spring and summer.

Northeast Species Notes

Compsilura concinnata is a good example of humans trying to control nature that went wrong. In the early 1900s these European parasitic flies were introduced in California and in the Northeast to control gypsy moths and tent caterpillars. They've become well established and not only attack larvae of gypsy moths, but over 200 hundred host species including beetle and sawfly larvae, other caterpillars, including swallowtail butterflies and silk moths, decimating populations of non target species. In one motion, females pierce the host with a larvapositor and inject a maggot. She repeats the process on the host a number of times, and in her life can produce 100 larvae.

One of the first tachinids to appear in the spring is ***Epalpus signifer***, a parasitoid of Noctuid moth caterpillars. Members of the genus ***Archytas*** are commonly seen on flowers in the summer and fall. Females lay eggs that hatch on vegetation where the host is present. When a caterpillar passes by, the larvae attach to it and quickly burrow into the body.

Billaea rutilans is often found on tree trunks, and is a parasitoid of longhorn beetles, including *Enaphalodes atomarius*. The cylindrical members of ***Cylindromyia*** are frequently found on flowers, and parasitize stink bugs. Another slender species, **Hemyda aurata,** uses predatory stink bugs as its host.

The **Feather-legged Flies (Trichopoda sp.)** are distinctive with the large combs on the hind legs. **Trichopoda pennipes** uses hemipterans, including plant bugs, leaf-footed bugs and stink bugs as its host. **Trichopoda plumipes** is more restricted in its choice of host, using stink bugs in the genus *Brochymena*. **Xanthomelanodes** look like small *Trichopoda* without the feather-legs. Their host is thought to be assassin bugs.

Gymnocheta are parasites of caterpillars in the Noctuid family. **Zelia** are often found on tree trunks in the summer, facing head down. They're parasitoids of beetle larvae. **Gymnosoma** are small hairless tachinids that are parasites of stink bugs and shield bugs. **Gymnoclytia** look similar to *Gymnosoma* are but have fine abdominal hairs. They frequent flowers and are known to parasitize stink bugs, Noctuid moths and Pierid butterflies. **Pararchytas decisus** is a common species found on flowers in summer throughout most of North America, but its host is still unknown. The large spiny tachinids of the genus **Juriniopsis** and **Hystricia abrupta** occur from late summer to the fall and both are parasites of tiger moth caterpillars.

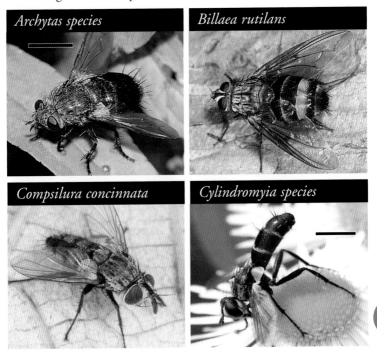

Archytas species

Billaea rutilans

Compsilura concinnata

Cylindromyia species

Epalpus signifer

Euclytia flava

Euthera tentatrix

Gonia species

Gymnocheta species

Gymnoclytia species

Gymnosoma species

Hemyda aurata

Hystricia abrupta

Juriniopsis species

Pararchytas decisus

Phasia aurulans

Trichopoda pennipes

Trichopoda plumipes

Xanthomelanodes species

Zelia species

Fruit Flies
Family Tephritidae

Appearance

Small to medium-sized flies, measuring ⅛ to ⅜ inch long. The wings are often ornately banded or spotted. Fruit flies are variously colored including brown. They have a small, tapered abdomen with females possessing a conspicuous ovipositor.

The Goldenrod Gall Fly causes this commonly seen gall.

Biology

Fruit flies are found in a variety of habitats where they lay eggs on many different plant parts and fruits. When found walking on surfaces, fruit flies often rhythmically move their wings slowly up and down. It is thought that distinctly patterned wings play a role in courtship rituals. Fruit flies are common from May to September.

Fruit Fly *Campiglossa (Paroxyna) albiceps*

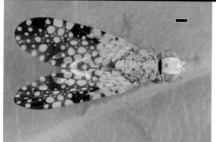

Campiglossa albiceps, formerly called *Paroxyna albiceps,* is a widespread species commonly found during the summer. It gets its name *albiceps* which is Latin for "white head." Females oviposit on aster flower heads, where the larvae develop.

Fruit Fly *Euaresta bella*

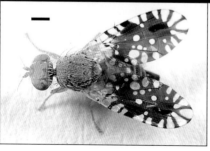

Euaresta bella is one of 3 eastern species in the genus, which is widespread through eastern North America. Females lay eggs only in seed heads of Common Ragweed *(Ambrosia artemisiifolia),* helping to reduce the bothersome weed. Larvae overwinter in the Common Ragweed seeds.

Fruit Fly *Eurosta comma*

Fruit flies in the genus *Eurosta* are represented by at least 4 of the 7 North American species that all form galls on goldenrod. *Eurosta comma* galls are not commonly seen because their galls are on the roots. From August to October adults of this widespread species can be found in fields containing goldenrod.

Goldenrod Gall Fly *Eurosta solidaginis*

Goldenrod Gall Flies aren't often seen, but their galls are a familiar sight in almost any field with goldenrod *(Solidago)*. Eggs are laid in the goldenrod stem where the plant creates a ball around the larvae, causing the large gall. Adults emerge in late spring after having overwintered as a pupa inside the gall.

Fruit Fly *Eutreta noveboracensis*

This is our most common species of *Eutreta* in the Northeast. Its wing pattern and the angle the wings are held, make this genus easy to recognize. The larvae live in root masses (rhizomes) of goldenrod. Look for these widespread flies in wooded areas from May to October.

Fruit Fly *Icterica seriata*

One of two species in the genus. *I. circinata* is similar, but has circular patterns on the wings instead of spots. This is a northeastern species that prefers damp habitats, where the larvae develop in beggarticks *(Bidens)*. Adult flies are out in August and September. They walk around on leaves, rolling their wings forward in display.

Fruit Fly *Procecidochares atra*

Procecidochares atra has a distinctive barred wing pattern with no spots, like some other Tephritids. There's two very different generations a year. The one in the spring has several larvae in a stem gall at the base of a goldenrod *(Solidago)*. The summer generation makes bud galls (inset photo) in goldenrod with a single larva in each one.

Rose Hip Fly *Rhagoletis basiola*

The Rose Hip Fly is a medium-sized fly distributed through most of North America. Adults are active during the summer months, where they can be found in gardens and other open areas with roses nearby. Larvae feed inside the fruiting bodies of roses *(Rosa spp.)*—rose hips.

Apple Maggot Fly *Rhagoletis pomonella*

This native originally fed on hawthorn, but in the last century it has included commercially grown apples and cherries where its maggots can be a serious pest as they bore into fruit. Adults feed on fruit juices and honeydew produced by aphids. Adults emerge in July and are active into early fall. Males wave their wings to attract females.

Four-barred Knapweed Gall Fly *Urophora quadrifasciata*

The Four-barred Knapweed Gall Fly was introduced from Europe to control knapweed *(Centaurea sp.)*, and is now widespread in the U.S. and Canada. Larvae overwinter in the gall formed on the knapweed, with adults emerging through the summer months.

Frit Flies (Grass Flies) Family Chloropidae

Appearance

Small, generally between 1/16 to 1/8 inch long, relatively hairless flies. Frit flies are often yellow and black or gray. All have a triangular patch on their head.

Biology

Frit flies are common in meadows and other grassy areas and are usually low on plants. They are often associated with living plants or decaying organic matter while some are predaceous and a few are gall makers. They are common spring and summer.

Grass Fly *Chlorops species*

Tiny but colorful. Grass flies are 3 to 5mm, and vary in color from bright yellows and blacks (like this one) to more subtle tans and brown combinations. This large genus lives in grasses from coast to coast, occurring from May to August. Eggs are laid in grass stems where feeding causes a lump called a gout.

Large Cigar Gall Fly *Lipara lucens*

This European fly was first discovered in Connecticut around 1990, and is expanding its range along the coast. Larvae enter phragmites at the shoot tip and mine down, where it forms a gall. At over 6mm this is one of the largest frit flies, and unlike most in the family, it's covered with hairs, even on the eyes.

Marsh Flies
Family Sciomyzidae

Medium-sized flies with noticeably long antennae and most have wing markings. Common on vegetation at the margins of virtually every body of water. 140 species in 20 genera are found in North America, with at least 15 genera occurring in the northeast. Larvae prey on or parasitize mollusks. Aquatic and terrestrial snails, slugs, slug eggs and fingernail clams are on their menu. Adults feed on nectar, dead insects and deer fly eggs.

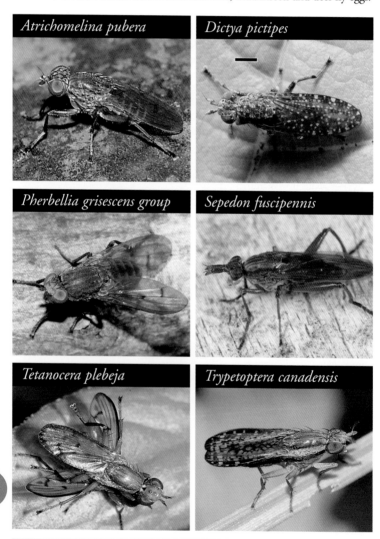

Atrichomelina pubera

Dictya pictipes

Pherbellia grisescens group

Sepedon fuscipennis

Tetanocera plebeja

Trypetoptera canadensis

Signal Flies
Family Platystomatidae

Appearance
Colorful and tiny flies that hold their wings outstretched. The wings are constantly in motion, as if signaling, hence the family name.

Biology
Mostly found in fields, some in woodlands. Larvae of *Rivellia* species develop inside the root nodules in legumes.

Signal Fly *Rivellia variabilis*

Rivellia is the most common and widespread signal fly with 34 species, having at least 10 in the Northeast. The 3 black wing bands are distinctive for the genus. *R. variabilis* has several color variations, waves its wings constantly as if it's signaling, and is differentiated from the other species by having bicolored legs and lacking long hairs dorsally on the thorax. Larvae develop singly underground in individual root nodules of legumes.

Signal Fly *Amphicnephes species*

Small flies with distinctly patterned down curved wings, shiny black abdomen and red eyes with blue–green highlights. Found on low vegetation in rocky or sandy habitats during spring and summer. The genus contains 2 widespread but uncommon species, with both occurring in the Northeast.

Picture-winged Flies
Family Ulidiidae

Appearance
Small flies, about ⅙ to ⅜ inch long. They typically have metallic colored bodies and wings marked with black, brown, or yellow.

Biology
Picture-winged flies are usually found in moist areas and can become quite numerous in a given area. The larvae feed on decaying plant matter. You can find picture-winged flies from May to August.

Picture-winged Fly *Chaetopsis aenea*

Small size and banded wings that are opened and closed are typical of most of the 7 North American species of *Chaetopsis*. *C. aenea* occurs on the East Coast around salt marshes, where it feeds on cordgrass. One other species inhabits salt marshes, but doesn't have reddish legs like this one.

Picture-winged Fly *Delphinia picta*

This is one of the most commonly noticed picture-winged flies. As it walks, its distinctively patterned wings are waved in a twisting fashion. It's the only member we have in the genus, and occurs throughout eastern North America, spring through fall. Larvae breed in organic matter, and are common in compost piles.

Picture-winged Fly *Eumetopiella rufipes*

This is the only member of the genus in New England. Their extremely slender body and black-tipped wings are unlike other Ulidiids. South to Florida and west to Ohio. Adults active June to September. Look in the grasses at the edges of farm fields where the larvae of these flies feed on barnyard grass.

Picture-winged Fly *Physiphora alceae (Musca demandata)*

A stout little fly with clear wings that it doesn't wave around like most other Ulidiids. Only 2 species north of Mexico; this is the only northeast species. Eyes are red with blue and orange stripes and the front legs are waved about like a wasp's antennae. Look along dirt powerline trails from August to October for these little flies.

Picture-winged Fly *Pseudotephritis vau*

Picture-winged flies in the genus *Pseudotephritis* are usually found in woodlands, raising their wings in courtship displays on dead logs. Five widespread species in U.S and Canada, 2 in the northeast. The more common *P. vau* has the mottled body typical of the genus, but the wing pattern is more pronounced with fewer and larger spots.

Picture-winged Fly *Tritoxa incurva*

Tritoxa incurva is one of the most common *Tritoxa* species in New England and New York. It seems to prefer grasses. Occurs throughout eastern North America from May through September.

Black Onion Fly *Tritoxa flexa*

The Black Onion Fly is one of the most common of the 5 species on our continent. Occurs throughout eastern North America from May through September. It is associated with wild onions and cultivated garlic, hence its common name. Look in fields, meadows and gardens for these flies that look like they're wearing a gas mask.

Thick-headed Flies
Family Conopidae

Appearance

Named for their large heads, thick-headed flies are usually found in open habitats on or near flowers. Many species resemble wasps.

Biology

Thick-headed Flies are internal parasites of wasps, bees, ants, cockroaches, crickets and flies. Once the victim is injected with an egg, the larva feeds inside the abdomen of the live host, and only when the fly is ready to pupate then the host dies, and its empty husk is a shelter for the parasitoids pupa. Host preference varies depending on which of the 4 subfamilies are involved. 67 species occur in North America, with at least 20 species in the northeast.

Thick-headed Fly   *Myopa species*

This *Myopa* species sits in its unique position, probably waiting and watching for the host species of bee or wasp. Adults fly from April to June and feed on flower nectar. Widespread in most of North America.

Thick-headed Fly   *Physoconops species*

Physoconops is a great wasp mimic that closely resembles its close relatives in the genus *Physocephala*, which lack ocelli, have a thickened base of the hind femur and a slight wing vein difference. Most often found around flowers where females look for an adult wasp or bee to inject one of her eggs into its abdomen while in flight. The host continues on its business and succumbs to the internal parasite at about the time of its normal lifespan. Found through most of the continent mainly during the months of June to August.

Thick-headed Fly   *Stylogaster neglecta*

An internal parasite of crickets, grasshoppers, katydids and roaches, the female impales the host with her ovipositor, inserting a harpoon-shaped egg with a barbed tip. Only 2 species of *Stylogaster* are found in North America, with *S. neglecta* occurring in the northeast. Look for them visiting flowers in open fields from June to October.

Leaf-mining Flies
Family Agromyzidae

Appearance
They range in size from 1mm to 5mm.

Biology
Female leaf-mining flies use their stiff ovipositors to deposit eggs between the layers of a leaf. Most are species specific, so knowing the host plant narrows down the choices of the fly species. Also the shape of the mine and where the frass is deposited are important clues. If you see the larva still in the leaf tissue it can be reared by placing the leaf in a sealed container and waiting for the adult fly to emerge. There are about 500 different North American species but not all Agromyzids deposit eggs in leaves, a few use roots, branches, stems, blades of grass and seed casings.

Poplar Twig Gall Fly   *Hexomyza schineri*

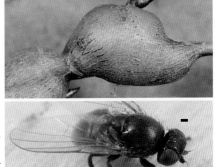

This native is one of the few species of leaf miners that doesn't mine leaves. Instead the female deposits eggs on developing aspen shoots near a bud. The feeding of the maggot causes the twig to form a gall that's noticeable by fall. Larvae feed all summer and overwinter as a maggot inside the gall and pupate either late winter or early spring. When the adult fly emerges in the spring they're just barely over 2mm long.

Stilt-legged Flies
Family Micropezidae

Appearance

Small to medium-sized flies, measuring from ⅛ to ½ inch long. They have an elongate body and very long legs, especially the second and third pairs, and an abdomen narrowed anteriorly to a stalk. Stilt-legged flies can resemble wasps or ants. These flies are usually light brown or blue black.

Biology

Stilt-legged flies are usually found around moist sites in wooded areas, meadows, marshes, and similar areas, where they are typically found on leaves. These flies can have elaborate courtship rituals and lay eggs in rotting wood, fruit, or other decaying plant matter. In addition to their similarity to wasps, some stilt-legged flies mimic wasp behavior to further the appearance. Look for stilt-legged flies during May to August.

Stilt-legged Fly *Rainieria antennaepes*

Rainieria antennaepes is widespread and common east of the Great Plains. It is the only member of its genus in North America. Look for them on logs and leaves along forest trails in summer. Watch them wave their white front legs, mimicking an Ichneumon wasp waving its antennae.

Stilt-legged Fly *Compsobata univitta*

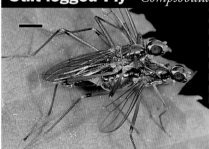

Foliage around wet meadows is where you can find *Compsobata univitta* in its northeast range. Adults are predators of small insects and are active from May to August. Larvae feed on decaying matter, including rotting wood. Unlike many of the other Micropezids, the front legs don't have white markings and are not often waved like wasp antennae.

Black Scavenger Flies
Family Sepsidae

Appearance

Small, ¹⁄₁₆ to ¹⁄₄ inch long, shiny black slender to medium-bodied flies. Black scavenger flies have a very round head, are ant-like or wasp-like and sometimes have a black spot on each wing near the tip.

Biology

Black scavenger flies are found in variety of habitats associated with decaying organic materials especially manure as well as carcasses and decay-

Black scavenger flies tend to spread and row their wings as they walk.

ing plant matter. They have the curious habit of "rowing" their wings outwards as they walk. Black scavenger flies are common spring and summer.

Black Scavenger Fly *Themira annulipes*

Themira is the largest genus of Black Scavenger Flies with 10 species, and are different from the other genera by their lack of wing spots and not having bristles on the dorsal thorax. *T. annulipes* has black legs with a yellow base on each one. Look for these flies near decaying matter and dung where they breed. Active spring and summer.

Glossary

Abdomen: The elongated, ten-segmented rearward body part.

Ametabolous Metamorphosis: A type of metamorphosis in which the adults are wingless and the only difference between nymphs and adults is size.

Arthropod: Animals that possess segmented bodies, a hard external integument (exoskeleton) and paired jointed appendages, e.g. legs and antennae (insects, spiders, ticks, mites, crayfish, centipedes and millipedes).

Caudal Filaments: Long appendages at tip of abdomen, a.k.a "tails" (mayfly nymphs).

Cerci: A pair of appendages on the last segment of the abdomen that usually function as sensory organs.

Crepitation: rubbing peg-like structures on their back legs against their forewing producing a low buzzing song or by making a snapping sound with their wings as they fly.

Femur: Portion of the leg closest to the insect's body; above the tibia.

Furcula: A forked appendage used for jumping. When not in use, a furcula is tucked up under the body, set like a mouse trap. When released, it extends down rapidly propelling the insect forward (springtails).

Grub: Inactive larval stage of some insects, especially beetles.

Hemielytrous Wings: Wings that are part leathery and part membranous (true bugs, cockroaches).

Hemimetabolous Metamorphosis: A type of metamorphosis in which the nymphs (sometimes called naiads) are aquatic and differ considerably in form from the adults which live on land.

Herbaceous Plants: Deciduous trees, shrubs and forbs; Non-coniferous.

Holometabolous Metamorphosis: A type of complete metamorphosis in which larvae look very different from adults, usually feeding on different types of food and living in different habitats. Last instar larvae molt into a pupa or resting stage.

Honeydew: A sugary sticky waste material produced by aphids . Honeydew can be a food source of other insects, especially ants.

Instar: The stage between molts in an insect's life.

Maggot: The legless larvae of flies.

Mandibulate: Possessing mandibles.

Metamorphosis: A change in form during development. Sometimes this change is gradual but many times it is very dramatic.

Nymph: Immature stage of some insects (mayflies, dragonflies, etc.)

Ocelli: Simple eyes (winter crane flies).

Ootheca: A case in which eggs are produced (cockroaches).

Ovipositor: The structure used by females to lay eggs in a suitable environment.

Palp: A segmented finger-like extension of the mouthparts.

Paurometabolous Metamorphosis: A type of metamorphosis in which the nymphs and adults are similar in form, differing chiefly in size, and typically live the same environment.

Proboscis: Extended, coiled mouthparts (butterflies, moths).

Pronotum: Plate-like structure (cockroaches, fireflies).

Prothorax: Front section of the thorax (e.g. the spined portion of a Spined Soldier Bug).

Puparium: Protective covering around the pupa (pl. puparia). The puparium often consists of the last shed larval "skin," darkened and hardened into a capsule-like envelope (flies).

Thorax: Mid section of an insect consisting of the prothorax, mesothorax and metathorax. There is a pair of legs on each thoracic segment.

Scutellum: A segment of the pronotum; often triangular (true bugs, beetles).

Stridulation: Sound produced by grasshoppers, crickets and katydids for mating, distress and aggression. Accomplished by rubbing specialized structures on two body parts together (orthopterans).

Tymbals: Sound organs located on the sides of the base of the cicada abdomen which vibrate and resonate into a cavity located inside parts of the thorax and abdomen (cicadas).

Tympanum: An ear in the tibia of the front legs (katydids).

Viviparous: Eggs develop inside the mother and she gives birth to live young (aphids).

Insect Websites

BugGuide www.bugguide.net
A great online resource for identifying your insect and spider photos.
Thousands of species covered with input from enthusiasts and experts.

Moth Photographers Group Google "moth photographers group"
The absolute best and most complete online resource for moth identification.

Nearctic Database www.nearctica.com
Lists of all North American insects (conifers and wildflowers too).

Canadian Journal of Arthropod Identification
Google "cdn jrnl arthropod"
Keys illustrated with excellent macro photos of pinned specimens. Also detailed
species accounts for Canada. For example, 38 (!) species of *Megachile* bees.

Crane Flies of Pennsylvania Google "crane flies pennsylvania"
Very detailed photo-illustrated keys. 415 species listed. Great photo gallery.

Discover Life www.discoverlife.org
An interactive encyclopedia about the taxonomy, natural history, distribution,
abundance & ecology of ALL species...including insects, of course.

Tree of Life www.tolweb.org/insecta
A bit clunky to use but does have videos of insects.

MCZ Type Database Google "mcz database"
Search the entire Harvard University Museum of Comparative Zoology online.

What's Bugging You www.arthurevans.wordpress.com
A folksy insect blog by author/entomologist Dr. Art Evans.

Bug Eric Google "bug eric"
The very well written and fun blog of Eric Eaton, co-author of the *Kaufman
Field Guide to Insects of North America.*

Photo Credits

Numbering begins at the top
left starting with "A" and pro-
ceeds clockwise around the page.

Amazingly, the vast majority of the photos were taken by the author. Tom
has photographed over 7,000 (!!) species of insects in the last 10 years. See
more of Tom's work at **www.pbase.com/tmurray74**. We filled in the very
few holes with images from the following photographers:

Dean Hanson: 38C; **Scott Nelson:** 152A;

Mike Reese [www.WisconsinButterflies.org]: 104C; **Larry Weber:** 50A

Lynette Schimming [www.flickr.com/photos/25980517@N03/sets/]: 133C

Sparky Stensaas [www.ThePhotoNaturalist.com]: 8, 14ACD, 33B, 40, 43C,
44BD, 50B, 66B, 69A, 72AB, 86E, 98A, 102C, 111BC, 116AB, 119B, 126A, 133B, 142A,
144A, 148B, 156ABC, 158B, 162B, 165AB, 167A, 170A, 173E, 216A, 218BC, 222A,
228ABC, 236ALL, 240BCD, 242CD, 246B, 247B, 248AB, 272C, 275A, 276A, 277A,
296A, 302, 308, 318B, 319B, 324A, 326C, 330A, 334DF, 340AC, 354A, 355B, 360A

Titles of Interest

Acorn, J. and I. Sheldon, 2003. *Bugs of Ontario.* Lone Pine Publishing. Edmonton, AB. 160 pp.

Arnett, R. H., Jr., M. C. Thomas, P. E. Skelley and J.H. Frank (editors). 2002. *American Beetles, Volume 2: Polyphaga: Scarabaeoidea through Curculionoidea.* CRC Press LCC, Boca Raton, FL. 861 pp.

Arnett, R. H., Jr. 2000. *American Insects: A Handbook of the Insects of America North of Mexico, 2nd Edition.* CRC Press LCC, Boca Raton, FL. 1003 pp.

Capinera, J. L., R. D. Scott, and T. J. Walker, 2004. *Field Guide to Grasshoppers, Katydid, & Crickets of the United States.* Cornell University Press, Ithaca, NY. 249 pp.

Cech, R., 2007 *Butterflies of the East Coast an Observer's Guide,* Princeton University Press, 345 pp.

Dunkle, S., 2000 *Dragonflies through Binoculars.* Oxford University Press 266 pp

Eaton, E. R. and K. Kaufman, 2007. *Kaufman Field Guide to Insects of North America.* Houghton-Mifflin. 391 pp.

Eiseman, C. and N. Charney. 2010. *Tracks and Signs of Insects and Other Invertebrates.* Stackpole Books, Mechanicsburg, PA. 592 pp.

Evans, A., 2007. *National Wildlife Federation Field Guide to Insects and Spiders of North America.* Sterling. 496 pp.

Hahn, J., 2009. *Insects of the North Woods: North Woods Naturalist Series.* Kollath-Stensaas Publishing, Duluth, MN. 245 pp.

Johnson, N. F. and C. A. Triplehorn. 2004. *Borror and DeLong's Introduction to Insects, 7th Edition.* Thomas Brooks/Cole, Belmont, CA. 864 pp.

Lam, E., 2004. *Damselflies of the Northeast.* Biodiversity Books, Forest Hills, NY. 96 pp.

Majka, C., D. Chandler, and C. Donahue. *Checklist of the Beetles of Maine.* http://www.chebucto.ns.ca/~aa051/maine.html.

Marshall, S. A. 2006. *Insects—Their Natural History and Diversity: With a Photographic Guide To Insects of Eastern North America.* Firefly Books Ltd Buffalo, NY. 718 pp.

Paulson, D. 2011. *Dragonflies & Damselflies of the East.* Princeton University Press. 576 pp.

Slater, J. A. and J. Alexander, 1978. *How To Know the True Bugs.* William C. Brown Company, Dubuque, IA. 256 pp.

Wagner, D. L., D. F. Schweitzer, J. B. Sullivan and R. C. Reardon 2011 *Owlet Caterpillars of Eastern North America,* Princeton University Press, 576pp.

White, R. 1998 *Beetles: A Field Guide to the Beetles of North America; Peterson Field Guide.* Houghton Mifflin Harcourt 384 pp.

Index

Quick Insect Finder

Other user-friendly guides from Kollath-Stensaas